Hours in the Dark

Hours in the Dark

Essays on Cinema

T.G. Vaidyanathan

DELHI
OXFORD UNIVERSITY PRESS
BOMBAY CALCUTTA MADRAS
1996

Oxford University Press, Walton Street, Oxford OX2 6DP

Oxford   New York
Athens   Auckland   Bangkok   Bombay
Calcutta   Cape Town   Dar es Salaam   Delhi
Florence   Hong Kong   Istanbul   Karachi
Kuala Lumpur   Madras   Madrid   Melbourne
Mexico City   Nairobi   Paris   Singapore
Taipei   Tokyo   Toronto
and associates in
Berlin   Ibadan

ISBN 0 19 563764 X

Typeset by Print Line, Greater Kailash II, New Delhi 110048
Printed at Rekha Printers Pvt. Ltd., New Delhi 110020
and published by Manzar Khan, Oxford University Press
YMCA Library Building, Jai Singh Road, New Delhi 110001

To the Burma-evacuee brothers, Pat and Purushot,
who first taught me to love the movies
and to
the late T.M. Ramachandran, of *Film World* and
Cinema India International, who first published my film essays

Contents

Preface

I have been a lifelong addict of films, graduating from being a film-goer
in the tent cinemas of my Thanjavoor boyhood to the diminutive
show parlours and multiplexes that now dot Western capitals. I have
always loved to sit right in front, as close to the screen as possible,
the middle-class drivel about this being bad for your eyes notwithstanding. And recently reading Aldous Huxley's *The Art of Seeing*, I feel
reassured that all along I have been doing the right thing. My tastes,
thank god, have not really evolved and, if anything, I am even more
in thrall of the American gangster film now — particularly those of
Brian De Palma — than I ever was. Then — I am thinking here of
the middle and late 40s — it was the smart exchanges in Howard
Hawks' *The Big Sleep*, Raoul Walsh's *White Heat* or Henry Hathaway's
Kiss of Death that moved me to near emulation. (You have to bear
in mind that I grew up to young manhood in Tamil-speaking Madras
where cinema *is* talk more than anything else as the career of Sivaji
Ganesan so clearly shows. I am not sure I have entirely outgrown
that sensibility.) First it was the fast cross-talk of the Hollywood co-
medians, Bud Abbott and Lou Costella, that captured my youthful
imagination, later refined into quotability in the throwaway lines of
the Marx Brothers, particularly Groucho of the leering eyes and quick-
silver sideways motion. English films — i.e., films from England —
were unwatchable, too insular, too British for my taste, except may
be something which featured Laurence Olivier, George Sanders or Charles Laughton. But Hollywood films had style and Humphrey Bogart's
loose-limbed walk and laid-back cynical humour seemed just the thing
for my Sait Colony fraternity where tempers frequently frayed and

brawls were pretty routine. You talked tough, laconic, like Bogart's Marlowe in *The Big Sleep* or his Rick Blaine in *Casablanca.*

By the 50s, Tamil films began to re-enter my landscape after a gap of some 10 to 12 years: the reasons are too complex to go into here, but they certainly had to do with 'decolonization', with finding my roots, as I realize now. As a professional teacher of English literature, I found myself in the late 50s and early 60s (when both 'Death in the Apu Trilogy' and the 'Denouement in Modern Films' were written and first published in Bombay and Calcutta respectively) in a bit of no-man's land. Serious film criticism was virtually unheard of (especially in the South) and I was even dissuaded by one of Satyajit's own cousins who pleaded with me not to waste my time on films. I should pursue my career, I was told, and deck myself out with a Ph.D. I had just edited the Shakespeare Quartercentenary Number for the *Osmania Journal of English Studies* at Osmania University and my dogged persistence in film criticism seemed rank folly. To make matters worse, there were few models to emulate. Like a drowning man, I clutched at garbled accounts in *Cine Advance* and at Dwight Macdonald's witty column in *Esquire* (which I picked off the pavement in Madras) where his essay on Antonioni's *La Notte* was a revelation. It was quite a while before the films themselves — one or two Bergmans, Polanski's *Knife in the Water*, Fellini's *La Dolce Vita* — arrived in India and caught up with my hitherto 'bookish' knowledge of them. Eventually when, in 1976, I did see *La Notte* at the National Film Archive in Pune, I surprised one of the professors there, who was sitting next to me, with my 'expert' knowledge of a film I was seeing for the first time in my life!

Some of my film criticism is rather 'literary' and 'bookish', I realize now, but, as in *Vamsha Vriksha* and *Chomana Dudi*, it seems to me entirely justified because most Indian art film-makers, including Ray who confessed to me his admiration for Thomas Mann, are very bookish, despite the cant that the cinema is a purely visual medium. Words will ever remain important in Indian cinema and when it self-consciously abandons them — as in the stylish freeze-frames that bring both Ray's *Charulata* and *Seemabaddha* to a close — the result is either a wanton and needless ambiguity or a stilted preciosity masquerading as moral judgement. Of course, cinema is a visual medium, too, and its chief purpose is to find suitable 'objective correlatives' (in T.S. Eliot's sense) for the various emotional states depicted. This is where 'art' cinema differs from its bastard cousin, 'commercial' cinema. Where 'art' cinema succeeds — as in Kasaravalli's *Mane* or M.T. Vasudevan Nair's *Nir-malayam* — the 'objective correlatives' are found and conveyed with surpassing excellence; where it doesn't, as in pseudo-art production, mere tedium results. 'Commercial' cinema is happily free of this obligation since it assumes the result and hence, instead of 'objective correlatives', it substitutes ready-made and stock melodramatic situations to achieve its ends. Hence, as in the runaway success of *Hum Apke Hain Kaun*, it reaffirms the governing ideological norms of the culture; it cannot, and will not examine them. However, there is a third category of film which is neither entirely artistic nor wholly commercial. I will place here films like K. Balachander's *Arangetram* and J. Mahendran's *Udhiri Pookal* — the latter, particularly, expertly scripted with a very good screenplay, although its principal protagonist is a repulsive figure. It is a minor classic, based on one of the late Pudumaipittan's stories.

After a lifetime of viewing films and writing about them, what, I may be asked, are the requirements of a good critic? He must be something of an artist himself (not a frustrated one, hopefully) for a good piece of criticism must be 'as well written and shaped as *mutatis mutandis*, a poem, a story, or a personal essay' (John Simon). Which means it can be read independently of the work in question. A leading Delhi publisher once told me some twenty years ago, 'Nobody wants to *read* about films', and I can only hope that these essays prove him wrong. To continue: the critic must not only have the ability to clinically describe the fulcrumatic moments (which are the real bearers of meaning) but also an evocative style that brings vividly alive moments of sheer splendour as those which occur in Ray's *Shatranj Ke Khiladi* or Benegal's *Junoon*. But style without a kind of nimble wit — the kind that can cut a feather in half — can be cloying, even annoying. Wit, which goes with worldly wisdom, signals an awareness of the present and is like seasoning to prevent style from growing stale. Sheed has this kind of wit in abundance and so has Simon but Simon is also something of a stylist who can, if he wishes, evoke memorably. His books taught me destructive criticism of which the *Gandhi* essay (my personal favourite, despite its unpopularity!), the two essays on *Chowringhee Lane* and *Paroma* and the Costa-Gavras piece are apt specimens.

I made more friends talking about films (only temporary enemies arguing about cricket!) than through any other activity. To all of them — too numerous to be listed here — I am in permanent and unrepayable debt. Love of the movies is a different thing altogether. I owe this to my Sait Colony fraternity referred to earlier. Especially to two Burma-evacuee brothers of the early 40s whose undiluted love of cinema and accompanying mimicry of whole snatches of dialogue (*The Black Swan, Blood and Sand, Kiss of Death, White Heat,* et al.) still ring in my ears and often move me to tears.

And finally, to the late T.M. Ramachandran (of *Film World* and *Cinema-India International,* both from Bombay), to K.N. Hari Kumar (of *Deccan Herald*, Bangalore), to Ramoji Rao (of *Newstime,* Hyderabad), to Chidananda Das Gupta (of *The Telegraph,* Calcutta) and Mrs Nirmala Lakshman (of *The Hindu*, Madras) my grateful thanks for letting me indulge an obsession. All the pieces here appeared in one or the other of these and other sundry publications.

T.G. Vaidyanathan
25 August 1995

Perspectives from the West

Towards a Century of Cinema

The beginnings of cinema are shrouded in some mystery. The popular belief is that the Lumiere brothers were the men behind the first showing of a projected film to a paying public on 28 December 1895 at the so-called 'Indian Room' at 14, Boulevard des Capucines in Paris. But even before that historic date, various people in various countries have laid claim to that invention.

Between 1826 and 1834, various kinds of equipment — the stroboscope, the zoetrope, the thaumotrope — were invented which showed moving images. Half-a-century later, in 1872, Eadweard Muybridge, with the aid of 24 cameras, demonstrated the movement of horses' legs. In 1877, the first projector, Praxinoscope, was developed. This was used in 1879 to project successive images on the screen. Between 1878 and 1895, a French physiologist developed various forms of camera to record human and animal movements. In 1887, Augustin le Prince produced the first series of images on a perforated film. In the same year, Thomas Edison, who had already developed the phonograph, took the first steps in developing a motion-picture recording and reproducing device to accompany recorded sound. In 1888, William Friere-Green showed the first celluloid film and patented a movie camera. The next year Edison invented the 35 mm film. In the following years he perfected his kinetograph camera and kinetoscope individual viewer, using perforated film. This photographic equipment was commercially produced in London, New York, and Paris. And in 1895, the Lumiere brothers, Auguste and Louis, projected to an audience a film of a train arriving at a station. History records that a section of that audience fled in terror.

Some of the best films were made in the infancy of the motion picture. We note, in passing, the tremendous achievement of those early pioneers, George Melies' A *Trip to the Moon* (1902) and Edwin S. Porter's *The Great Train Robbery* (1903), before pausing to pay tribute to the immortal D.W. Griffith for his Civil War classic, *The Birth of a Nation* (1915).

With Alan Crosland's *The Jazz Singer* (1927), the movies acquired a voice. A brief look at the plot of this film — the first of the 'talkies' — will reveal that at least popular cinema has yet to find a better box-office formula. The hero of this film, Jakie Robinowitz, is deeply attached to his mother but offends his cantor father by singing popular songs at a public bar. He runs away from home but is reconciled to his dying father by sacrificing a first night appearance to stand in for his father at the Passover service. Now, have we improved on this for a commercial success?

The coming of sound was seen — and still is, by many theorists — as an impediment to true cinema. Purists lamented the intrusion of sound and saw it as a regressive step, pushing cinema back towards its theatrical origins. The great Chaplin himself refused to budge until *The Great Dictator* (1940), understandably, drove him to the use of speech! But who will deny that the *silent* Chaplin is the true Chaplin and, incomparably, the greater artist than the *wordy* Chaplin of the later years — with the shining exception of *Limelight* (1952). Even Alfred Hitchcock was caught in the crossfire between sight and sound. Making *Blackmail* (1929) initially as a silent movie, he switched to sound midstream and the film proved to be an outstanding success as the first British all-talkie film. Still, two versions of *Blackmail* — one silent and the other with sound — are to be found in the cinematheques for the benefit of the connoisseur. Hitchcock himself clearly welcomed the coming of sound and, indeed, his greatest triumphs like *Psycho* (1960) are almost inconceivable without sound.

So the 'talkies' — as many of our older cinema houses in India are still called — have been with us only for about 60 years or so. Less than 100 years after the invention of the motion picture, it is still too early to say whether what we have is the seventh muse after literature, painting, sculpture, music, dance, and drama, or merely a mongrel muse parasitical on the established six. That is why arguments about what is cinema (the title of Bazin's famous volumes) sound somewhat premature, if not downright misleading. There are even rumours afloat that the movies are dying now that we have the video and cable TV.

Still, when I was asked at a national seminar on cinema what, for me, constituted a good film, I was flummoxed for a satisfactory answer. I began by emphasizing the importance of plot and characterization and, if I had allowed myself to think of Indian requirements only, I should have included music as well. After all, hadn't even the dour, unsentimental Naipaul of *An Area of Darkness* positively melted on hearing the sad, haunting strains of *tumhin ne mujhko prem sikhaya*? Well, I didn't and went on to underline the importance of a strong denouement and gave the examples of Adoor Gopalakrishnan's *Kodiyettam* (1977) (where fireworks go off in the sky as the various strands in the plot come together in the stirring finale) and Fassbinder's *The Marriage of Maria Braun* (1978) (where the telecast of the World Cup final punctuates the final sequence of the film culminating in the accidental death of the title figure). My choice of plot and characterization may sound unfashionable to a generation bred on Godard who once observed: 'I too believe in a beginning, a middle and an end but not necessarily in that order.' To broaden the scope of the discussion, let me cite from the decennial *Sight and Sound* poll of 1952, 1962, 1972, and 1982. Let me first summarize the findings of these four international .polls. De Sica's *Bicycle Thief* (1949) (which fascinated Satyajit Ray so much) topped the poll in 1952, slipped to the seventh spot in 1962, and went out of favour subsequently. Two Chaplin masterpieces, *The Gold Rush* (1925) and *City Lights* (1931) tied for second place in 1952, just below *Bicycle Thief*, but have not found favour subsequently: the current favourite is Chaplin's contemporary Buster Keaton's *The General* (1927).

Along with De Sica and Chaplin, many old reputations have fallen by the wayside: Carné, Flaherty, Lean, Clair; Visconti came into favour in the 1962 poll with *La Terra Trema* (1947) and so did Jean Vigo with *L' Atalante* (1934). Both have sunk into the same oblivion as Bergman and Dryer after the 1972 poll where they figured. In the last poll in 1982, serenely on top, were Welles's *Citizen Kane* (1941) and Renoir's *La Règle du Jeu* (1939) followed some way behind by Eisenstein's *Battleship Potemkin* (1925) and, rather unexpectedly, by Hitchcock's *Vertigo* (1958) and John Ford's *The Searchers* (1956). Film classics are a bit like champion race horses: here today, gone tomorrow — to the stud in the case of horses or, in the case of films, down the devouring jaws of cinematheques. And one might note in passing about the new favourites — *Seven Samurai* (1954), *The Searchers* (1956), and *Vertigo* (1958) — that they are strong in narrativity (i.e. plot) and characterization. A brief consideration of the Welles, Renoir, and Eisenstein films may take us nearer an answer to the question: What is good cinema as of, at least, 1982?

To start with *Battleship Potemkin* (1925). It has come under attack from many quarters (V.F. Perkins in England and Christian Metz in France) and in the pages of *Sight and Sound* itself. It seems unlikely to occupy the place it once did. It will remain, along with T.S. Eliot's *The Waste Land* and James Joyce's *Ulysses*, as a memorial to the 20s; a monument of high modernism from which the world is in so many ways retreating, if not actually recoiling. When one thinks of *Potemkin*, it is not for subtlety of plot or for any depth of characterization. It is always for those well-known filmic devices: the Odessa steps sequence which has inspired a host of imitations, ranging in quality from Brian De Palma's *The Untouchables* (1987) to that popular Kamalahasan pot-boiler whose name escapes me. More dated, perhaps, is the device of the shot of the three stone lions awakened by editing to some un-specified emotion (suspicion? alarm? anger? or watchfulness?). This cinema of a 'thousand cuts' (as Perkins has characterized it) employs editing as an end in itself, unlike, say, Hitchcock in *Psycho* (1960) where the famous cutting in the shower-bath murder sequence — 70 camera set-ups for 45 seconds of footage — is at the service of the film as a whole.

Renoir's *La Règle deu Jeu* (1939), with its astringent pessimism, will endure as long as 'everyone has his reasons' — to quote the film's most celebrated line. It is precisely this humane understanding and intellectual compassion that distinguish Renoir from Eisenstein. In *Potemkin* , Eisenstein idealizes the proletariat and cruelly caricatures the military whereas Renoir, in *La Règle deu Jeu*, dramatizes his affection for a way of life — the aristocracy's — which he actually criticizes deeply. That he was able to maintain the two opposed claims in equilibrium (the test of a first-rate mind, according to Scott Fitzgerald) is a sign not only of his artistic but also intellectual integrity. In his celebrity lecture at the London Film Festival in November 1967, he said that in the making of the film his 'ambition was to find a certain elegance, a certain grace, a certain rhythm which is typical of the eighteenth century'. Certainly this triumvirate is the aesthetic and cinematic fulcrum of the film. Only the hunting sequence resorts to rapid cutting, otherwise all is elegance, grace, and rhythm. But let me leave to Bazin, his greatest *rasika*, the last word on *La Règle deu Jeu* :

In this film, so extraordinarily audacious in subject, story, and technique, Renoir gave to French art on the threshold of the war something comparable to what *The Marriage of Figaro* had been to the French Revolution ... it implicitly translates the entire crisis of consciousness of a civilization on the verge of destruction.

Which brings me to Welles's *Citizen Kane* (1941) which has retained its pre-eminent position since 1962, polling 14 more votes than Renoir's masterpiece in the 1982 *Sight and Sound* poll. Its story of the newspaper tycoon whose dying utterance — Rosebud — sends the magazine reporter on his endless search is so full of lapses in characterization and gaps in narrative line that it would seem to disprove the importance of my preferred criterion! Still, its form is that of a mystery, reminding us of Borges' observation that *Citizen Kane* is like 'a centreless labyrinth'. Or, as Winston Churchill observed in another context, 'it is a riddle wrapped in a mystery inside an enigma'. Since Welles's *The Magnificent Ambersons* (1942) figures both in the 1972 and 1982 polls it seems necessary to say something of this lesser known work of Welles. *Ambersons* is a lament for a lost epoch, for vanishing values; and its style is so fluid that the cuts are almost invisible. Truffaut thought there were less than 200 shots in the entire film. Based on the well-known novel by Booth Tarkington (there's plot and characterization for you!), *Ambersons* was a favourite of Andre Bazin. It contains some fine examples of what has come to be known as the sequence shot. Welles's own favourite is the celebrated kitchen scene (which he rehearsed over and over again) which runs some four-and-a-half minutes without a cut. But while *Kane* has a memorable denouement, the ending of *Ambersons* was mutilated by Radio-Keith-Orphenm and, indeed, was the work of Welles's assistant, Freddie Fleck. No wonder that Manny Farber has complained of its 'hearts-and-flowers' finish.

It is indeed a puzzle why Satyajit Ray never figured in any of the *Sight and Sound* polls despite being widely admired in England. He might well have figured in the 1962 poll but thereafter it was all Antonioni (*L'Avventura*, 1960) or Fellini (*8 1/2*, 1962) or any one of the sombre Bergman masterpieces (usually *Persona* ,1966). The great Russian, Tarkovsky, was slowly gaining in status, and in the 1982 poll we find his *Andrei Roublev* (1966) among the runners-up. We shouldn't be surprised to see him figuring among the top ten in the 1992 poll. Surprisingly, Jean Luc Godard, the high priest of cinema, doesn't figure in the polls through any of his films. He is eighth in the 1982 poll of great directors, an honour he shares with Buster Keaton. But in James Monaco's influential 1979 survey of great European films of the 1970s, Godard doesn't figure at all! The top place goes to Eric Rohmer's *Claire's Knee* (1970) which polled twice the number of votes polled by all five others including Rohmer's own Pascalian *My Night at Maud's* (1969). *Claire's Knee* is about an adolescent's knee which provides the sublime focus of the hero's passion. *O tempora! O mores!*

2

Denouement in the Modern Film

John Howard Lawson writes in his *Film: The Creative Process:* 'The climax concludes *what happened* in a particular system of events; it is also a judgement on *why* it happens, *what* it means and *how* it affects our lives and conduct. The *what, why* and *how* are embodied in every part of the story; the end refers back to every part and summarizes the total result. Since the climax is the key to the story, it reveals the creator's purpose — or his confusion or lack of purpose — in the sharpest form. The limitations of the modern film are most evident in the climax.' This essay is an attempt to analyse some contemporary film climaxes in the light of these observations.

Critical discussion of films often founders for want of proper criteria and it is hoped that the ensuing discussion of an easily isolable part of films will help to focus attention on similar easily recognizable features and in doing so, throw useful light on the nature of meaning in films. What is suggested is that omnibus terms be dropped, especially when we are concerned with questions of meaning; what we need instead is more serviceable, descriptive terms like denouement. Borrowing from the sister arts is inevitable, but we may do so without necessarily accepting all the implications of this term from dramaturgy. We should particularly guard against the temptation to regard the denouement as in any sense the definitive solution of the problems posed by the preceding action, for the structure of a film need not be dramatic at all and, in such a case, the denouement cannot be expected to provide any ready-made solution. We may say at this point that the structure of the denouement should reflect the structure of the film and be, in an important sense, the most complete statement of it. But even to this there are important exceptions as we shall see. The most that we can expect of any denouement is that it should terminate the action while revealing the creator's purpose. Whether, in addition, it should show us, as Lawson demands, 'how, it affects our lives and conduct' will be one of the things investigated in this essay.

Nothing reveals more clearly the difference of the modern film from the film of a decade or so ago than the nature of the denouement. The older type of film (and this species will apparently never be extinct since it has had, and will have an endless lease of life in the commercial film of yesterday, today, and tomorrow) had only two versions of the denouement: the 'they-lived-happily-ever-after' ending and its radical opposite which involved the death of one of the principals. But death itself as a general rule was avoided, except for the unwanted or the bad characters, and in this way it has helped to round off many Westerns and American gangster films. But both the happy ending and the climactic ending through death (with important exceptions) are evasions of the whole question of meaning. We might adapt Aldous Huxley's observations on the novel and say that a film should begin with marriage and not end with it; similarly, it should begin with death, as in *Hiroshima, Mon Amour* (1959) where the destruction of Hiroshima and the general fact of World War II cast their grim shadows over the action, or as in the Japanese film *Ikuru* (1952) which begins with the certainty of a particular death. Happiness and death are at the terminals of human experience: the first is an ideal postulate and the second is an incomprehensible mystery, and the concern of art proper is not with these but with the spectrum of possibilities in between. Of course, the quest for happiness can be the theme of a film as the fear of death can be the theme of others (*Wild Strawberries* [1957] comes immediately to mind), but to realize imaginatively the achievement of happiness or the attachment to life can be no subject for a film. The conventional film closing on the note of an impossibly naïve happiness or a problem-terminating death cannot serve as a vehicle for any kind of meaning or any kind of reality for, as Kracauer has rightly said, the nature of the cinematic art is the redemption of physical reality. The film for Kracauer fulfils its true function when it shows 'physical existence in its endlessness . . . continuum of life or "flow of life" . . . which of course is identical with open-ended life'. It is obvious that the conventional film closing on the note of happiness or death is not dealing with open-ended life but with an artificially created world which moves like clockwork to its predestined end. It is my contention that the modern film is distinguished chiefly by its open-endedness, and nothing reveals this more clearly than the nature of the denouement.

Before approaching our principal task of analysing some climaxes in contemporary films, a few preliminary remarks are necessary. We may distinguish, instead of the conventional death-or-happiness ending, three different types of denouement employed by contemporary film-makers. There is, first, what we may call the static end, which leaves the principals with their problems relatively unsolved. The climax merely mirrors and poses the central problem in the clearest possible terms without in the least suggesting how it can be resolved or whether there is any possibility of resolution. Secondly, we have the kind of denouement where we witness a qualitative leap at the end, and the problem is not so much resolved as surmounted. A dynamic and un-expected solution is offered that often appears to question the very *données* of the film, and, clearly, the extremity of the solution is a measure of the difficulty encountered in reaching a satisfactory denoue-ment. The criticism can be made that these denouements are theatrical *deus ex machina* and not cinematic devices at all. We shall examine this criticism later. And finally, we have the third kind of denouement that deliberately employs a radical kind of ambiguity. In this category the doubt engendered at the end is not merely due to a refusal to arrive at conclusions but either due to a radical uncertainty on the part of the creator himself or the intrusion of the subjectivity of the creator into the material of his art or both. We are here dealing with an almost Heisenbergian uncertainty in the realm of the film that surely portends a new era in films.

The best example of the first kind of denouement mentioned above is furnished by the films of Antonioni. There is some irony in this because Antonioni is a dedicated Marxist and he certainly is, as William Whitebait has observed in *The New Statesman*, 'in the impossible position of a Henry James who is "committed" '. Some of the difficulties of Antonioni are apparent in his *Il Grido* (1957). The denouement here is reached when Aldo returns to the industrial town where his ex-wife is now living with her new husband. He arrives when there is a mass uprising against the installation of an American air base, but Aldo is cut off in his loneliness from all this display of human solidarity, and when he reaches the home of his former wife he finds her changing the diapers of the new baby. Unable to bear it all, Aldo rushes to the plant where he used to work and, climbing a tower, plunges to his death as his ex-wife, who has followed him, screams in horror.

The scream, which gives the film its title, is melodramatic and seems out of key with the theme of alienation that is otherwise so beautifully realized in the film through the melancholy and misty landscape of the Po valley as Aldo wanders across it with his daughter Rosina. But Antonioni's Marxism, rather obtrusive in this film in the somewhat unnecessary scenes of the popular demonstration, is never allowed any free rein in his later films and the only commitment discernible hereafter is to art. His *L'Avventura* (1960) completely avoids melodrama in its denouement and is probably the best example of the particular type of denouement under discussion for, as we shall see, it poses the moral issue at the end incisively — almost geometrically. The situation at the close of *L'Avventura* is almost too well-known to need any summary. Claudia is aware that Sandro has betrayed her, yet the two come together at the end in a recognition of mutual need and weakness. The woman gently strokes the man's hair and the episode is over. Antonioni himself has discussed the composition of the last scene:

One side of the frame is Mount Etna in all its snowy whiteness, and on the other is a concrete wall. The wall corresponds to the man and Mount Etna corresponds somewhat to the situation of the woman. Thus the frame is divided exactly in half; one half containing the concrete wall which represents the pessimistic side, while the other side showing Mount Etna represents the optimistic. But I really don't know if the relationship between these halves will endure or not.

This lucid balance between pessimism and optimism struck in the final frame serves to summarize the plot of *L'Avventura* and expresses the creator's purpose: the breakdown of permanency in human relationships ('But I really don't know if the relationship between these halves will endure or not'), with its corollary of a failure of love and a failure of communication between human beings. To have gone beyond this, to any hope in the future, would have been untrue to the premises of the film which is concerned not so much with the search for the missing Anna as with the human situation. The close of his next film *La Notte* (1961) is less convincing and more contrived, seeking to prove Antonioni's thesis about the barrenness of marriage. Again it is a man and a woman (the wife in this case) who face each other in the grey, sombre dawn on the links of the millionaire's golf course. Their movements are stylized (as Dwight Macdonald has pointed out) as the woman tells the man that the friend they had visited in hospital that morning has just died. As if this disclosure is not obvious enough in its implications, Antonioni further underscores his meaning by making the woman read a passionate letter that she says a man once wrote to her. At the end the man asks 'Who wrote that?', and the woman replies 'You did'. As the camera draws away from the couple, the man begins to make love to the woman. She protests: 'But I don't love you any more.' 'Be quiet,' he says, and Antonioni closes his film by giving us a wonderfully melancholy shot of the dawn (an Antonioni speciality) landscape. In bringing us to accept that the husband is insensitive enough not to recognize his own writing, Antonioni undoubtedly strains our credulity. Instead of the subtlety of *L'Avventura*, Antonioni reverts to a form of melodrama: the faintly glimpsed sexual act taking the place of Aldo's fatal plunge at the end of *Il Grido*. This apart, the climax of *La Notte* sins by being tediously verbal. Although only the woman speaks, several minutes are taken up as Lydia reminisces and analyses the reasons for the failure of the marriage. Antonioni himself has admitted that 'it is really a soliloquy, a monologue by the wife. The woman is still willing to discuss, to analyse, to examine the reasons for the failure of the marriage.' Still we are entitled to ask: Does her speech add anything to what we already know about Giovanni and Lydia? It merely verbalizes what has already been achieved in the long party sequence in Lydia's walk through the streets of Milan. *L'Eclisse* (1962) has a much more abstract theme than its predecessors, and its denouement is consequently equally abstract and somewhat uncertain in meaning. We have a series of abstract, or at any rate semi-abstract, sequences terminating in the moment of darkness when the sun is obscured at the end of the film. The sequence, which is otherwise beautifully executed, is unfortunately marred by the shot of the man reading a newspaper carrying the huge banner headline: GUERRE ATOMICA. Still the function of the denouement remains unchanged in Antonioni's films which is: to summarize the action that has gone before in a static sequence fully expressive of the author's purpose. Antonioni's purpose in *L'Eclisse* is to state the eclipse of human feeling, and this he achieves through a series of visual metaphors right through the film (the reduction of man to an object being memorably rendered in the scenes on the Stock Exchange), and the denouement is merely the most abstract paraphrase of the same theme. There is no need to argue, as Lawson does, that the ending of *L'Eclisse* 'presages a new direction in Antonioni's work, an attempt to break out of the circle of despair that has enclosed his characters'.

The denouement in Antonioni's films have always been contained in the action. He never goes beyond it, and in this sense he is a purist. But at the same time there have been a number of modern films in which the denouement is in no sense a paraphrase of the action but (to borrow Marxist terminology) a qualitative leap into another domain. This we have described as the second type of denouement. In this type there is a strong element of surprise and even improbability in the solution, but the audience is literally seduced into accepting it. A strong element of wish-fulfilment is certainly involved in these climaxes, but there are wishes and wishes so let us, after Aristotle, call these the impossible probabilities. My first example is Tennesse Williams' *Cat on a Hot Tin Roof* (1958). In the revised ending that Elia Kazan gave the play (and the film), Maggie prepares to make good her declaration to Big Daddy that she is pregnant. The audience is persuaded to accept the improbability that Brick, hitherto assumed homosexual and/or impotent, will make good Maggie's declaration. The immense popularity of the play on Broadway proves that the improbability of a denouement is no barrier to a story's appeal. At a very much higher level, the films of Ingmar Bergman make the same qualitative leap at the end. Even the sceptical *Wild Strawberries* (1957) closes on a note of tranquil happiness as the Professor sits, basking in sunlight, on the bank of a lake, fishing — a scene that has been variously interpreted. But it is *The Magician* (1958) and *The Virgin Spring* (1960) that furnish the best examples of the qualitative leap at the end. As the magician, a disappointed man now, prepares to leave the town in pouring rain, he suddenly receives a summons from the court for a command performance: the rain suddenly vanishes and the town is bathed in the most resplendent sunlight (Harris Dienstfrey has noted in his article on Bergman in *Commentary* that *The Seventh Seal, Wild Strawberries* and *The Magician* 'end with parallel scenes: their victorious heroes bathed in the bright warmth of a peaceful sun'). Bearing in mind Bergman's religious propensities and the similarities in structure between *The Magician* and Kafka's *The Castle* (the arrival in town in the middle of the night, the interrogation sequences, etc.), the denouement in Bergman's film is of the greatest interest. What we are witnessing here is nothing less than a Kierkegaardian leap from the empirical to the transcendental plane, and if it is objected that this is theatrical and not cinematic, all one can say is that one's ideas of the cinematic have to be enlarged to accommodate such original departures from the conventional as in Bergman. It is true that Bergman's theatricality — particularly the theatricality of his climaxes has alienated a great many of his admirers. Bergman's climaxes are optimistic (optimistic, that is, in the sense in which religion is optimistic), but they fit the requirements of Lawson's definition that the denouement should reveal '*how* it affects our lives and our conduct', for nothing does this more comprehensively than an assertion of a belief in the Divinity. *The Virgin Spring* is blatantly religious, and there is little for the imagination to seize upon in the final scene where the spilled blood of the virgin turns into holy water, for she has in fact become a sacred spring. The device is theatrical and religious, and casts a retrospective light on what has gone before (the first requirement of Lawson's definition) provided of course one accepts Bergman's religious premises. Bergman's numerous admirers and the great vogue he has enjoyed till recently establishes the admissibility of this type of denouement which I have termed the qualitative leap. It can be easily abused, as it is in every film that makes use of a surprise ending — especially when the surprise does not spring from ignorance of facts but from our being asked to accept total moral regeneration in an individual presented throughout the film as depraved and incapable of change.

We now come to the final category of modern denouements: the climax with multiple meaning or the ambiguous ending. The most obvious way in which ambiguity can be introduced is through the use of the frozen shot in the last sequence (although a frozen shot can also be employed to state the meaning of a film in the clearest possible terms, as in Truffaut's *The Four Hundred Blows* [1958] which closes on the face of the young boy whose first glimpse of the sea merely destroys the fond delusions he has had about it). The distinguishing feature of this category is the intrusion of the radical subjectivity of the creator in some way, into the very structure of the film, thereby affecting the denouement so that there is a deliberate denial of objective truth in preference to a more subjective interpretation of reality. Reality is redeemed but is ringed around with the personal fantasies of the creator. As Robbe-Grillet observes of *Last Year at Marienbad* (1961): 'The story of *Marienbad* doesn't exist apart from the way it's told.' The projection of ambiguity is well employed at the close of Roman Polanski's *Knife in the Water* (1962). The car of the returning couple is frozen in front of a fork in the road in the last shot of the film. The husband has the choice of believing himself to have sent to his death a young man they had picked up during their pleasure cruise or believing his wife who reports that the young man is alive because she has, in fact, spent the night with him. The climax is right because doubt is part of the essential furniture of the world of *Knife in the Water*. The husband's predicament in not knowing whether he is a murderer or a cuckold is an apt summary of the predicament of modern man with his intolerable guilt (for what nameless crimes?) in a world where transcendence is denied and man is faced with the choice of choosing between intolerable alternatives.

Satyajit Ray's *Charulata* (1964) makes use of the ambiguous ending less justifiably. This film also closes on a frozen shot with the extended hands of Charulata and Bhupati striving to touch and unite or remain forever suspended in mid-air. The end of a film, according to Lawson's definition, 'refers back to every part and summarizes the total result'. In what way does the end of *Charulata* do so? The truth is that the doubt engendered by the close is not organic and continuous with the world of *Charulata* for we have been led to take the essence of Bhupati's character to lie in trust, and there is nothing for him to disbelieve in the evidence of Amal's letter or his wife's hysterical break-down on hearing of her lover's intended departure to England. The votary of Mazzini and Garibaldi, of Gladstone and Disraeli, is shown as confronted for the first time in his life by something he doesn't comprehend. Comprehend he cannot, but this would never in him lead to indecision to which he is essentially a stranger. Surely a man like that would react vehemently, either with a complete forgiveness or with an equally total rejection. But Ray will have none of this, although he does appear to be driving towards the assertion that the 'public' life of action and politics (around which Bhupati's life and values have been so irrevocably built) is ultimately a fraud. If this was Ray's intention it is surely weakened by the twilight ambiguities of the end with its twin suggestions of imminent reconciliation but essential alienation. *Charulata* shows Ray's historical and political imagination at work, probing the gradually awakening mind of nineteenth century India by pitting the certainties of the 'public' mind against the agonies of the private heart. But because at the end it renounces historical objectivity in the interests of modern, if somewhat continental, dilemmas, it will remain in the Ray canon as his most splendid failure. Ray's *Kanchenjunga* (1962), which is very Chekovian in its structure, has also a rather ambiguous end, as Monisha's father shouts for help. It is unclear whether he has had a stroke, just as it is unclear what Monisha and Ashok will do at the end of the film. It is interesting to note that just before the end, the little Nepali boy who has been dogging the unlucky Banerjee like the Eumenides, breaks out into an incomprehensible song as he helps himself to the bar of chocolate that he has just been given by Banerjee. The lovely Himalayan peak hidden in mist all through the film emerges for a fleeting moment but is glimpsed by nobody except us in the audience, and Ray surely intends this as a major irony on the nature of happiness. Since the characters in *Kanchenjunga* are all shown in quest of happiness and peace, the unglimpsed peak serves as a fit comment on the elusive nature of happiness. The end is therefore completely justified, so delicately preserving the uncertainties of the characters. Each character is more or less left where he was at the beginning of the film.

Andrzej Munk's *Passenger* (1963) makes excellent use of the frozen shot to suggest ambiguity as Lisa, a former SS guard, catches a glimpse of Martha, a former political prisoner, on the gangway as the ship she is travelling on docks at Southampton. Munk unfortunately did not live to complete the film, but the rapidly changing expression on Lisa's face is captured by the camera in a series of frozen shots as she moves all the way from astonishment to a sudden doubt at the end about whether it is actually Martha she has seen. The end takes us to the beginning, and the circle is adroitly closed. We are left perfectly in the dark. Doubt of a very different kind is introduced at the end of Bunuel's *Viridiana* (1961). In the original ending of the film Virdiana enters the room where her cousin Jorge and Ramona are playing a game of cards, and it is apparent that the two have just made love. Quick to perceive the change in Viridiana (who looks haggard and bewildered), Jorge promptly dismisses Ramona from the room, but the maid spies from the keyhole. To appease the Spanish censor Bunuel changed the ending. In the revised ending of the film, Jorge does not send Ramona away, the three settling down to a game of cards to the accompaniment of a crude rock 'n' roll record (the use of popular music to heighten the irony at the end is also employed very effectively in Stanley Kubrick's *Dr Strangelove* [1963] where we see the huge mushroom cloud signifying the end of the world to the accompaniment of a sentimental song, 'When Johnny Comes Marching Home').

But ambiguity and the desire to be profound can often be the undoing of a film. The close of Fellini's *La Dolce Vita* (1960) is marred by ambiguity of a very unfortunate kind. The weakness in the structure of the film is glaring, as Lawson has pointed out, because it is not clear whether Fellini intended the film as a psychological study of Marcello or as a panorama of social corruption. The weakness of the

main structure is transmitted at the end to the denouement when
the guests at Nadia's all-night party gather round the enormous fish
on the beach which stares leadenly out of its dead eyes. Whatever
meaning we may attach to the episode, the entire burden of meaning
is not carried solely by it. There is another episode worked into this
last sequence when, quite suddenly, a young girl whom Marcello had
met earlier at a restaurant, calls to him across a sheet of water. Salvation
for Marcello seems tantalizingly near, but the wind obscures her words
and he walks away with another girl after a half-hearted attempt at
establishing communication. Fellini's own explanation of the end is
of interest. He tells us that it is 'a remembrance of childhood. I was
walking along the sea by Rimini in the early morning when I saw
that the sea had vomitted a monstrous fish.' We reach a new dimension
of ambiguity here when the personal biography of the creator becomes
necessary to explain the denouement. But Fellini is not content with
the fish and the sea, and he introduces the girl with the Mona Lisa
smile, thus compounding the ambiguity. A radical uncertainity on the
part of the creator is certainly responsible for the ambiguity at the
end. Fellini himself has confessed: 'I haven't found a solution myself
and I would consider myself finished if I had found it. *I don't have
any certainty or clarity myself*' (emphasis added).

I should like to close this examination of the nature of the denouement
in modern films with a final example from the third category of denouement. My example is Alain Resnais' *Last Year at Marienbad* (1961)
because the descent into uncertainty here seems as far as film art can
at present go. The relationship between A, M and X (merely the initials
of the principals are given in Robbe-Grillet's script, while the film
doesn't mention them at all), which forms the substance of the film,
receives the subtlest kind of treatment and the nature of the sex triangle,
forming the basis of the plot, is unlike any that we have been accustomed
to so far in films. In the final sequence of the film, as A and X enter
the formal garden adjoining the baroque hotel in which most of the
action of the film takes place, we hear X's voice:

It seemed at first glance, impossible to get lost here ... at first glance ... down
straight paths, between the statues with frozen gestures and the granite slabs,
where you were now already getting lost, forever, in the calm night, alone
with me.

One really doesn't know quite what to make of the last part of
the quotation: '...where you were now already getting lost, forever,

in the calm night, alone with me.' It defies grammar, our sense of before and after, and marks a radical departure from the concept of linear time which gave the denouement of the older type of film its mythic simplicity. In what way, one may ask, does this denouement fall within the scope of the definition quoted at the beginning of this essay? The answer is, frankly, that it doesn't, for we do not really know *what happened* in Marienbad and therefore we do not have any clue as to *why* it happened. The natural consequence of this is that we do not know if the denouement of *Marienbad* summarizes the preceding action or not. The tense employed by X is, intriguingly enough, the past tense and the speech, in asserting the pastness of *what happened,* cannot therefore be labelled as part of the denouement. Even the force of the 'now' in X's speech is weakened by the accompanying 'forever', but this destruction of the time sequence in the words hurls us forward into the implacable reality of the garden, towards that looming mass in the background with its friendly lights. And so we return to Kracauer's definition of the film quoted at the beginning of the essay — that the art of the cinema is the redemption of physical reality. Shall we say that because *Marienbad* appears to doubt the very existence of objective reality, it does not redeem reality but damns it? Or shall we rather say that because it forces us to question the reality of human relationships, it returns us even more irrevocably to that physical reality which Kracauer has described as its true domain? Is that not why the film is so meticulous about physical details? Kracauer himself has observed that the film should be edited in such a way as to go beyond the boundaries of the intrigue towards the realm of objects so that they appear in their 'suggestive indeterminacy'. 'Suggestive indeterminacy' is indeed the phrase we should employ in describing the twilight world of *Last Year at Marienbad.*

3

Western or Anti-Western?

The choice of films for the Western Retrospective at the Hyderabad Filmotsav (1986) makes one wonder if the Delhi Film Directorate knew what they were doing. For none of the nine films chosen belongs to the classic period of the Western which sent the likes of Robert Warshow and Andre Bazin into raptures. Starting with *Cat Ballou* (1965) and closing with *The Great Northfield Minnesota Raid* (1972) and *Rooster Coghburn* (1975), all eight films debunk the pretensions of the genre. Only Clint Eastwood's *High Plains Drifter* (1973) comes to us trailing clouds of glory as 'No Name' dispenses a kind of Old Testament justice in the infernal town which shamelessly watched its marshall die. John Ford's films were probably left out because the 1979 Delhi festival had a retrospective of his films, but how can you tell the story of the Western without that climatic gunfight at the OK Corrall told, oh, by so many of its countless votaries. And since John Wayne cannot be left out, was it not possible to have one of his better films — Hawks's *Rio Bravo* (1959) for instance rather than the dismal *Rooster Coghburn* (1975) where the once great Duke makes a campy fool of himself.

The truth is that, historically speaking, you simply can't tell the story of the Western by leaving out its dazzling youth and its sturdy young manhood. The particular segment of history that the early Westerns took in their stride was from about 1865 to about 1890 — to the period, you might say, when the West was really won. This twilight era was a truly momentous one; within its span we can tick off a number of frontiers in the sudden rush of mining camps, the building of railways, the Indian wars, the cattle drives and, of course, the great trauma of the Civil War itself. This is the era of those epic figures — Daniel Boone, Kit Carson and Buffalo Bill Cody — in whom the historian Henry Nash Smith has seen the agents who changed the desert face of America into a garden: an image that had dominated countless novels, political tracts, and popular magazine stories. The Western in the hands of people like John Ford celebrated America by elevating the contrasting images of Garden and Wilderness into the dimensions of a national myth. And so in *My Darling Clementine* (1946) a half-built church embodies the spirit of pioneer America. Moreover, that famous dance of Wyatt Earp and Clementine, marking the marriage ceremony, unites the best qualities of the civilizing East and the rugged West. It is one of the great moments of American cinema and has been the subject of as much scrutiny as anything in Welles or Eisenstein.

In his seminal essay 'The Evolution of the Western', Andre Bazin found even a film like *Clementine* an example of 'baroque embellishment' of the classicism of *Stagecoach* (1939) which he declared the archetypal Western. If one can borrow the terminology of Northrop Frye in his *Anatomy of Criticism*, we could say that by the 50s the Western was already working its way from the levels of myth and romance towards the ironic level which it eventually reached in the 70s. Westerns like *Clementine, High Noon* (1952) and *Shane* (1953), were in the high mimetic mode. The superhuman heroes of the earliest Western in the epic mode (which led Bazin to see the cowboy as a 'knight in arms') are superior both to other men and to their environment. In the high mimetic mode which followed in the 50s, the hero is still superior but subject to social criticism and natural law. In the low mimetic mode the hero is just one of us and, finally, in the ironic mode of, say, *Cat Ballou* (1965) the hero is inferior to ourselves and we look down at the absurdity of his drunken plight. So the Western, which, in its heyday, treated the Civil War with the epic splendour of the Trojan War, is today ridden with self-doubt and pitiless parody.

The Western has, indeed, come a long way from its early W.S. Hart, Bronco Billy Anderson, and Tom Mix days. The vogue for psychology turned it first Freudian, and then sociological, and, finally, in films like *Soldier Blue* (1970) and *Little Big Man* (1970), explicitly political. With a general decline in the belief in good and evil, the Western — in its classic form — was bound to give way to other alternate heroic types like, say, the secret agent and, of late, the space merchants of modern science fiction films. But the ironic mode of the 70s Westerns cannot be regarded as the elegy of the Western. The rise of the spaghetti

Westerns in the 60s and 70s (both in Italy and America) shows that everyone has grown tired of parodying the gunfighter and the ironic mode may give way to the mythic, and the Lone Ranger of old may ride again. Ayn Rand in a very perceptive essay 'Bootleg Romanticism' has argued that 'the failure to understand the nature and appeal of Romanticism is an eloquent measure of the modern intellectual's epistemological disintegration'. Those intellectuals at Delhi who chose these nine Westerns must be held similarly guilty of an inability to understand 'the nature and appeal of Romanticism'. And the people of Andhra Pradesh who, by choosing such a romantic hero as NTR as their Chief Minister showed how they understand, accept, and live by the appeal of Romanticism, cannot be expected to flock to their 'anti-Western' retrospective if ever there was one.

The Welles Charisma

Andre Bazin writes in the Foreword to his famous book on Welles: 'Orson Welles has made eight films with his right hand (*Kane, Ambersons,* the three Shakespeare adaptations, *Immortal Story, The Other Side of the Wind*) and films with his left hand (the thrillers). In the right-handed films there is always snow, and in the left-handed films there are always gunshots; but all constitute what Cocteau called the "poetry of cinematography".' It is difficult to fault this judgement except to observe that, as with Graham Greene who also wrote 'serious books' and 'entertainments' — the two categories sometimes overlap with startling results. Recent criticism has elevated *Touch of Evil* (1958) — apparently a thriller — to the status of a classic, and certainly Stephen Heath's 115-page shot-by-shot analysis of it has already become the starting point of the new semiotic analysis of cinema. But *Touch of Evil* — and I'm not thinking merely of the astonishing and virtuoso opening shot, surely the greatest crane-cum-tracking shot in the history of cinema — thematically also important for its central protagonist, Quinlan, is organically related to all the major creations of Welles. Following Robin Wood, one can abstract a master-pattern in the films of Welles on which individual films constitute interesting variations. All of Welles's films are constructed on a dominant relationship between a corrupt older man and a pure younger one, and the film moves towards the betrayal of the older man by the younger one, although the former is the locus of all the film's emotional energies and is invariably played by Welles himself. Of course, no film exemplifies this pattern exactly and point-to-point. For instance in *Citizen Kane* (1941) the two men are roughly the same age; in *Confidential Agent* (US title: *Mr Arkadin,* 1945 — a name inspired, we learn, from the actress Irina Arkadina in Chekhov's *The Seagull*), the younger man is far from pure in a story which seems a repeat of *Citizen Kane*; in *Lady From Shanghai* (1948) (which Bazin bracketed rather generously with *Kane* and *Ambersons* [1942] as fit to be carved on any 'Arch of Triumph celebrating the history of cinema'), Welles plays, for once (and unsuccessfully, too), the younger man, giving his usual role to Everett Sloane; in *Othello* (1952) the corruption and purity are reversed and, of course, in *Touch of Evil* (1958) the two men are not friends. The theme of betrayal is clearest in one of Welles's saddest testaments, *Chimes at Midnight* (1967) scripted by Welles from four Shakespearean plays. The film centres around the Falstaff—Hal relationship, the rejection of Falstaff in *Henry IV, Part II* being one of the most poignant sequences in Shakespeare. In Welles's film it is even more so than in Shakespeare, where the treatment is more ambiguous. The pattern underlies *The Immortal Story* (1969) (based on a novella by the late Baroness Karen Blixen whom Welles adored — if Kenneth Tynan is to be trusted — as much as Chou en-lai and Robert Graves) where the Wellesian hero (from Kane to Falstaff) is almost, inevitably, vanquished by his illusions. Welles failed with Kafka's *The Trial* (1963) because, as Truffaut has pointed out, the true domain of Welles is pride and dominance whereas Kafka is an archaeologist of weakness, humility, and submission. The larger-than-life Welles came a cropper with the smaller-than-life Kafka. Parenthetically one may note that Welles's world is strictly a homosexual one like that of Howard Hawks. Women have a very subordinate role in this world of power relations, and when they do appear at all, they are passive creatures outside the central grid of action.

   Citizen Kane — Welles's first film made when he was barely 26 — is generally acknowledged to be one of the masterpieces of world cinema (it has twice topped the *Sight and Sound* poll among international critics as the greatest film of all time — ahead of such champions as *Potemkin* and *Règle deu Jeu*). My remarks here will be confined to the structure of the film as the main *theme* of his film has already been dealt with.

   Told from the viewpoints of five different people, the movie uses the thread of the reporter Thompson's search for the meaning of Rosebud, Kane's dying words — to stitch the stories together. The sections are, for the most part, chronological and overlapping; with the exception of Thatcher, each narrator begins his story a little before his predecessors and carries it past the point from which the next narrator will begin. Some events — like Susan's rise and fall as an opera singer — are shown twice, but from different perspectives. The only objective viewpoint used in the film is the early 'News on the March' sequence which, in eight and a half minutes and 121 shots, summarizes Kane's entire life. It is like that extraordinary pillar in the temple at Belur in Karnataka — the whole of *Citizen Kane* in miniature.

The film's complexity arises from the narrators' conflicting judgements, their varying summations of Kane. Each sees a different side of Kane at a different stage of his life, yet each takes his estimate to be definitive. To Thatcher, Kane is an arrogant smart alec who becomes 'nothing more or less than a Communist'. Berstein's Kane is a man of high principles, with a sharp business sense and a love off the common man. Leland's Kane, only in love with himself, is a man of no convictions, a betrayer of the masses. Susan sees Kane as a selfish but pitiful old man. And Raymond's story of Kane as a lonely hermit betrays the cold detachment of his own nature. Each judgement leaves out something essential, and so the more we see of Kane the harder it becomes to judge him. Understanding goes beyond simple praise or reductive condemnation.

It is this complexity, from Welles to Godard, that is central to contemporary cinema and the secret of *Kane*'s own originality. A film that begins and ends with a NO TRESPASSING sign is really a warning to critics to beware of interpretation. Joseph McBride begins his section on *Kane* in his marvellous book on Welles with a quotation from Jose Luis Borges. *Citizen Kane*, observes Borges, is 'a labyrinth without a centre'. Truly, *Citizen Kane*, like Shakespeare's *Antony and Cleopatra*, is a critique of judgement.

5

Fassbinder: Breaking the Heart Without Betraying the Mind

As Siegfried Kracauer has shown in his seminal study of the German cinema, *From Caligari to Hitler*, 'melodrama need not strain realism of its inner weight as Stroheim's classic *Greed* (1924) demonstrated'. Pabst was the most distinguished practitioner of the 'Neue Sachlichkeit' ('new objectivity'), a term coined by Gustav Hartlaub, director of the Mannheim Museum. Pabst eschewed any romanticism because he felt 'real life is too romantic, too ghastly'. Fassbinder, too, is interested in creating a 'new realism' which is to come about 'through a collision between film and the subconscious'. It is this 'new realism' that can act as a catalyst of social change. What this means is that Fassbinder is a Marxist, but of the non-dogmatic type. He has no use for Eisenstein. Making the masses into an epic hero, as the great Russian did, does not break with the epic—heroic mode and has the further disadvantage of devaluing the individual.

As an artist, Fassbinder is primarily interested in the individual. Not in the great, the distinguished (*Petra* [1972] and *Maria Braun* [1978] being the exceptions here), but in the castaways of society, those who don't make it and are outside the pale of the German 'economic miracle'. All his principal characters reach the point of no return in their lives and are plunged into a bottomless despair. There is the ageing Petra ruled imperiously by Karin reaching the very nadir of nothingness in *The Bitter Tears of Petra von Kant*; Hans in *The Peddler of Four Seasons* (1969) drowned in drink and self-destruction; Emmy and her Moroccan lover in *Fear Eats the Soul* (1974), hounded by an unfriendly and hostile society. Every one of these characters reaches the end of his/her spiritual tether.

Despair is indeed Fassbinder's forte, his stock-in-trade. He has himself said that 'the only thing I can accept is despair'. And so most of his films are depressing but only, as he has said in an interview in *Time*, 'to fulfil the principle of hope'. The endings of *Petra von Kant* and *Peddler of Four Seasons* are full of despair but not so the end of *Fear Eats the Soul* where there are only hints of disintegration. *Maria Braun* which ends on the accidental explosion that kills Maria is quite simply numbing as is the grim suicide of the transsexual Erwin-Elvira at the end of Fassbinder's *In a Year with Thirteen Moons* (1978). All are victims of an unattainable love which seems to be the sole refuge of the embattled individual, where, as Matthew Arnold has said, 'ignorant armies clash by night'. Even the terrorist and bomb specialist Walsch, in the nightmare world of the *The Third Generation* (1979), is mowed down by police bullets as he grieves inconsolably at the death of his love who has taken her life in despair.

To achieve this heightened realism, Fassbinder bombards the spectator with a torrential sound-track. His denouements are, among other things, epics of sound. The screaming commentary of a World Cup final where Germany are world champions crowns the climactic scene of *Maria Braun*, as Maria seems at long last so close to her happiness with her Hermann. In *Third Generation* (1979) the dialogue seems to be engaged in a losing battle with the sound from an insistent television set. In *Maria Braun*, even the innocent click-clack of a typewriter assumes menacing proportions as Maria quietly reduces to tears Oswald's terrified secretary. Erwin-Elvira's long abrasive monologue in *Thirteen Moons* is punctuated fiercely by the bleeding of freshly-killed bulls in a slaughter-house. The ascendancy of mute objects or sound *per se* is, arguably, an indicator of irrational powers and authoritarian forces, but whether Fassbinder's films are symptomatic of such forces in present-day Germany we must leave to the sociologists of the cinema. If they can be shown to be so — and one thinks of the Bader-Meinhoff — Fassbinder's films would join the distinguished company of Fritz Lang's *Mabuse* (1922) and *M* (1931) as a mirror of the times.

When the Young German Cinema was born some ten years ago, the excitement matched the enthusiasm with which the world greeted the Golden Age of Murnau, Lang, Pabst, et al. in the years before Hitler. Alexander Kluge appears to have faded out after his sole master-piece *Artists at the Top of the Big Top: Disoriented* (1968), and of the early group Herzog alone seems to have vitality. But his *Nosferatu* (1979) seemed to derive its inspiration wholly from Murnau's silent classic (it had the blessings, too, of Lotte Eisner, the German film historian, to see whom Herzog is reported to have walked 600 miles from Munich to Paris where Eisner was lying ill in hospital).

Both Satyajit Ray and Youssef Chahine told me they found it inferior to the Murnau original. Of the other great German film — makers of the present, perhaps Straub alone is Fassbinder's peer. But between Straub's hermetic formalism and Herzog's beleaguered humanism, Fassbinder alone seems to have found a way 'to break the heart without betraying the mind' (in Andrew Sarris's arresting phrase). His vigorous, 'melodramatic' cinema is made in the best traditions of Hollywood and hence occupies the middle ground between art and commerce, between the mandarins and the masses, and achieves the near impossible mix of ideology and humanism.

The frequency of suicide in Fassbinder's films now seems — after his own tragic suicide from a mixture of drugs and alcohol on 10 June 1988 — not just morbid but eerily prophetic. It looks as if he was quietly foretelling his own grim end. Kenneth Tynan once observed that men of the Left tended to love their mothers while those of the Right were closer to their fathers. If this is true, then Fassbinder's desperate longing for love and affection in all his films should leave us in little doubt about his political leanings. Yet Fassbinder was not a political man in the conventional sense. He once said: 'No man who thinks according to an ideology that comes outside himself can like my films.' His dream of making a film 'beautiful and extravagant and fantastic and nevertheless able to go against the existing order' remains still largely unrealized. Unrealizable too, because it involves the impossible union of art and commerce.

Querelle : Fassbinder's swan song

The interest of *Querelle* (1982) for the student of Fassbinder is twofold. First, it is the last film he made before his own tragic suicide on 10 June 1988. Secondly, it is based on a novel by Jean Genet and hence raises all the old questions of the relation between literature and film. Fassbinder himself has observed: 'The cinematic transformation of a literary work should never assume that its purpose is simply the maximum realization of the images which literature evokes in the minds of its readers ... Any attempt to turn a film into a substitute for a piece of literature must inevitably result in a compound fantasy based on the lowest common denominator and will therefore, by definition be a mediocre and lifeless product.'

Querelle's story, sketchily told, looks on the surface the most third-rate kind of story of a criminal imaginable. Querelle, a sailor, disembarks at Brest, smuggles opium with the help of a fellow sailor, Vic, and later murders him. He puts the blame on Gil who is eventually hanged for the crime. But the film — Fassbinder's swan song — is really a film about love. The original screenplay by Fassbinder himself has a title card carrying a quote from Plutarch's treatise 'On Love'. The eponymous hero of the film is a murderer where murder is the ultimate metaphor for isolation. He is the object of love for several of the film's characters — Nono (the brothel-keeper), Mario (the cop), Lysiane (Nono's wife, played by the great Jeanne Moreau) and, most of all, Lt. Seblon (played by Franco Nero). But Querelle himself is basically a Narcissus figure, initially incapable of love. Towards the end he does move from being a passive object of love to an active lover of the Polack, Gil Turko. But — to my mind at any rate — he is so damned a soul that he betrays his love to Inspector Mario. The celebrated line of Oscar Wilde's *The Ballad of Reading Gaol* ('Each man kills the things he loves') comes at once to mind. For that, too, was a story, like *Querelle*, of doomed homosexual love. The art direction by Rolf Zebetbauer — who has created some fascinating surrealistic sets — is outstanding.

6

Bergman's Swan Song

I want to be one of the artists of the cathedral that stands above the plains.
Bergman, *Cahiers du Cinema*

Probably no European film-maker is so widely and universally admired as Bergman. It is true that Godard has a more fashionable following — but Bergman, like the salesman in Arthur Miller's famous play, is not only liked but 'well-liked'. The reasons are varied. Bergman has that cold, northern Protestant seriousness that is so congenial to the Indian temperament. When *Wild Strawberries* (1957) was first shown here in the 60s, everyone was rapturous about its arcane symbolism: that faceless corpse, that clock without hands, and that heavy silence all seemed at once to speak to our Freudian unconscious.

The *Seventh Seal* (1957) had a less universal appeal with its setting in the Middle Ages, but still its influence on Indian cinema was considerable. Few probably know that it was a viewing of that film in England that inspired U.R. Anantha Murthy to write his celebrated *Samskara*. Even the Pattabhi film (based on the novel) owes its opening — with the vultures hovering in the sky — to it. And *The Virgin Spring* (1959) sealed Bergman's early reputation here with its gruesome rape and its healing miracle at the end. The middle period Bergman has not had quite the same impact, being smothered in the miasmas of cultish film society viewings. But *An Autumn Sonata* (1978) stoked the dull embers, and *Fanny and Alexander* (1983) burst into a consuming flame. It was a fitting swan song for the Swedish master whom even the pernickety John Simon had described as 'the greatest film-maker the world has seen so far'.

Ernst Ingmar Bergman was born at Uppsala, about 50 miles north-west

of Stockholm, on 14 July 1918. The son of a Lutheran clergyman,
Bergman grew up in a very claustrophobic setting. A Swedish critic,
Marianne Hook, in her book-length study of Bergman, has brought
out the reservation-like character of Bergman's childhood home: 'An
island in a secularized society, a reservation where a more or less conscious
wish to preserve an earlier generation's ideals and customs accentuates
the antagonism to the outside world and increases the demands of
those who belong within this milieu.' All this probably accounts for
Bergman's lack of flexibility and temper tantrums. 'His exasperating
allergies,' observes the Black American novelist James Baldwin, 'extended
to such things as refusing to work with a carpenter, say, to whom
he had never spoken but whose face he disliked. He has been known,
upon finding guests at his home, to hide himself in the bathroom
until they left.'

Bergman himself has testified in a *Cahiers* essay to the influence
of his upbringing on his later thought: 'Anyone who, like myself, was
born in the family of a pastor, learns at an early age to look behind
the scenes in life and death. Whenever Father has a burial, a marriage,
a baptism, a mediation, he writes a sermon. You make an early acquaintance with the devil and, like all children, you need to give him
a concrete form.' It was the cinematic rendering of the devil in
'concrete form' that was to be one of Bergman's outstanding achieve-
ments in cinema.

Bergman spent much of his childhood in the University town of
Uppsala, staying with a widowed grandmother in a huge 14-room
apartment which was left unchanged as it had been in 1890 when
his grandmother had first come there as a bride. Bergman's only other
companion in the house was an old servant, full of tales of fantasy
and country yarns . He acquired his first cinematograph from his older
brother during Christmas, when he was nine or ten years old. He
exchanged this for half his army of tin soldiers, although he was well
aware that in future he would lose all his battles to his brother. His
formative years as an artist coincided with the emergence of a new
generation of Swedish writers known as the 'fortyists', who, drawing
their inspiration from such writers as Kafka, Sartre, and Camus, produced
a credo of pessimism and despair. Little wonder then that Bergman's
early work looks so heavy, difficult, and deterministic — 'a riddle
without a sphinx' in William Pechter's telling phrase. Particularly, the
concept of a silent and unreciprocating God — of God as need but
not as fulfilment in his films upto, say, *Winter Light* (1963) — appears

to have been clearly derived from Kafka. Strindberg, too, was a lasting influence. 'In my own life,' he writes in the Preface to *Four Screenplays of Ingmar Bergman*, 'my great literary experience was Strindberg ... And it is my dream to produce "A Dream Play" some day. Olaf Molander's production of it in 1934 was for me a fundamental dramatic experience.'

The year 1944 was a turning point in Bergman's life. He did the script for *Torment* which was made into a film by the leading film production company in Sweden — the Svenska Filmindustri — and he was appointed director of the City Theater in Halsingborg. During the next 11 years he directed seven of his own plays on stage, but by 1955 he stopped writing plays. His first film was *Crisis* in 1945, but it was not as well received as *Torment*. His most notable early film is perhaps *Prison* (1949) — mistitled in America as *The Devil's Wanton* — made when Bergman was 30. The film-within-a-film device used here appears again in the Prologue to one of Bergman's later masterpieces *Persona* (1966). Bergman became director of the prestigious theatre at Malmo after the success of his film *Summer Interlude* (1951), and it was here that he assembled the great team of actors and actresses — Harriet Andersson, Bibi Andersson, Ingrid Thulin, and Max Van Sydow. During his tenure at Malmo, Bergman directed 11 films in addition to his formal duties as theatre director. This was the great decade that produced *The Seventh Seal* (1957) and *Wild Strawberries* (1957). In 1959 Bergman left Malmo to accept the directorship of the Royal Dramatic Theatre in Stockholm. In 1966 he resigned his post to devote more time to films.

There is no doubt that Bergman will be best remembered for the remarkable films of his middle period beginning with *The Seventh Seal*. Not surprisingly, these films all deal, in their different ways, with questions of faith. This did produce some extraordinary films — particularly *Winter Light* (1963) which many regard as Bergman's greatest film (it appears in Pauline Kael's list of all-time greats) — but the attendant desire to make the 'perfect film' did not always produce happy results. Bergman has himself confessed that 'the enormous desire to make the best film in the world' was behind the making of such films like *Through a Glass Darkly* (1961) and *Winter Light*, and it is only when he gave up the ambition 'to make the perfect creation' that he became (as he told Charles Thomas Samuels in 1971) 'un-neurotic'. The period beginning with *Persona* (1966) led to an altogether different kind of film from the early period. Jung took the place of

Freud in Bergman's new exploration of personality and interpersonal man—woman relationships. This led to the now famous 'marriage scenarios' — *Scenes From a Marriage* (1973), *Face to Face* (1975), and the incomparable *An Autumn Sonata* (1978), featuring that other illustrious Bergman — Ingrid Bergman.

Fanny and Alexander (1983) is unlike the marriage scenarios — less intense, apparently more diffuse, but, actually a reprise of all the famous Bergman themes. 'The sum total of my life as a film-maker', is how Bergman himself has described it. *Fanny And Alexander*, set around the turn of the century, begins on a deceptively joyous note as the Ekdahl clan come together to celebrate Christmas. Of Helena Ekdahl's three sons, Oskar is the actor married to Emilie — also an actress — and it is their children, Fanny and Alexander, who give the film its title. Gustave, the second son, is a garrulous restauranteur, used to the good things of life, which include, of course, Helena's accommodating and willing maid, Maj. And, finally, Carl is the failed professor whose wife, the German-born Lydia, cannot speak Swedish after twenty years in the country. Carl's own speciality is flatulence on demand, a demonstration of which one gets quite early in the film. Bergman's published screenplay is positively hilarious in describing the performance which occurs during the course of the Christmas dinner which climaxes the film's joyous opening:

Professor Carl Ekdahl attracts Alexander's attention. He is red in the face and sweating copiously; his blue eyes are bleary and slightly squinting behind the gold-rimmed pince-nez. Alexander signals to Fanny and Jenny, who are rather tipsy from lemonade and Christmas excitement. The professor rises carefully from the table, excusing himself with a bow, and vanishes round the corner of the serving passage. Alexander, Fanny and Jenny sneak after him unnoticed, following close on Uncle Carl's heels with expectant faces. Now they have reached the hall. Professor Ekdahl has a lighted candle in each hand and he gives them to Fanny and Jenny. Soundless he opens the door to the wide, echoing staircase with ceiling paintings and sportive cupids, red carpets and brass fittings, marble-clad walls and window mosaics.

Uncle Carl makes hushing movements. A trifle shyly he loosens his braces and unbuttons his trousers and under-pants. The children's faces are pale with expectation. Professor Ekdahl bends forward, grasps the banisters, and grunts violently. As if by a miracle, a series of deep organ tones rise from Uncle Carl's fat bottom, ending in a clap of thunder. Fanny and Jenny hold their lighted candles close to the Professor's behind. A moment of tension. Then loud gunfire booms through the Ekdahls' staircase. The candle flames flicker and go out.

A passage — and a situation — worthy of Rabelais himself! But this is Bergman land, and dark, sinister shadows soon envelop the Ekdahls. And Death — like a perfect Swedish gentleman — arrives quietly to claim Oskar, leaving his wife, Emilie, disconsolate and vulnerable. One of the most disturbing scenes in the film occurs on the night of Oskar's death as Fanny and Alexander tiptoe to the room where they espy, through a half-open door, their mother hysterically weeping beside their father's coffin. Momentarily, as it were, we are plunged into the terrifying world of *Cries and Whispers* (1972).

The gloom and the ugliness persist through Emilie's second marriage to that cold monster of a man, Edvard Vergerus, the officiating bishop at Oskar's funeral. Rescue comes mysteriously through Isak (a Jew who was once Helena's lover), who smuggles the children out of the bishop's household in an absolutely fairy-tale sequence. Edvard, himself, is given a terrible — almost Biblical — death as he is engulfed in flames when his obese and bedridden aunt — the forbidding Elsa — rushes into his room at night, her clothes a moving ball of fire.

But soon joy returns to the Ekdahl household by the end of the film with the birth of Emilie's child and Gustave's illegitimate child with Maj, the maid. The film which began in winter gloom ends as summer is in full bloom. The officiating clergyman is bribed by Gustave into shutting his eyes over the dubious lineage of Maj's child. Helena herself sums up the summer mood of joy as she reads from Strindberg — Bergman's lifelong admiration — 'Anything can happen, anything is possible and likely. Time and space do not exist. On flimsy ground of reality imagination spins out and weaves new patterns ...' Isn't this the Shakespearean sunset world of *The Tempest*? Don't we hear the Prospero strains of 'Our revels now are ended...'? Only there is an ironic twist at the end. Through Prospero's famous speech at the end, Shakespeare is definitely taking leave of the theatre. Perhaps Bergman, too, is doing the same (although there are rumours of his return, and he has already done a television play) with the difference that at the end of the film the ageing former actress, Helena Ekdahl, is contemplating a return to the stage!

Filmography

As screenwriter — 1944: *Torment/Frenzy*; 1947: *Woman Without a Face* 1948: *Eva* (story, co-sc.); 1950: *While the City Sleeps* (synopsis only); 1951:

Divorced (story, co-sc.); **1956**: *The Last Couple Out* (story, co-sc.); **1961**: *Pleasure Garden* (co-sc.).

As director-screenwriter — **1945**: *Crisis*; **1946**: *It Rains on Our Love*; **1947**: *The Land of Desire/A Ship to India/Frustration*; **1948**: *Night is My Future, Port of Call*; **1949**: *The Devil's Wanton/Prison, Three Strange Loves/Thirst*; **1950**: *To Joy. High Tension/This Can't Happen Here*; **1951**: *Illicit Interlude Summer Interlude*; **1952**: *Secrets of Women/Waiting Women*; **1953**: *Monika/Summer With Monika. The Naked Night/Sawdust and Tinsel*; **1954**: *A Lesson in Love*; **1955**: *Dreams/Journey Into Autumn: Smiles of a Summer Night*; **1957**: *The Seventh Seal, Wild Strawberries*; **1958**: *Brink of Life/So Close to Life, The Magician/The Face*; **1960**: *The Virgin Spring. The Devil's Eye*; **1961**: *Through a Glass Darkly*; **1963**: *Winter Light/The Communicants, The Silence*; **1964**: *All These Women/Now About These Women*; **1966**: *Persona* ; **1967**: *Stimulantia* ('Daniel' episode; also phot.); **1968**: *Hour of The Wolf. Shame/The Shame*; **1969**: *The Ritual/The Rite* (originally made for TV), *The Passion of Anna/Passion*; **1970**: *The Faro Documentary* (doc.); **1971**: *The Touch* (Swl.US); **1972**: *Cries and Whispers*; **1973** : *Scenes From A Marriage* (originally a TV series); **1974**: *The Magic Flute*; **1976**: *Face to Face* **1978**: *The Serpent's Egg* (Ger./US), *An Autumn Sonata* (UK/Norw.); **1983**: *Fanny And Alexander*.

7

Michelangelo Antonioni, *Blow-up* (1966)

Pauline Kael in reviewing *Blow-Up* in *The New Republic* describes the expressionist finale of the film, the mimed tennis match, as one of those 'fancy finishes' that seem to say much without really meaning anything precisely. Fancy it may be, but this is not to deny that it says anything. It is into the nature of what it says that we will have to look before any final evaluation of the film can be made.

Let us go back to the mime group. In the very opening sequence of the film, after a brief shot of a tall, modern structure, we are introduced to the group who, in their jeep, go round and round a deserted closed-in thoroughfare, waving frantically at a nonexistent audience. They get off the jeep and swarm through a sidewalk, brushing past the guard on duty and two nuns walking in the opposite direction. They encounter Thomas returning from an all-night session of photography and he gives them some money. It is fairly early in the morning. Exactly twenty-four hours later (and this shows how strictly the Aristotelian unities have been adhered to), Thomas meets the same mime group at dawn in the fatal park, and here again they repeat their lunatic circle round the asphalt track before they stop, apparently on seeing Thomas. Then follows the mimed tennis game that ends with Thomas throwing back the imaginary ball, and he hears, and we hear, the click-clack of the game in progress. The question to be asked here is: Has the second and latter Thomas lost his hold on objective reality or not?

The current critical orthodoxy on the film says he does. Thus Robin Wood in his book on Antonioni argues that the final park scene is the decisive point in the film. Thomas retrieving the ball, it is argued, marks his final surrender and his subsequent hallucination of the sound of a tennis ball hit by a racket points to the total breakdown of his grasp of objective reality. This Thomas ceases to be a 'photographer' and joins the legions of the damned souls watching through the wire-netting, the imaginary tennis match. This view is certainly plausible and Wood makes out a very able case for it. But the theory does not wholly fit the facts. For it can be shown that even before this scene Thomas was never very secure in his grasp on reality. Consider his reactions after he has seen the corpse in the park for the first time. He hears a noise that oddly disturbs him, and hereabouts he seems very unsure of himself. He returns to the studio, touches the tip of the propellor to reassure himself of the reality of objects, goes home and stares at himself in the mirror, and even the bells which he jogs accidentally startle him. He goes out to see his friend Ron and across the street from his parked car he sees Vanessa Redgrave, but in a beautifully photographed sequence she mysteriously vanishes. Is not his hold on reality already weakened here, we may ask, long before the disappearance of the corpse and the hallucinated tennis ball?

We can push this line of thinking even further back if we want. Take that first long scene with Vanessa Redgrave in the studio. When the phone rings he is momentarily quite paralysed and then impulsively dives across the room and gives the receiver to her. He first says it is from his wife, and then modifies this remark: it is someone he lives with. They just have kids, he says, and quickly withdraws even this. Not even kids, he says, it just feels as if they have kids. He then describes his mistress as not beautiful but just easy to live with. Then: she is not easy to live with, that is why he doesn't live with her. What are we to make of all this? Does it not point to the very thin line that divides reality from illusion for Thomas? Did this man have to wait for the case of the vanished corpse before he throws up?

We can see how this line of thinking would seriously imperil the Wood hypothesis, that Thomas loses his hold on reality only at the end. Perhaps Thomas had no hold on reality to start with. Remember his remark to Vanessa Redgrave in the park: 'There are other things I want in the real.' The same Thomas remarks to a shaken Vanessa later: 'There is nothing like a disaster to sort things out.' This Thomas is unhappy, disillusioned, 'fed up with the bitches', the homosexuals and the queers; it is this Thomas who wants to leave London because 'it does not do anything' for him, who wants a lot of money to be free even if he has no clear conception of the kind of freedom he wants. This Thomas it is who goes to take photographs in the park, finding it peaceful, suddenly comes upon reality, a murder, a death, and at once his well-ordered, carefully constructed but nevertheless illusory world collapses. He had lived from day-to-day, a Tuesday following a Monday, without a moment to pause, to reflect. As he tells the teenage girls who want just two minutes: 'If I had two minutes, I could have my appendix out.' In this scene also the connection is made between time and money, which are, for a worldly person, interchangeable quantities: time *is* money. Thomas is shown sliding a coin on his knuckles, and he tosses it carelessly aside as he tells the girls about how busy he is. He has had early in the day (and also in the film) two strenuous photographic sessions with his models, and we also know that he spent the previous night photographing in a doss-house. He negotiates the purchase of an antique shop and, in between negotiations, goes to the park and has his rendezvous with Destiny. The walls of his secure if unreal world cave in and he has his moment of truth.

We should remember that it is not at once that he discovers the truth. At one moment he actually thinks he has saved a life, and it is only after the romp with the teenage girls (a very unsatisfactory sequence, if I may say so) that he discovers the corpse in the picture. So it is death that awakens him to reality and to the world around him. It is a sadder and a wiser Thomas who watches Sarah Miles make love without any involvement. His whole demeanour in the following scene with her shows him vulnerable, sensitive, sceptical, and alive to the sufferings of others. Contrast this scene with his earlier scene with her which shows him narcisstically self-indulgent, wanting to be pampered by others. We have indeed a new Thomas, and his reactions at the discothèque and the pot party merely confirm the birth of this new Thomas. Ron, with his 'What did you see in the park?' is what Thomas was before his world crumbled. He is alone with the truth now. He goes to the park to confirm his truth and finds that the corpse has gone.

The fact that the corpse has disappeared meanwhile does not, on the view taken here, materially alter the nature of the truth that Thomas has experienced. Nothing happens to Thomas in this scene which has not already happened. It only confirms him in his isolation and saddles him with the responsibility for creating and maintaining the illusion of reality. The return of the mime group at the end is thus chiefly therapeutic. The tennis match they mime is for Thomas's benefit: it is a version of group therapy. Thomas is *instructed* by the group on how to play the game. It is a game of tennis, it could be the game of life. Life may ultimately be illusion, but it is real in so far as we make it so, Antonioni seems to say, like so many thinkers and poets before him. The American poetess Marianne Moore once spoke of real toads in imaginary gardens, and likewise the tennis at the end may be real tennis in an imaginary world — or as it appears to us, unreal tennis in a real world. Thomas's disappearance before the credits at the end parallel the disappearance of the corpse: both are unreal, if you like, only if you have already specified and defined a standard for reality. This, the film shows to be an impossibility. And in this Antonioni seems to have lined up with existentialists like Camus and Sartre in underlining paradoxically the impossibility of objective knowledge but the recurring necessity of living. It is in this climate of gloom, in this dawn without hope, this twilight mood of the permanent possibility of existence but its equally permanent elusiveness, that the mime group invites not only Thomas but us, too, in the audience to play the game of life.

8

Costa-Gavras, *Z* (1969)

There is a sequence towards the end of *Z* when a carpenter (a friendly witness, so to speak) is in hospital with an ice pack on his head. His injuries are inconsequential and he is clearly a comic turn in the great tradition of French masters like Harry Baur or the incomparable Raimu. But what is he doing in this film? The entire ward with its innumerable beds is mysteriously empty and there is not a single doctor or nurse in sight.

However, there are visitors galore: a sobbing, loving mother, a raging mini-skirted sister, the General with his squeaking calf leather shoes, the Colonel, the Magistrate, his Assistant, and, of course, the ubiquitous photographer. Each of these scenes is played for laughs while the poor plot languishes outside in the cold. The audience which had come to jeer, rage, and fume at Rightist paranoia, CIA meddling and at the brave, handsome Deputy (Yves Montand), in his immaculate brown suit, being struck down by hoodlums is slavering now for a bit of the good old box office entertainment. And, of course, Costa-Gavras is not going to refuse them a little fun, just a little fun, you understand. The plot, creaking now from rust and disuse, doesn't really recover from this farcical interlude, whose traces are found even later, in the treatment of the indictment of the top brass (which ought to have been the film's moral fulcrum). But, meanwhile, see how they run down that predictable corridor! More laughs. And then that cartoon summary at the end ('The Trial', a caption reads and the screen expands to reveal a sketch of watching heads) till the final trick is turned.

Now that slimy muckraker of a photographer — with his fast wisecracks, his smooth line with women, and his Nikon — has his come-uppance. The audiences laughs in superior, knowing amusement.

And so the seeming triumph of Justice sputters out into the triumph of reaction *and we don't give a damn*! Our response is one of lazy acceptance rather than anguish or rage. And then that witty rag-bag of things and oddments and authors that your true-blue Leftist will no doubt welcome and nurture in his Utopia — never mind what China and Cuba and the USSR actually did historically — further dulls the edge of anger and *Z* is over. Not *he*, then but *she* — as William James called the Bitch Goddess — lives.

The trouble is that, like so many of us, Costa-Gavras (whose father fought on the EAM or the losing side of the Greek Civil War) grew up with a fondness for American gangster movies of the thirties and forties, and it is difficult for him now to shake off that old love while attempting at the same time to hate US imperialism. This is the paradox of the Leftist film-maker today who is anxious to carry his audience along with him emotionally as well as politically. But these very same techniques could be used by a Fascist film-maker against the Left or Centre, and certainly this has been done in innumerable Hollywood films like *The Green Berets* (1968) and others of the same ilk. Ironically, it is these very techniques, employing an abrasive pace, fast staccato cutting with mini flashbacks and the overall percussive rhythms of the music score verily drenching the soundtrack (the music composed by Mikos Theodorakis — one of the folk heroes of the Greek Resistance — is very, very effective), that numb the senses so thoroughly that we hardly know what is happening to us on this particular 'trip'.

For instance, why do the police want to get rid of the Yves Montand character? We know only from the wall posters what his speech is all about, but amidst the raucous blare of the loudspeaker we hardly hear the speech of Superman. Olympic champion at 20, liked by his students, loved by the women (a bosomy young blond with a peace button pinned on her billowing sweater literally drinks him in hungrily as he begins his faltering speech), he is the hope of the Opposition. Saviour and Redeemer, an all-but-God figure, his arrival on the Olympus airline is heralded by tumultous musical chords — a veritable choir of the angels. He shakes hands with a passing porter (wouldn't a fascist demagogue have done likewise?) and as Faithful await him in the lounge, three scrawny teenagers gawk at him with bated breath. And, now, scorning the Secretary's suggestion that they lunch first, he asks to be driven to the office of the Director of Security to get clearance for the hall. They draw a blank there but he is unflappable. Alighting from the car a bit later, he is momentarily distracted by an attractive shop assistant who is fixing the wig on a mannequin. He is reminded of his young mistress back home who, too,wears a blond wig. Ah, *mon cherie*! Time, now, to look into the draft of his speech which, like other unheard melodies, must be presumed to be sweeter than the usual heard ones. But not before getting on the line to *mon cherie*. Who else? Bears need to eat before they dance, he now confides cosily to the lawyer Deputy as he goes in for that delayed lunch in a friskily bearish mood. He is pretty hungry now.

Is he a communist? No, of course not! He is an ex-Olympic champion, that is what he is, the man with the brave and fighting heart which the doctors apostrophize three times in ten minutes. Is that carpenter a communist? No, of course not! He hates politics and loves pears. Also wants to get his picture in the papers. Is the Examining Magistrate a communist, then? For why else is he bringing down the whole rotten structure? No, we regret to inform you, he is not a communist. If you really want to know, his father was a Colonel in the National Police. We are shown the extreme Right all right, but where is the bloody Left? The communists are, as a matter of fact, nowhere in sight! It is merely the paranoid Right that has created them. Of course the Russians are there with their famed Bolshoi. Thank God, they haven't been able to change that, says the rabbit-faced Public Prosecutor to his lovely young wife after opening night. The Public Prosecutor has been reading the History of the Paris Commune. Still, he is not a Communist either or even a fellow traveller. He is a 100 per cent bourgeois with his tastefully decorated house hung with wall paintings of the great tenth-century masters. He has his little jokes about the Chinks and the kamikaze, but damn it, he is human after all! If you really want to meet the boors in Government, come this way please. Meet the General of the National Police who can twist and turn the evidence at will and whose only response to the news of the Deputy's death is a matter of suitable terminology to couch it in. He is terrible indeed in his opening speech (a brilliantly edited sequence set off by the *tabla*) about the sunspots of socialism and anarchism, a proof that even God refused His light to these movements! He can hardly breathe in the stark, scholarly study of the Examining Magistrate, this man of God. He waves cheerfully to the busload of the Bolshoi girls while at the same time despising the Bolshoi as degenerate. On top of it all, he is a rabid anti-Semite whose attitude to the lawyer Deputy is of a piece with his attitude to the Dreyfus case.

The good people are unbelievably good and the bad people un-

believably bad: one of the killers is actually called Iago! The Examining
Magistrate doesn't smoke, drinks only orange juice, and is thoroughly
unflappable while ferretting out the truth, whereas one of the hired
assassins is a leering homosexual who'd make a pass at anything in
pants. When the demonstration is in full swing he looks adoringly
at an athletic-looking young man leaning over in the balcony. This
shocks even Iago who exclaims: 'By God, that is all you think about?'
And two passes later, we learn that he was once nabbed for rape which
momentarily puzzles the Magistrate, 'You?' he quizzes. During the early
mêlée he kicks at women brutally but he too, in time, becomes a
comic turn as the film lurches helplessly towards farce. (Orson Welles
once remarked that since Shakespeare all tragedy in the West had
become inseparable from melodrama. Perhaps we should modify this
to read that all melodrama today ends up as farce.)

If the assassin becomes a comic turn, what about the victim's wife?
She is Irene Papas in all her resplendent glory who, too, like her late
(if not exactly lamented as we shall see) husband is heralded into town
in a beautiful overhead shot to the same celestial background score
that welcomed him. What is eating her up is not so much Montand's
critical condition in hospital, as tormenting images of that nubile young
brunette in her husband's consulting room about to unbutton her
blouse. We are told by Montand himself that he doesn't see his children,
that he and his wife have not aged together in the same way, but
that 'this does not alter the essentials'. But there is an unmistakable
look of alarm on Irene Papas's face twice in the flashbacks. Do Montand
and Papas have, after all, a different set of 'essentials'? She doesn't
entirely break down after his death, but merely walks distractedly about
the room, sniffing his aftershave lotion, before retiring to the peace
of the blue Mediterranean. How does all this add up to an understanding
of Montand, his marriage, and the Cause for which he dies a martyr.
We are not meant to ask such questions, but merely respond to the
frequent changes of scene.

For instance, how does our martyr—hero not survive the solitary
blow from a speeding kamikaze while the other two Deputies outlive
an infinitely worse clobbering from stationary positions? Why, because
he is the Christ-figure who has to die once more in order to live
in the hearts and minds of the Faithful. In thus apparently reversing
the practice in commercial films where the hero is indestructible, *Z*
still remains faithful to the origins of its inspiration. For it is as slave-
bound to the unwritten laws of commercial cinema as is any *Sholay*

(1975). It worships not the Cause (as all progressive cinema should) but the Star (Yves Montand) and pays proper homage to the Star System by elevating the Star to its title (Z— 'He lives'). But his tinsel martyrdom is nothing compared to the fearless and tireless pursuit of truth of the Examining Magistrate. Isn't this what we really should applaud in the film? It is the self-effacing Magistrate rather than the philandering ex-Olympian who is worthy of our respect and admiration. It is he who lives or ought to live in our memories. But the film-maker decrees otherwise. Perhaps we in our country who have witnessed the apotheosis of Sanjay Gandhi and the virtual oblivion of his impeacher, Justice Shah, shouldn't in the least be surprised at this tragic eclipse of justice in art as well as in life. The King is dead! Long live the Queen!

9

Milos Foreman, *One Flew Over the Cuckoo's Nest* (1975)

There is a scene towards the end of *One Flew Over the Cuckoo's Nest* that is crucial to an understanding of the film. Billy Bibbit, a sexually starved young man cursed with a terrible stammer, has had his first woman — the delectable Candy — thanks to the imaginatively compassionate McMurphy who puts off his own escape from Ward 34-B to infuse hope and life into the starry-eyed, if spineless, Billy.

Comes the morning and the sinister Ratched enters the ward to find it in a shambles. A search reveals the missing Billy, soporifically happy in the arms of the still delectable Candy. In the ensuing interrogation, Billy is initially full of an unaccustomed aplomb, and even the stammer is momentarily gone. But when the terrible Ratched threatens to tell his mother who happens to be her friend, his stammer returns and he breaks down hysterically. Left alone in a room temporarily, he commits suicide.

What makes the episode so crucial is that up to this point, the nurse, Mildred Ratched, had appeared — mind you, appeared — merely routinely efficient and perhaps overly duty conscious, but certainly not malevolent. And now she suddenly turns on the full panoply of the Machiavellian diabolism of her demented and repressed self, unheedingly sending Billy to his doom. She will first goad him to the admission that the girl dragged him in there by force; that, indeed, everybody did. Then she will drive him to the betrayal of McMurphy, his only true friend. Then she will play her trump and threaten him with telling his mother. The rout and destruction is complete. And all this, mind you, in the name of getting to the bottom of his first suicide attempt!

In an earlier group therapy session, she had ferretted out of him details of that Sunday when he had proposed to his girl Sylvia. She had asked him not only why he had wanted to marry her ('Because I love her' is his brief reply) but why he hadn't told his mother about it! And she had blatantly suggested to him that it was his guilt over the concealment that had led to his first suicide attempt.

So we come to the latter scene fully armed with this knowledge and realize that the nurse's threat of telling his mother is, to this highly strung man, as good as issuing a death warrant. And a death warrant it turns out to be in the hideous scene of his self-immolation.

Is not Ratched then a killer, a castrator and a maniac more dangerous than all the ones in her charge? Peter Cowie is surely right when he observes that 'she is more mentally ill than any of the men in the ward'.

In the light of this, McMurphy's attempt to throttle her, vexed by her inhuman calm after Billy's death ('The best thing we can do is to go on with our daily routine,' she declares to the stunned inmates) is probably the kindest thing he could have done to her. Bravo McMurphy!

That Ratched's 'mania' has sexual origins is also brought out in the way she deals with Harding's problems with his wife. That Harding himself is an egoist whose relationship with nearly everyone is queered up is brought out in ever so many ways. But the fact remains that Ratched shows no comprehension of anything, least of all sex, when, confronted by Harding's fears of his wife's infidelity, she can only say that he was not patient enough and in her talk of Harding's wife not providing him 'adequate mental satisfaction'.

You see the stress on 'mental satisfaction' when the patient himself talks freely of sexual difficulties! No wonder Ratched is quick to change the subject when McMurphy, fresh from electroshock, comes up with: 'When I get out of here, the first woman that takes on Ol' Red McMurphy, the ten-thousand watt psychopath, she's gonna light up like a pinball machine and pay off in silver dollars.' No lighting up for good Ol' Ratched. No thank you! It is not for nothing that she has on one of those wartime coiffures, an Army Nurse for whom the war never ended and who never grew up.

McMurphy identifies her character type accurately when he tells Dr Spivey that the nurse likes 'a rigged game'. She is a killjoy who will not let the inmates watch the World Series on TV on the pretext of having adjourned the meeting at the vote of 9 to 9. Her belief in democratic procedures is sham through and through, as is her concern with McMurphy's welfare when the other doctors want him sent back to Pendleton Work Farm.

It is clear that she feels him to be Enemy No. 1 (her double in the film, the black attendant Washington, feels this too) who must be destroyed before her hegemony is re-established. And in the tragic denouement of the film McMurphy is initially destroyed by lobotomy, the Establishment's neutron bomb. His actual death which follows in the film's most pathetic sequence is actually an act of mercy, euthanasia really, and like a latter-day Christ he takes on the burden of others and dies a heroic death. The twin marks we see on his forehead are the stigmata of his martyrdom. It is in every sense a Crucifixion.

But this death is life-giving to others and is surely one of the most liberating sequences in cinema. The Chief smashes one of the ward windows with the water regulator panel at which McMurphy's faith had, earlier in the film, striven in vain. But Faith, which the Gospel says moves mountains, now moves the intractable instrument through the Samsonian arms of Chief Bromden. And in the last magical sequence of this extraordinary film we see the dazzling 'one' who flew over the 'cuckoo's nest' gliding like a languid ghost over those paradisal valleys of freedom.

McMurphy embodies all the positives in the film excluded from the Ratched *Weltanschauung.* Primarily he is a healthy being sexually (he himself admits his trouble is 'fucks and fights'), but he is no millionaire like Rocky Marciano who fought 40 times to his own modest 5. His defence of the statutory rape charge brought against him is that no man alive could have resisted that 'red beaver'!

At the end of his session with the psychiatric panel (after the fishing escapade), his only question to Dr Spivey is (showing the doctor one of his porno cards): 'Where do you suppose she lives!' He is seen as fundamentally liberating throughout the movie. He is never daunted by ugly circumstance, as witness his imaginative running commentary of an imaginary ball game.

This surely is the film's most euphoric moment, a signal triumph of the heart's desire over the desert wastes of the Ratched empire. McMurphy is unselfish to a fault, and never more heroically so than in the melée at the end following Billy's terrible death when he gloriously forgoes his chance to escape. He is magnificent here and he is a man. This is the second time that night that he forgoes freedom, answering a call greater than freedom — for what doth it profit a man if he gains the whole world but has lost his soul.

The film gives a grim portrait of those who have lost their souls, and in doing so have also lost their freedom. One and all they are buried in the bottomless pits of their own devouring egoism. In response to McMurphy's outburst questioning their enduring it while complaining about it *ad nauseam*, Scanlon can only ask about the locked dormitory, Cheswick about his cigarettes, and Martin about how they are going to win their money back after the closing down of McMurphy's little 'gambling casino'. The card game at the end suggests that they will remain locked in their private hells, McMurphy or no McMurphy. As McMurphy himself sums it up at one point: 'That's what your schedule does to you!'

Jack Nicholson as McMurphy is near perfect, and both he and Louise Fletcher as Nurse Ratched, with her baby-blue eyes and dead-pan expression, fully merit the Oscars they received for their performances.

The music is imaginative with the waltz strains of *Charmaine* and the *Medication Valse* indoors giving way to the vacation time open-air notes of the Hawaiian *Alsha Los Pescadores*. The beginning and end of the film are held together by that eerie flute and musical saw music cut diagonally by the lone cuckoo.

Haskell Wexler's photography catches the sinister fascination of those warm, off-white walls (painted specially for the movie instead of the regulation green at the Oregon State Hospital whose actual Superintendent, Dr Dean K. Brooks, plays the imperturbable Dr Spivey), and the film's calm sea opening and night-drenched open valley ending are miracles of composition and lighting.

Milos Foreman, whose *Taking Off* (1971) had a cool reception in India some three or four years earlier, directs with a surer-hand this time to make Ward 34-B a microcosm of our own demotic world. Ken Kesev's vision of Menlo Park in 1962 becomes transformed in the film into a veritable portrait of an age.

For *Cuckoo's Nest* is not about mental hospitals at all. It is about the condition of man in modern industrial societies, getting used to deadening routine and subsiding like a vegetable incapable of raising his voice in protest. More, it is a tidy little metaphor about us, about those of us who, in fear of freedom, have handed over our destinies to the Ratcheds of this world.

10

Francis Ford Coppola, *Godfather Part II* (1975)

Paramount's *Godfather Part II* is an extraordinary film with a most unusual ending. After Michael has coldly despatched his 'enemies' — Hyman Roth as he lands in Miami, all doors of safe exile now remorselessly closed to him, Frankie Petrangeli by his own hand, like his beloved Roman emperors and Michael's own brother, the feckless Fredo, as he is out fishing to the strange litany of a Hail Mary — we see him in ghostly silhouette behind the French windows of his Lake Tahoe home in Nevada.

But the film doesn't end here as it well might have. Coppola adds two more flashbacks to serve as comment before returning us once again to a brooding Michael at the end of the film. We see him now sitting alone amidst the giant firs, in the late evening light, on the far right of the frame, unseeing eyes staring into the void. 'You are blind, Michael,' Kay had said just before leaving him, and Michael seems just that now. We have come a long way indeed from the young Vito Corleone staring longingly at the Statue of Liberty in one of the film's most arresting images. What does Coppola mean to tell us? For his elliptic end is surely more ambiguous than the relatively more straightforward end of *Godfather I* where Michael, after having lied to Kay about the death of Connie's husband, quietly occupies the throne left vacant by the death of his father.

First, those flashbacks. Significantly, all the five earlier flashbacks in the film were concerned with the rise and fortunes of Vito Corleone, but these are exclusively concerned with Michael. The first shows us the young Corleone clan gathered round a table waiting for the father to return for his birthday party in 1941. The Japanese have just attacked

Pearl Harbour and 30,000 Americans have enlisted in a single day, and so has Michael much to the disappointment of the family.

As the others leave the table to greet their father, Michael is left alone, brooding and stoic in his decision. The second flashback shows Vito Corleone asking his infant son Michael to say goodbye to the Sicilian clan that has gathered on the station platform at Corleone. What is the significance of these flashbacks? John Hess in an otherwise excellent essay in *Jump Cut* ('*Godfather II*: A Deal Coppola Couldn't Refuse') takes the hard Marxist line that since the first flashback directly associates Michael's 'individualism' with bourgeois values, his values were always the same as the system he lived by. Michael was always America and his indictment in the film equals the indictment of the corporate values of capitalist America. Writes Hess:

Michael's goals are those of any other businessman: security for him and his family, respectability and opportunity for his children. Thus the connection between Michael and the usual businessman is not hidden. Michael's individualism is directly associated with bourgeois values in the final sequence, the flashback to the 1941 birthday party of Don Vito. Michael has enlisted in the Marines against his father's wishes because he has his own plans for his life ... At first Michael wanted to lead a different kind of life, but since the values he lived by were those of the system, and since the values of the Mafia are not substantially different from corporate American values, Michael couldn't ultimately leave the system, or really understand what was happening to him.

This seems to me a drastic simplification since it wholly distorts and falsifies Michael's intransigence in refusing to join the family concern by flatly equating it with the unbridled individualism of the bourgeois value world. But Coppola himself has said of Michael that 'at one time [he] had been an innocent. He was caught up in events that he couldn't and didn't turn...they turned him.' And, indeed, the whole point of the first flashback at the end is to show Michael at a time when he was an 'innocent', when he could and did turn events by quitting college to join the Marines. When Sonny cynically remarks that only saps fight for their country and risk their lives for strangers, Michael snaps at him with: 'That's pop talking.'

At this point he is clearly dissociated from his father's values and, indeed, is in clear opposition to it. Isn't this why this scene dissolves into the Sicilian sequence when, in marked contrast, Michael, as a child, is asked and made to say goodbye by his father? But then he saw through a glass darkly, but now he is old enough to decide for himself, to make 'his own plans for his life', which, in the first instance, involves fighting for his country. To equate this with bourgeois 'individualism' is to miss the individual trees for the Marxist wood of an undifferentiated overall determinism.

Indeed, throughout the film, Coppola is at pains to show us that Michael is not morally dead, and that his regeneration is something more than an abstract moral possibility. Early in the film, while dancing with Michael during the celebrations attending Anthony's First Communion, Kay complains that he has not yet gone 'legitimate' although it is seven years since he promised to do so. Michael says he is trying. And, soon after, when in Havana for the Cuban deal, he sees the Cuban freedom fighter immolating himself rather than give in, he still has enough of his older altruistic self— 'the Marine self' — left in him to see that the rebels have a chance of winning against the Batista regime (both Hyman Roth and Johnny Ola dismiss the rebels lightly) because they are not fighting for money. And, immediately after the Cuban 'fiasco' (Michael's judgment of events here proving correct), there is the bitter blow of Kay's 'miscarriage' (Michael is badly mistaken in this) and a very confused Michael seeks the sanctuary of his mother's counsel.

This is his night of Gethsemane. Will he perhaps lose his family by being too strong for its sake? The poor woman thinks he is referring to the loss of the baby, and he derives little comfort from her. 'Times are changing,' he muses wistfully more to himself than to her and, certainly, they are for him as we see him nearly cornered before the Congressional committee and lying his head off to save his skin and that of his family. It is this ghastly business that leads straight to the confrontation with Kay — the film's nerve-centre and moral fulcrum — when she tells him that it wasn't a miscarriage but an abortion — 'just like our marriage' — because she felt it was 'unholy' and 'evil' to bring another child of his into the world. 'There's no way you could forgive me now,' she says bravely and unforgettably, 'because of this Sicilian thing that has been going on for more than 2000 years.'

The force of this scene derives from our unquestioning faith in Kay's moral purity and incorruptibility. The moral indictment of Michael would get short-circuited if one took the position of Pauline Kael in her *New Yorker* essay that if Kay doesn't know that Michael lied at the end of *Godfather I* it is 'because she doesn't want to'. This is a whole lot worse than the position at the end of the Mario Puzo book where Kay allows herself to return to Michael, persuaded by Tom and seeking solace in the Catholic church. No, Kay is never an accomplice to his corruption in spite of the slight ambiguity at the end of the earlier film. It is only *now* that she does know for sure (and Coppola is careful to show her beside Michael during the Congressional hearings), and she doesn't hesitate in the least to act on her knowledge. After such knowledge, what forgiveness? His empty promises to change, to start a new life with her ('I learnt that I have the strength to change') fall on deaf ears now and she gives up husband, home, and children without a moment's hesitation. With Kay gone, Michael's moral collapse is complete. Significantly, it is only now that he orders all the three killings that bring the film to a close.

The contrast with Michael's sister, Connie, is revealing: Connie who knew that Michael had her husband Carlo killed and who, after a brief fling with Merle, is back with the family at the end. If Kay were not present as a moral agent, the film would lack a moral centre and, indeed, the whole edifice of the moral/political critique of the Mafia/corporate capitalist America would crumble and collapse. But for Kay to be a moral agent it is absolutely essential that Michael not be wholly corrupt right from the outset of their relationship. For otherwise Kay would have to be a mindless moron unable to see through Michael's dauntless duplicities. Truly, then, Kay represents the 'permanent possibility' of Michael's salvation. But, tragically, the World War II marine who was awarded the Navy Cross became, in time, the new Godfather. The two flashbacks at the end of the film, by showing us a time when he consciously set his face against such a possibility, squarely lay the blame on him for his final predicament.

John Hess has, with pardonable exaggeration, called it 'the greatest Hollywood film since *Citizen Kane*'. Still, one wonders how Coppola struck his Promethean spark from the Puzo trash which does not in the least live up to its epigraph (a celebrated line from Balzac which Marx admired very much). It has such mind-blowing lines as '*The young rascal's hot loaf would be in its oven, Nazorine thought lewdly ...*' (emphasis Puzo's!) simply because Nazorine happens to be a baker. But Puzo or no Puzo, Coppola only borrows the young manhood of Vito Corleone in New York and the Fanucci and Roberto episodes from the book, and has got electric performances from his cast. Al Pacino is hard and granite—like in his awesome power, a will of iron behind a face of steel. His movements are cagey and wary like an animal's and so when he explodes, it is dynamite. The watchword is always absolute control. Robert De Niro is stylish in a very modern American way and his voice a masterpiece of cunning Sicilian masquerade (he reportedly went to Sicily to master the nuances of the dialect). He is lordly and humble by turns and, unluckily for us, the scenario does not permit him to appear together with Pacino for the full display of the Italian—American grandeur in acting.

The supporting stars are truly of first magnitude in a very crowded galaxy indeed. Michael Gazzo as Petrangeli has one or two absolutely dazzling moments. Gaston Moschin, with his flashy gold tooth and white fedora plays Fanucci with a panache that bring to mind Laird Cregar in *Blood and Sand* (1941), and Leopoldo Trieste is Signor Roberto to the life ('The rent stays like a buffalo' bleats this once greedy landlord!). Spradlin's Senator Geary is well-honed and carefully observed, a perfect satiric portrait, and the legendary Lee Strasberg plays Hyman Roth from the back of his hand. John Cazale, as Fredo, is lizard-like and darting in his movements but his essential impotence comes through in moments of iceberg immobility. Coppola's sister Talia Shire, as Connie, is all molten fire beneath those brilliant eyes and her smouldering sensuality is clearly every man's oasis in the surrounding desert of love. Diane Keaton, as Kay, has of course, her one great scene. Nina Rota — Fellini's wizard — does his haunting waltz theme (which the usually sagacious Page Cook has, somewhat unaccountably, seen as 'a sad signpost of his crumbling musicality') in *legato* (simultaneously nostalgic and melancholy, chilling and menacing) to evoke the old Mafia epoch of the great Al Capone days.

Gordon Willis's camera captures the lyricism and sunlight of Sicily and the squalor of Little Italy in New York, but in the interiors of Michael's Lake Tahoe home, it is all heavy muted tones, sickly yellows but mostly Rembrandt browns. A great film, truly epic.

11

James Ivory, *Roseland* (1977)

James Ivory's *Roseland* is a metaphor alright but, like all good metaphors, it is tantalizingly ambiguous. As if to beguile us, it is flanked at either end by two episodes, 'The Waltz' and 'The Peabody' which are lightweights really, transparent, lucid, almost too lucid. May, the pleasantly senile if well-bred widow in 'The Waltz', can relate to the gruff, unremittingly cheerful Stan only through her pathetic longing for Eddie and his spotless elegance ('You don't have old-world elegance') while the dour, solipsistic, almost Bismarckian Rosa in 'The Peabody' is somewhat rougher on meek, mousy little Arthur ('All you Americans know is movies'). But between Stan, who finally shakes May out of her obsession with her 35-year textbook marriage to Eddie, and Arthur, who never makes it back to Roseland for the Champagne Hour Peabody Contest, there is more than the difference of age or ethnic background or dancing ability. The women, however, are more alike in their strenuous preoccupation with the past, and this is probably why the two episodes featuring them lack the resonance of felt life. Lilia Skala alone, with her bravura Marlene Dietrich imitations and her European *grand dame* manner, saves the last episode from collapsing into outright sentimentality. Even so the final episode, with its dance of death end, is too 'aesthetic', too 'finished', to really tell us what can happen in this eerie urban outpost, this 'seedy Shangri-La' (Sarris) on 52nd Street.

But the central episode, 'The Hustle', hums with unexpected life. Even Pauline Kael, in an otherwise hostile review of the film (*New Yorker*, 5 Dec. '77) has to concede: 'In the middle section, the writer got on to something, but maybe because of being locked into the short form, she didn't develop it ...(The) gigolo's courteous nastiness gives the film its only magnetic force — it's the only emotion in the movie (except for the m.c.'s) that isn't fully comprehended, chewed and swallowed.' But then *she* goes on to comprehend, chew, and swallow Russel up so thoroughly that she misreads his final action in staying behind with the dying Pauline. 'Both the girl and Cleo are trying to force him to be more than he is', she observes correctly, but then goes on to infer wrongly that 'because the emphasis is on his betrayal of the naive girl, rather than on the betrayal of his talent (and of his partner), the episode never becomes dramatic.' But the emphasis is Kael's, not Ivory's, and certainly Cleo (played with a world-weary charm by Helen Gallagher) was never in the running.

When I met Ivory in Madras and asked him about Russel, he said that Russel was 'a very positive character'. He didn't think Russel was, in any way, manipulative, playing the three women off against each other: 'He doesn't need to calculate.' When I asked him about the end when Russel stays with Pauline, he said, 'It is his feeling for Pauline. She is his family. He talks of his mother, remember.'

A New York-based Indian critic, Sreekumar Menon, derides Russel for his 'oedipal fixations', suggested no doubt by Russel's remark to Cleo about Marilyn: 'She reminds me of my mother; my mother would have liked to talk like that, wear that kind of clothes.' But Russel's initial interest in Marilyn (a depressed divorcee played by Geraldine Chaplin) is on Pauline's account, not independent, and he is quick enough to wean himself from her growing possessiveness. His 'narcissism' again is on the surface: his compassion for his women is genuine enough. Oddly, though, his critics are mostly women: 'polite veneer ... chilling self-sufficiency' (Kael); 'chilly arrogance' (Kathleen Carroll); 'chilling portrait ... of a kept man ... (who) through his kindnesses hands a little heartbreak to three women' (Judith Crist). It is certainly a tribute to Christopher Walken's low-keyed acting that he has drawn such fire from the women, but these judgements must be set beside his uniform courtesy to everyone, and even after his argument with Marilyn it is he who takes the trouble to ring her up.

It is his relationship with Pauline, really, that reveals the essential Russel. When he kisses her perfunctorily she playfully admonishes him to do better. For Pauline he is 'like John Barrymore' (for Pauline Kael he is rather more like Valentino!). When she invites him home 'for an hour of backgammon', Russel is non-committal with his poker face. But this is enough to frighten Pauline (whose aging desperation Joan Copeland captures so well) into the mumbling apology of 'Oh, darling Russel, I'm spoiling your whole day'. We know from his subsequent conversation with Marilyn, when she deliberately misses her bus, that Pauline is on the phone to him 'six times a day'. Yet he doesn't feel imposed upon, this 'stoic gigolo'. He visits Pauline in hospital unlike the selfish and ungrateful Marilyn — remember it is Pauline who takes her under her wing and brings her to Roseland — who doesn't because, as George puts it, she 'hates hospitals'. She would. And, despite tempting offers of support from both Cleo (who has her own dreams of setting up with him, of winning the Harvest Moon Ball), and Marilyn (who is willing to work overtime as a waitress at night to pay for Russel's dance fees), Russel sticks with Pauline, deciding that 'the socially disreputable choice is the more honourable one'. Perhaps this is not such a wholly selfish decision. He gives rather more than he takes and, certainly, between the clasp he gives her for her birthday at the opening and the gold watch she gives him at the end there is no simple equation. Russel's loyalties actually go beyond Pauline. He won't insult his old friend Cleo in front of the brash Marilyn who wants to make everything 'clear'. His answer to Marilyn could well serve as his motto in life: 'I have known them all my life. There is no need to make anything clear.' Certainly, in these brassy days of one-upmanship, this likeable stud who 'looks like the Hapsburg Empire and speaks like Brooklyn' (*Variety*, 5 Oct. '77) has claims to be regarded as something of a modern saint.

'The Hustle' is a quartet with all the strings attached. In it all the latent ambiguities of *Roseland* are writ large. Nothing is clear-cut: May and Eddie, May and Stan, Rosa and Arthur are cardboard cut-outs when held against the shimmering Roseland-haze of the Russel—Pauline—Cleo—Marilyn quartet as they do the real hustle to the strains of Elton John's 'Super Cool'. Each of the characters reflects on the other and, in turn, is reflected on by the other. Cleo is bitchy about Pauline ('Does she keep you on cigarettes?') who, in turn, is bitchy about Cleo ('Watch her hips'); Cleo thinks Marilyn is 'stuck up', and Marilyn wants Russel 'to make it clear to Cleo and Pauline'. Even the unflappable Russel, momentarily off guard, complains about Pauline to Marilyn: 'Pauline is my curse.' We are in a deliquescent world where every judgement is undercut since no character is privileged, including the narrator herself, who, for once, is caught up in the action herself. Cleo, dangling between the has-been George and the would-be Russel, with her little sentimentalities about poor George and Georgina who had 'a taste for good things'. Cleo, wise and knowing, but really over the hill: 'I never quite found out what happened to Georgina.'

We could adopt this as our own motto, too, about this tantalizing fragment. Did the Hustle couple ever make it? Whatever happened to Marilyn? Did Russel quite become like George? Did Russel and Pauline make that winter cruise?

Roseland may not be the great film that the audiences at the New York Film Festival found it to be (the ovation at the end lasted fully seven minutes, one learns) but it is that much rarer thing, the kind of small, quiet film that we have come to expect from the Merchant—Ivory team. Its decline and fall theme (treated comically in *Savages* [1972]) derives from their earlier films, particularly from the elegant and masterly *Shakespeare Wallah* (1965). But the pathos here is more sublime, because more personal, more shatteringly real than that of the beleaguered colonials in the Shakespeare film.

12

Vittorio and Paulo Taviani, *Padre Padrone* (1977)

Romain Rolland's remark (a favourite of Gramsci's, by the way) about 'the optimism of the will, pessimism of the intellect' could well serve as our guide to the Taviani brothers' masterpiece, *Padre Padrone*. The film, originally shot on 16 mm for Italian television, deals with the growth of a young mind from 'the culture of silence' (in Paulo Freire's evocative phrase) to the culture of speech and, hence, of liberation. And yet it isn't naively optimistic — and hence my quotation from Rolland — although a growing optimism accompanies Gavino's gradual if painful mastery of his oppressive environment. The environment here is the south (of Italy), 'the south as the national unsolved problem, as an epic if not of mythical patrimony, as the coagulation of explosive forces that condition our future'. I have been quoting from the joint directors of the film for whom the South is in a way our *Moby Dick*. And, like the great white whale of the Melville masterpiece, Sardinia, too, provokes very ambivalent reactions in Gavino. Attempting to migrate to West Germany along with fellow Sardinians, young Gavino spits at the land of his birth and, in an even more robust gesture of desecration, proceeds to piss from the moving transport that is carrying them. But, at the end of the film, a now triumphant Gavino (the author of the autobiography on which the film is based) decides to stay behind in his native Siligo and not to go to the mainland (where, as a glottologist, he would have more opportunities) because, as he puts it, going away 'would be the triumph of my father'. Love for the native land reverses the earlier loathing and, indeed, the film is built on a series of such dramatic reversals. Visually and thematically the most striking reversal is the shot of Gavino's classroom which is repeated at the end of the film. The film opens here as Gavino's father comes to take him away to mind the sheep. As he leaves the room with his son, derisive laughter is heard and Gavino's father angrily returns and warns the boys that their turn will soon come. Shots of the faces of four boys are held as everyone of them fantasizes some harm, each to his own father, to prevent the catastrophe of being taken away from school. And now, at the end, the same shot is repeated and we return to the terrified class and to the class teacher with averted gaze held momentarily in stop motion. The camera returns to the once terrified faces, but Gavino's success is there between then and now, and a mischievous look of impending triumph is writ large on the impudent young faces as Gavino's victory tune over Sardinian cir-cumstance — the joyous *Fledermaus* waltz — is heard yet again and the victory of history over nature, of sound over silence, of freedom over tyranny, of son over father seems permanently assured. The scene is one of many such 'epiphanies' in the film.

Johann Strauss's *Fledermaus* is cunningly used throughout, inter-woven into the very structure of the film, and functions as a metaphor for Gavino's gradual liberation. There is the scene, for instance, when during the period of his compulsory military service he is shown as-sembling a wireless set in class. The instructor going round the classroom comes to Gavino's desk and turns on the set. There is an ominous moment of deafening silence — and we know Gavino has promised himself he will study further only if he succeeds here — before the accordion strains of the Strauss waltz are heard, the music of liberation for Gavino. The Strauss waltz was encountered first in the desolate fields of the Siliga fastnesses of his youth. Two bandits are making their way to the feast at Muros, accordion strung across the back of one of them. Gavino, now twenty, and numbed in the stupor of loneli-ness, is squatting inside a pit, and into the peaceful soporific valley comes the strains of the Viennese waltz. Gavino, overcome with emotion, trades two lambs for the accordion and comes in, while mumbling in his sleep, for much searching scrutiny from his father. But the unwieldy instrument, which initially Gavino treats like one of his own refractory sheep, becomes a metaphor for all his yearnings for the excluded outer world. The Strauss waltz is heard at crucial moments in the film, notably at the end as already mentioned, and as a discordant counterpoint in the scene when Gavino (now returned from military service to com-plete his studies, much to his father's chagrin; he doesn't want to stay in the army because, as he puts it, 'I don't want to become a social executioner') strikes his father defiantly as his father taunts him to do.

Lest I have given the impression that *Padre Padrone* is a glum, lugubrious film about a father—son tussle, let me hasten to add that much of it is done in high humour. There is the scene where Gavino milks a sheep which keeps dropping turds into the pail. Gavino's ensuing anger here is given point by making the equally irate animal talk back! But in this vein, perhaps none is funnier than the scene at sunset when the entire village — boys, men, and women — seems to indulge in one massive orgy of sex! Young shepherds mount their sheep, the younger boys assault their chickens, while the men entice their women who are in the midst of domestic chores. In this incredibly funny scene, the soundtrack alone, significantly, in this very aural film, is left to record, with its *mélange* of sighs and panting, the tumultous results! Indeed, no scene is too grave for the film's overflowing and abundant humour. Carrying aloft a statue in a religious procession, Gavino's friends exchange notes about whores whom they find un-satisfactory because (unlike their cherished *burros*) they lack tails! Then there is the scene where Gavino returns shamefacedly from an attempted escape to West Germany and the whole family is shown in stitches of laughter — because Gavino's secret efforts have been foiled by his father who has not given his approval by signing the required application form!

But *Padre Padrone* escapes easy classification. Pauline Kael has said that it 'may be the only fully consciously animistic movie ever made outside the Disney films'. This has some unexpected consequences. One is compelled to 'hear' this film as much as 'see it'. Certainly the images are stunning in their pared-down simplicity; the compositions are spare, with mostly one or two figures picked out in that awesome landscape dominated by the sacred oak tree whose brooding presence, in a couple of nocturnal shots, is certainly malevolent. But the sounds provide an even more accurate barometer of the film's main theme. The serene, unclouded classroom singing gives way to four ominous sounds struck on a gong (they could well be the percussive clanging of Gavino's own suppressed rage and hence subjective sounds) as Gavino is left alone in his sheep pen. He rocks back and forth in a gesture of helplessness, a gesture that is repeated two more times in the film. Again, after Gavino's father has thrashed him into senselessness for attempting to run away, he puts his son on his lap and we hear an ancient chant from far-off which sounds like some half-forgotten lullaby.

Farts are heard, most innocent of nature's sounds, before Sebastiano is cruelly hacked to death by his enemies. But always there is the wind, now low and deep, now whistling in winter's deep as the bitter frost destroys the Gavinos' precious live crop and, at the end, yet again, enveloping and overseeing Gavino's solitary meditation.

Gavino's education, indeed, begins and ends with sounds. As he is taken to the sheepfold by his father (we don't see either of them, a subjectively tracking camera merely captures the oncoming darkness over the road's metallic glint), he is taught now to listen to the wind, now to the murmuring oak and the rushing torrent, and also to prowling bandits. And to the generation now growing up on Castaneda, this must sound like the right kind of education, better, certainly, than the one Gavino was getting at school! In any case, it is perhaps one of the major ironies of the film that it is the same ear that is bewitched at last by the *Fledermaus.* Simple sounds of nature graduate imperceptibly into the Italian he learns during Army service, followed by Latin and Greek, and, in one sequence, he is even seen magisterially reciting the fate of Dido from Book II of Virgil's *Aeneid*! Perhaps both the natural and logical culmination of these studies is the thesis on Sardinian dialects that Gavino obtains by the end of the film.

Still *Padre Padrone*'s final impression is not one of unqualified optimism. 'The pessimism of the intellect' (or better still, the spirit) that Rolland and Gramsci have spoken about is evident in the closing shot of the film which returns us to the real Gavino Ledda, author of the book on which the film is based. A long shot shows him with his back to the wall but a closer shot reveals him rocking back and forth in the now familiar gesture of helplessness. (Anil Saari in his article on the film in *Screen,* 13 Jan. '78, comically misreads it as an allusion to Gavino's excessive masturbation!) The authors of the film seem to say that the real Ledda 'can never be like those who haven't experienced a childhood of solitary confinement' (Kael). By thus undercutting its own bracing optimism symbolized by the blazing *Fledermaus* at the end, the film merely draws our attention to the recurring human dilemmas even while reaffirming the possibilities inherent in the human spirit. The eternal wind (Nature) which we hear as we see Gavino rocking need not be thought to prevail over the Strauss waltz (History), for the film is nothing if it has not celebrated the cumulative, if miniscule, victories of the human spirit over the brute and stupid forces of nature.

13

Steven Spielberg, *Close Encounters of the Third Kind* (1977)

Columbia's blockbuster *Close Encounters of the Third Kind* — which cost 19 million dollars to make — begins with what the high priest of UFOlogy, Dr Hynek, has called a 'close encounter of the second kind'. Here UFOs interact with the environment and/or with witnesses without there being any actual contact.

In dusty and windy Mexico, a team of scientists and technicians examine some World War II naval bombers dropped off by mysterious but friendly space voyagers. Missing since 1945, these are the famous torpedo bombers that vanished into the mysterious Bermuda triangle. Questioning a wizened old peasant, the scientists begin their Holy Grail in search of the benign UFOs. From Mexico we move predictably to the mystic East, to Dharamsala, India, where a vast congregation of devout Hindus point upraised forefingers at the sky to indicate the source of the five-note chant they are all singing in unison. This kind of encounter clearly transcends Dr Hynek's drily perceptual categories and is presumably a 'close encounter of the sonic kind'. Thus are we readied for the bizarre happenings in Muncie, Indiana, to Roy Neary and his family and to Jillian and her four year old son, Barry. Not blessed by Hindu wisdom or Mexican innocence, Roy and Neary are entitled only to 'close encounters of the first kind', the kind where you merely physically sight the UFOs. The film moves from encounters of the first and second kind to encounters of the third kind where you encounter not just UFOs but actual UFOnauts. And this is where all the problems really begin. In the film's grand *son et lumiere* finale, the giant mother ship — clearly the Big Mama of the sprawling UFO family — looking rather like a gargantuan birthday cake, disgorges — guess what? — dazed US Navy men, the famous lost patrol of the Bermuda imbroglio! This chillingly anticlimactic moment, then, is the emotional prelude to the arrival of the mysterious aliens whose skinny and bald chief looks like one of Modigliani's nudes. But Spielberg fumbles the magic moment by foregrounding the banal instead of the sublime.

The film's climax (using 2000 floodlights and six arc lights, says *Time*) has led *New Yorker*'s Pauline Kael to more than her customary hyperbole. 'This is one of the peerless moments in movie history,' she declares, 'spiritually reassuring, magical, and funny at the same time.' Funny, perhaps, but 'spiritually reassuring'? Indeed, most American critics seem to have gone overboard at the sight of the mother ship. One expects and accepts this sort of thing from *Time* and *Newsweek* and, sure enough, they run true to form. *Time's* reviewer found the climax of the film 'almost mystical' while the *Newsweek* man likened the impact of the last 40 minutes to 'a kind of cushioned trauma that's close, I think, to that grandiose old idea of the sublime'. Cushioned trauma close to the idea of the sublime? What's happening to the sublime these days? The climax claimed more distinguished victims. *Saturday Review's* Arthur Schelesinger Jr. had to work in that passage about the 'transitory enchanted moment' from *The Great Gatsby* to do justice to the Spielberg finale, while the usually sober Stanley Kauffmann of *The New Republic* got mushy with his talk about the film 'feeding some of the hungers of our time with manna from the heavens'. Some hunger, some manna! Only Martin Gardner of *The New York Review of Books* in an essay cryptically entitled 'The Third Coming' sounded a warning note and hoped that Spielberg would soon grow up.

Close Encounters is indeed for those who haven't grown up. Its fake religiosity, its occultism masquerading as science, is certainly more lethal than all the benign fakery of *Star Wars* (1977). *Star Wars* had saving humour to protect its prognostications of the Force but *Close Encounters* is bug-eyed, humourless, and downright silly except when that technical wizard Douglas Trumbull gets busy. Worse, it is marred by an ethnocentric bias that I personally find repelling. For, granted that the aliens had to prove their *bona fides* by doing us humans a good turn, did they have to return the lost aircraft and the lost airmen of the Bermuda mystery? In their magnificent agelessness and Shangrila-like immunity from the ravages of old Father Time, why couldn't the mother ship have brought back some survivors from the lost continent of Atlantis which Plato mourns in his *Timaeus and Critias*? Or, perhaps, still better — as a gesture of goodwill to India for supplying the crucial musical clue — why not our own dear Subhas Chandra Bose who also mysteriously disappeared in an air crash during World War II? No, it has to be those US airmen to placate American vanity and round off the Spielbergian plot. After all, doesn't the naval wing of US Air Force deserve to be amply rewarded for its support to UFOlogy?

The script is banal and the Sphere paperback brings home the banality almost painfully. The bathos, in places, is simply stupefying. As the lost airmen disembark from the mother ship someone says, 'Lieutenant, welcome home. This way to debriefing.' The French scientist, Lacombe, played by Francois Truffaut (yes, Francois Truffaut!) is so dumb that he has to leave it to his American translator to figure out that the number series received from the aliens represent the latitudinal and longitudinal coordinates of Devil's Tower, Wyoming! Defending Neary to the Project Security Officer, Lacombe says, 'I believe that for every one of these confused people, there must be hundreds also touched by the implanted vision but never made it thus far. *How many others missed the television news and never made the ... psychic connection'* (emphasis added). Is this his comprehension of the 'implanted vision'? Does Neary, then, owe his climb up the purgatorial mountain to the accident of Walter Cronkite on the 6 o'clock news? Little wonder that Lacombe confesses to Neary: 'I envy you.' He has good reason to. Not that Roy Neary (near what? the truth?) is a particularly distinguished specimen of Homo sapiens. Even such a doughty champion of the film as Ms Kael has to concede that Spielberg can't create characters or develop them in a writer's way. 'Richard Dreyfuss's Roy,' she observes, 'waddles in rear view and becomes misty-eyed when he longs for knowledge ... Barry, the toddling light-worshipper ... is closer to the heart of Spielberg's vision than Roy.' Yet it is Roy who is central to the film's meaning. He is supposed to be the ordinary man in extraordinary circumstances but would such a man, I ask you, leave his life and three children for a space voyage without so much as batting an eyelid? For this Spielberg is to blame, as the whole conception of Roy is thin and bloodless. His total lack of inner conflict here betrays, as Schoenbaum has pointed out in his *Times Literary Supplement (TLS)* review, 'the psychological poverty of the script'. And the script, needless to say, is pure Spielberg. Is it any wonder, then, if we get close encounters of the Spielberg kind?

14

Hugh Hudson, *Chariots of Fire* (1981)

Chariots of Fire proved a disappointment. In spite of the picture-postcard photography (chopped up, I'm afraid, into some pretty gooey bits in Terry Rawling's hectic editing), the generally uplifting and inspirational music and the old world beauty of Cambridge, the film is hollow at the core. Liddell and Abrahams are cardboard cut-outs and their textbook exploits have long been the staple of schoolboy fiction. Truly, where there is a British will there is no doubt an Olympic way ! Only the ways of Liddell and Abrahams are never allowed to cross (except once), and the Sabbath comes in handy at the end to ward off a possible Liddell defeat. Result· there is not one but two parallel plots that never really come together. Since there is no conflict, neither character shows any growth: at the end they are both exactly as they were in the beginning. Even Liddell's 400-metres victory in the Paris Olympics ought properly to be chalked up to the credit of the Christian God. And, likewise, even Abrahams' 100-metres triumph belongs to the deeps of his Lithuanian Jewishness. Are there, then, any *ordinary* sportsmen in this *divine* film?

None except Lindsay, and even he is too good to be true. His stepping down on behalf of Liddell doesn't sound so good when you realize that he is a wholly fictitious character. The record books for 1924 don't mention any Lindsay finishing on the board in the 400 metres hurdles — the actual winner was Morgan Taylor (USA) followed by Eric Valen of Finland and Ivan Riky of the USA. Liddell himself, despite his Christian God, wasn't exactly Mr Invincible and finished an unspectacular third in the 200 metres, behind Charlie Paddock and Jackson Scholz who won in 21.6 secs. The pro-Liddell film ascribes this defeat quite gratuitously to Abrahams who is then allowed, almost

as a consolation for his Jewishness, to win the 100 metres — in a
record 10.52 secs, by the way, although the film is too sublime to
go into such mundane details. Liddell does eventually win the 400
but, in a curious sequence. Paddock — although he never ran this
particular race is seen hanging his head down in shame as the victorious
Scot is carried aloft by his delirious colleagues. But, stranger still, before
the start of this particular race, which brings the proceedings to a
merciful close, there is dissension in the American camp. Although
the American coach is confident of victory ('After 300 metres *rigor
mortis* will set in,' he remarks to one of his boys of Liddell's prospects),
Scholz — the 200-metres US hero — walks up to Liddell on the track,
for all the world to see, and hands him a personal message. 'It says
in the old book — he that honours me I will honour.' Clutching the
note in his palm like a talisman, Liddell strides — to the accompaniment
of much fanfare and more quotations — to a truly Christian victory.

The entire Olympiad resolves itself into a Great Britain vs USA
tussle with the Union Jack coming out trumps. There is simply no
mention of the great Finnish runner, Paavo Nurmi, who won five
golds in all — unequalled to this day by any track athlete — or the
great Johnny Weissmuller (remember Tarzan?) who picked up golds
too. The film's monomaniacal obsession with Liddell and Abrahams
forbids any mention of the only other gold medallist for Great Britain
in the 1924 Olympiad, Douglas Lowe, who won the 800 in 1 minute
52 seconds. He was to repeat the feat in 1928. Instead of these immortals
of sport, the film treats us to a long sequence in a Parisian palace
of a colloquy of British worthies — Lord Cadogan, Lord Birkenhead,
the Duke of Sutherland and the Prince of Wales. The whole point
of the scene (although its ostensible purpose is to persuade Liddell
to run on the Sabbath) is, I take it, to caricature the Old Guard
— men like Lord Cadogan and Lord Birkenhead. 'In my day, it was
King first, God after,' he remarks with more than a touch of asperity
to the God-intoxicated Liddell, only to draw from young Sutherland
the rebuke, 'And the war to end wars bitterly proved your point.'
Likewise, the Blimpish Birkenhead, sodden in a complacent jingoistic
pride, is pulled up short by Sutherland again who reminds him that
patriotism — especially patriotic sacrifice fuelled by a guilty national
pride — is simply not enough. The now familiar Blimp figure is the
target all through. The pompous Master of Trinity and the Master
of Caius (played gloriously by John Gielgud and Lindsay Anderson,
respectively) swilling their port and trotting out platitudes about *esprit*

de corps are figures of fun as is that sinister Jew-hating hall porter, Rodgers, whom Abrahams puts in his place early on in the film. There is indeed a quiet revulsion in the film to all that led to 1914 and it is significant that although Abrahams enlisted and gained a King's commission, he didn't see action in France. Against the warmongers are set the new, younger aristocracy, the Duke of Sutherland, the excellent (if fictitious) Lindsay, and of course the suave, persuasive Prince of Wales. But these honourable men, too, blundered and couldn't prevent Munich. In any case this sub-theme doesn't jell with the Liddell—Abrahams main theme.

The film's best moments are those featuring Sam Mussabini (played to perfection by the veteran Ian Holm) who plays Abrahams' coach His best scene comes (after Abrahams' 100-metres win) in a French café where Mussabini celebrates their victory in a rain-drenched voice that speaks volumes of his own lonely life. Lindsay, too, is superbly cast, eternally boyish, an aristocrat who practises on his country estate with overflowing champagne glasses perched precariously on all the hurdles. And — not to forget the one authentic woman in the film, Sybil (Alice Krige), who walks into my pantheon of the most kissable women encountered on or off the screen. But unfortunately, in spite of all these ancillary charms, it is, in the final reckoning, Liddell's film. And Liddell is a man of God. Now the Kingdom of God may not be a democracy and God may be in the fortunate position of not having to seek his re-election, as Liddell's father once observes magisterially. But, alas, the kingdom of man is merely democracy with all its attendant pitfalls and liabilities. By removing Liddell to a wholly non-tragic plane where even the possibility of failure doesn't exist, the film deprives him of citizenship in the perhaps lesser but all too human kingdom of man.

15

Jonathan Demme, *The Silence of the Lambs* (1991)

Anyone who watched the Academy Awards presentation in 1992 will remember that the biggest applause was reserved for Antony Hopkins' Oscar for his portrayal of Dr Hannibal — 'the Cannibal' — Lecter in Jonathan Demme's *The Silence of the Lambs*. The film's success — it picked up five major Oscars, only the third film in motion picture history, after Frank Capra's *It Happened One Night* (1934) and Milos Forman's *One Flew Over the Cuckoo's Nest* (1975) to do so — has dismayed some observers here who cannot understand how a Hollywood film which has almost no 'entertainment' value could be singled out for so many honours.

They probably have in mind a film such as Hitchcock's *Psycho* (1960) featuring yet another Anthony — Anthony Perkins — who plays a transvestite killer. *Psycho* drew a blank at the Oscars and gained but a single nomination for Janet Leigh who plays the luckless girl, butchered in that unforgettable shower-bath murder sequence. Incidentally, her co-star, John Gavin, who later became US Ambassador to Mexico, was too embarrassed to play his opening hotel-room sequence without a shirt! But times are a-changing, as that Bob Dylan song goes, and today many people would find Gavin's reservations positively corny. And, like it or not, it is the same people who enjoy the black humour of *The Silence of the Lambs* where Dr Lecter's idea of fun is to cook his victims and serve them up as dinner for unexpected guests.

'Haven't you ever had people coming over and no time to shop?' he matter-of-factly tells Clarice, the young FBI trainee-investigator, like a housewife swapping recipes with a neighbour. 'You have to make do with what's in the fridge, Clarice.' This is when he had cooked the thymus and pancreas of one of his patients — Raspail — and served them as sweetbreads to the President and the Conductor of the Baltimore Philharmonic (Lecter being a connoisseur of classical music, with a marked partiality for Bach's *Goldberg Variations* played by Glenn Gould) on the evening following Raspail's disappearance. All this, however, is in the Thomas Harris book of the same name. In the film, we are spared these horrors, but not entirely. Lecter merely informs Clarice casually, in their first encounter, that he once ate a human liver with some fava beans and washed it down with a bottle of Chianti.

The reader who has not thrown up so far might yet be startled to learn that the same Dr Lecter had once had a big psychiatric practice. He even wrote for several psychiatric and gourmet journals, and responded to serious correspondence from students even in fields un-related to his own. Now, in what lies the secret appeal of such a man to the likes of the young female investigator, Clarice Starling, who otherwise seems so normal? It is clear, both in the book and the film, that the Lecter—Starling relationship has several parameters. It is simultaneously an analyst—analysand relationship, a teacher—pupil (or guru—*shishya*) relationship and, most intriguingly, a romantic relationship, unless we invoke the psychoanalytic notions of transference and counter-transference to explain the third aspect.

However we view this personal side of their relationship, the fact remains that at their last face-to-face meeting in Memphis, when Starling goes to see Lecter on her own, the now clearly bewitched psychiatrist remarks at once, 'People will say we're in love'. And just as she is about to leave, wrenching herself free from protesting officers of the law, she dashes back to take Lecter's proferred file, their forefingers barely touch (the film, rather melodramatically, converts this into an outright Lecter caress) and the scalding moment leaps to life in a film so ostensibly devoid of the tender emotions. As if to confirm the buried implications of this moment, in the following scene before Lecter kills the two policemen, the camera pans to a charcoal sketch of Lecter's depicting Clarice with a spring lamb.

The other two aspects of the Lecter—Starling relationship merit rather more scrutiny. To begin with, the teacher—pupil (or, guru—shishya) relationship. This is made rather more explicit in the film when Clarice straightaway confesses to Lecter that she has come to learn. By steady progression we reach the crucial Memphis sequence when this aspect of the relationship becomes unmistakable. Quoting the Roman Emperor, Marcus Aurelius, Lecter lays down first principles: 'Of each particular thing ask: What is it in itself, in its own constitution? What is its casual nature?' Applying this principle rigorously, he is able to show that the fundamental nature of the killer that Clarice seeks is to covet, not to kill. Therefore, he kills the women he does because he seeks to be like them. Clarice, needless to say, is duly impressed. Towards the end of the film, we see her repeating Lecter's words to her room-mate, Andelia.

However, it is the analyst—analysand relationship between Lecter and Starling that is most intriguing. Though Lecter mocks psychoanalysis — referring to it in the novel as 'the dead religion of psychoanalysis' — it is clear that the therapeutic procedure he adopts with Clarice is well within orthodox Freudianism with a Christian bias. He makes Clarice confess her recurring nightmare: the screaming spring lambs which she could not save from being slaughtered in the Lutheran ranch in Montana where she went to stay after her father's death.

The film, indeed, bristles with Christian symbolism. Apart from the implied reference to Christ as the sacrificial paschal lamb, one of the brutally savaged policemen is strung up above Lecter's cell like Christ on the Cross in an obvious mockery of the Crucifixion. Lecter's obsession with the Crucifixion is also evident in his desire to acquire a 'crucifixion watch', as he tells Clarice. Lecter is obviously the new anti-Christ whose obsession with Christianity is such that he even draws Golgotha after the Deposition, after Duccio. Also, in the book if not in the film, he asks Clarice if she has read the Gospel of St John which is the only Gospel to refer to Christ as the paschal lamb. Significantly, his final question to Clarice is: 'Have the lambs stopped screaming?' They certainly do in the book, whose closing sentence informs us that 'Clarice ... sleeps deeply, sweetly, in the silence of the lambs'. In the film, Lecter walks away from us in quest of his next victim — Dr Chilton — his 'dinner' as he quietly tells Clarice over the phone.

The fictional predecessor of Lecter is, of course, Sherlock Holmes with whom he has a good deal in common. Both are connoisseurs of classical music: Holmes of Mendelssohn and Lecter of Bach. Both are great inferrers, of course, and use the method of 'retrospective prophecy' employed in several physical sciences. But, unlike Holmes who, apart from his phenomenal powers of observation, is a bit of a philistine, Lecter's interests are wide-ranging. He likes poetry, especially Donne, whom he quotes in a condolence note to Crawford, and is clearly interested in the history of painting: he refers to Titian's *The Flaying of Marsyas* as well as to the anatomical studies of the eighteenth century, and to the French painter, Theodore Gerricault's *The Raft of the Medusa*. In addition to all this, Lecter has an acute sense of smell, and at their first meeting is able to tell Clarice that she uses Evyan skin cream and her perfume is L' Air du Temps.

What about Lecter's reasoning? Is it logical? Possibly he hits off Buffalo Bill but otherwise, like Holmes, it is all a bit of inspired guess—work. While Hugh Kingsmill described Holmes as an 'inspired imbecile', Dr Joseph Bell, the Edinburgh surgeon who taught Sir Arthur Conan Doyle, referred to the Sherlock Holmes stories as 'a cataract of drivel'. Drivel or not, they are appealingly human. In a recent lecture at the Institute of Psychiatry, London, Dr Michael Shepherd has redeemed the reputation of Holmes by claiming that his method has inspired Sigmund Freud, no less — as Freud himself acknowledged in a private letter to Jung which Dr Shepherd quotes.

In any case, Lecter is clearly an amalgam of Holmes and Freud, although he has probably more in common with Joseph Mengele and the Nazi doctors at Auschwitz and Buchenwald ('Hannibal Lecter' is clearly a German-sounding name). Already, after two films (he appeared first in *Headhunters* based on Thomas Harris' *Red Dragon*), he is a mythopoeic character, like James Bond, slipping readily into the collective unconscious. We eagerly await his filmic return, to savour yet again the soaring intellect behind the cold, cannibalistic infamies.

Martin Scorcese, *Cape Fear* (1991)

It is an unmitigated disaster, by far the worst movie ever made by Scorcese in an otherwise distinguished career. Nearly all the major critics — all the way from the magisterial John Simon to his *bete noire*, Rex Reed — have panned it, with Simon even calling it 'one of the costliest and most elaborate duds to come out of Hollywood'. So what's new? Only the question: Why does *Cape Fear* (a remake of the '61 thriller by J. Lee Thompson with Gregory Peck and Robert Mitchum in the lead roles) fail so comprehensively? After all, it has Robert De Niro, the Marlon Brando of this generation, who sparkled in *Godfather II*, *Scarface* (1983), in Scorcese's own *Raging Bull* (1980) and, more recently, in the same director's *Good Fellas* (1993). It has Jessica Lange, no mean actress by any standards; it has the shining new star, Nick Nolte, and a host of supporting talent on the technical side: the brilliant Freddie Francis (photography), Bernard Herrmann's original score from the '61 version (albeit souped up to '91 requirements by Elmer Bernstein), hyper-kinetic editing by Thelma Schoonmaker. Why, it has even the great Saul Bass (assisted this time by his wife, Elaine) to do the opening titles which you mustn't miss if you are going to see the film. To cap it all, it brings back Peck and Mitchum to do little cameos. Why, then, does *Cape Fear* not deliver?

The answer to the question posed in the foregoing paragraph, quite simply, adds up to the perils inherent in 'remakitis'. Consider first the technical side. Freddie Francis may be a good cameraman (he has directed several horror films himself) and he has told us at great length about his experiments in *Cape Fear*. How he used only Eastman Kodak 5428 or 5296 and nothing else, and the fast stock exclusively for 80 per cent of the film; how he used half-a-key lighting and three-quarters lighting and what he euphemistically calls 'customer's lighting' for the storm sequence when De Niro and Nolte battle it out at the end. But, pray, what does all this add up to in the final analysis? Very little, I'm afraid, except sound and fury signifying that Scorcese is the real star of this movie. In one sequence, De Niro is seen hanging upside down (he is obliged to repeat this feat later for a rather more discernible reason) talking to young Danielle on the phone pretending to be her new drama teacher. Then, suddenly, he flip-flops and, for a change, the rest of the room is seen upside down — *but for no earthly reason!* Then, again, an ordinary game of squash between Nolte and his office girl-friend is photographed to simulate a sexual encounter: gratuitous mid-court collisions but little squash. We have X ray shots galore, swish pans, ugly close-ups (evidently designed to make the characters look repulsive) indeed, all the cinematic bag of tricks. The film's editor, Thelma Schoonmaker, joins in the fun by avoiding the usual cuts with the result that the characters often walk into the camera, blacking it out with alarming frequency.

The acting is no better. De Niro may well be the best-dressed ex-con to be seen from Hollywood after Victor Mature's Nick Bianca in Henry Hathaway's *Kiss of Death* (1947). His leisure wear is sharp enough to cause envy in Armani, and as he cruises by in his brand new red convertible sporting a natty Hawaiian shirt he could well be doing a commercial for General Motors. His prison education is no less impressive. It ranges from modern American literature (Thomas Wolfe's *Look Homeward Angel* to Henry Miller's notorious trilogy) to philosophy (Friedrich Nietzsche's *Thus Spake Zarathustra*, no less, from whence derives, no doubt, the demonic will-to-power). If we are to go by the evidence of the numerous tattoos on his body, he has picked up several quotations from the *Bible*, although the 'Loretta' over the splintered heart-shaped tattoo in front hints at something else altogether. Why, the man is so bookish he can even declaim the seventeenth—century German mystical poet, Angelus Silesius, after being beaten almost to death by Sam's hired thugs. Earlier he had cited from Paul's 'Epistle to the Galatians' ('Have you suffered so many things in vain?') in his efforts to educate Sam about the meaning of Suffering. Clearly, his 14 years in the state penitentiary have done him more good than Harvard or Yale. Not to speak of his knowledge of law, on the side as it were, to match wits with Sam Bowden. His years in prison — seven of them for murdering a fellow inmate, presumably after being sodomized by co-prisoners in a gang rape — have wonderfully toned up not only his mind but his muscles as well which could give even Arnold Schwarzenegger a run for his money. He is virtually indestructible, like Rasputin on whom he is clearly modelled. Also, he has taken a few quick lessons from Dr Hannibal, 'the Cannibal', Lecter from *The Silence of the Lambs* but lacks the Master's enormous chewing powers, as is clear from Lori's paltry facial injuries. To sum up, he is so improbable a mix of abilities as to fully merit the wry comment of the police chief (played by Robert Mitchum with his customary leaden-eyed melancholy): 'I don't know whether to look at him or read him.' The answer is obvious: you can only attempt to read him because Robert De Niro as Max Cady doesn't come alive as a real flesh-and-blood character like all the rest. He is a bloodless abstraction, an unrealized idea in the mind of the scriptwriter (Wesley Strick). He is probably devised as a messenger of God, an Angel of Death, or whatever to vent his pentecostal fury on the guilt-ridden, sinful Bowdens. But Max Cady never comes to screen life despite his hillybilly accent, his seersucker suits, his cigar-chewing, his love of classical music, his ghoulish grimaces, and his mirthless hyena laugh. He remains an impossible cross between Christ and anti-Christ (a large pin-up of Stalin adorns his prison cell, together with a varied assortment of books, icons, and symbols).

Sam Bowden (Nick Nolte), the New Essex lawyer with alimony briefs, is a philandering husband teetering on the edge of an affair with a law clerk, Lori (so repellantly played by Illeane Douglas that the Sunday audience I saw the film with in Madras laughed gleefully at her comeuppance). He has already sinned twice, first by that earlier marital indiscretion at Connecticut and then by suppressing evidence in Cady's favour: that the girl who was assaulted was promiscuous. Ergo, Sam deserves what he and his family get. This is the film's implacable logic on which everything is built.

Bowden's wife, Leigh (played edgily with a hint of neurosis by Jessica Lange) seems not to give a damn for anyone or anything around except her English terrier, Benjamin, whose sudden death reduces her to near hysteria. She is clearly a sexually frustrated woman (kneading her forehead and applying lipstick listlessly just after lovemaking) saddled with a husband who plays cat and mouse with her (asking for an encore of the way she brings down her shoulder straps at night but ignoring her attempts at a wifely kiss the following morning). She is a graphic designer, trying to do a logo for a travel agency but is clearly unstable emotionally. Her big scene comes when she overhears her husband talking to Lori on the phone, but thereafter she seems to become a mere appendage to the plot. Only at the fag end does she come to life again, confronted by Cady's immediate threat to Danielle. In this scene, she is truly magnificent.

Against all minuses, we have to place the A-plus performance of Juliette Lewis as Danielle Bowden, the sole progeny of the bickering Bowdens. In what is arguably the film's finest sequence, the wily Cady has lured the unwary Danielle into the deserted basement where he sits inside a make-believe gingerbread house — clearly the set of Little Red Riding Hood ('I am the big bad wolf' says Cady for starters). He first charms her by offering her a joint. Probing her about the Thomas Wolfe she is carrying with her, he describes it, in a parade of learning, as a *roman a clef* before introducing the subject of Henry Miller's *Sexus*— a copy of which, sure enough, turns up under the geranium pot on her doorstep the next day. Then he proceeds to shove his thumb into her mouth not once but twice and lets her suck it suggestively in a clear mimesis of you know what before moving in for a regulation kiss. In the ensuing mix of dread, fascination, and possible sexual arousal, we sense both Danielle's burgeoning sexuality as well as her utter vulnerability. Both the tension and tautness of the scene make it pure Scorcese. If a movie as disappointing as *Cape Fear* can be redeemed by a single scene, then this is it.

Scorcese being an incorrigible film buff (it is said that he employs a full-time archivist and the VCRs work overtime), there are tributes as well as quotes from several Hollywood films. Max Cady's much-tattooed torso (words, images, et al.) derives from yet another Mitchum starrer, *Night of the Hunter* (1955). The gruesome kitchen murders at *chez* Bowdens are pure Hitchcock and, of course, Bernard Hermann's score is an incessant reminder of that late master's *Psycho*. There is, too, a stylish quote from Douglas Sirk. Still, all this doesn't add up to a satisfying whole and *Cape Fear* remains a congeries of dazzling fragments yoked together without achieving unity. With the result that it is never clear what *Cape Fear* is all about. Is it about the threat to the nuclear family as with *Fatal Attraction*? But this film is far too ambitious for just that. Is it about the return of the repressed in the person of Cady? Martin Scorcese himself has gone on record that the film is about 'guilt, obsession. All the old stuff. All my old friends.' Mighty good intentions from a man who once wanted to be a priest ! But these intentions are either insufficiently or sometimes inartistically realized. In the words of the *Newsweek* reviewer, *Cape Fear* remains 'a small B-movie dressed up in haute couture'.

Some Aspects of Modern Indian Cinema

1

The Problems of Post-colonial Cinema

The peculiarity of 'our place in the world' which isn't to be confused with anybody else's. The peculiarity of our problems which aren't to be reduced to subordinate forms of any other problem. The peculiarity of our history, laced with terrible misfortunes which belong to no other history. The peculiarity of our culture which we intend to live and to make live in an ever more real manner.
Aime Cesaire *in his letter of resignation to the French Communist Party*

V.S. Naipaul's *An Area of Darkness* is not a popular book in India and its author is a much misunderstood man. His experience of India, however, is relevant to any understanding of the 'colonial experience' where you learn 'to live with the idea of subjection' — live within 'our lesser world', as he so aptly puts it in his more recent *A Wounded Civilization*, and learn 'to pretend it was whole because we had forgotten even that it had been shattered'. There is a short chapter towards the end of his earlier book that seems to me to encapsulate the whole post-Independence, post-colonial experience so marvellously that it is worth recalling here before we go on to the problems of the Indian film-maker since Independence. Naipaul makes a half-reluctant, duty-inspired journey to the ancestral village which his maternal grandfather had left several decades earlier to work as an indentured labourer in Trinidad. The first phase of the visit, as he approaches the village by jeep, is characterized by a sense of tremulous awe. Gone is the petulance, the constant sense of being perpetually on edge that India seems to have brought about in him when for a whole year, as he says, 'I had not learned acceptance'. But now, as he approaches his village, in spite of himself he is 'held'. The shrines built through the charity of his grandfather look 'reassuring'; a man clad in loincloth and sacred thread who is bathing looks elegant. 'How,' Naipaul muses, 'in the midst of populousness and dereliction had such beauty been preserved?' This is the apogee of the first stage, a stage which I have characterized as being dominated by a sense of tremulous awe. The second stage is characterized by embarrassment caused by encounter with the 'fabled' reality, a reality embodied for Naipaul in the person of the derelict Jussodra who knew his Trinidad grandfather and who now sentimentally recalls the past. Naipaul offers her money and even arranges for a *katha*. This phase culminates eventually in a feeling of almost guilty nostalgia symbolized by the old Hindi film song which Naipaul, now back in his hotel, identifies as a long-forgotten song of the thirties. The third phase of Naipaul's visit to the village is signalled by an abrupt return to the now familiar-irritation and disgust of much of the book. Naipaul feels overwhelmed by the poverty that he cannot do anything about, by the psychological demands made on him by Ramachandra's nagging importunacy. He leaves the village in a frenzy of 'futility and impatience', and because Naipaul is the humanist that he is, even this frenzy is qualified by a certain amount of self-reproach.

I believe that Indian cinema has since 1947 traversed all these three phases in its attempt to cope with Indian reality. Tremulous awe has been followed by embarrassment disguised as nostalgia which, of late, has been giving way to mounting irritation. But basically it has been a post-colonial cinema defined at all levels of sensibility and expression by its starting points and initial premises. My phases are not necessarily historical, although it is useful to construe them historically. So that not merely does Indian cinema as a body reflect these changes over the last thirty years but, sometimes, even a single film-maker, like Ray, reflects these changes in his attitudes and his entire corpus falls almost conveniently into these phases. The early trilogy is characterized almost entirely by this sense of tremulous awe. It is not surprising that the India of the trilogy is seen through a child's eyes, suffused with sentiment and a child's exaggerated sense of reality. It is almost as if India has been *rediscovered*, visually at any rate, after centuries of foreign rule and hence the sense of almost terrifying novelty. This is fundamentally the India of the anthropologists, emerging after the long night of colonialism and, not surprisingly, there is little or no evil in this world. Except for the would-be seducer in *Aparajita* (1956), there is no character in the trilogy who is anywhere near evil, and even he is associated visually with the monkeys who, even as they

are a menace in the Apu household, are a *natural* menace. It is this
Ray whom the West cherishes; it is this Ray who is dear to the heart
of the colonized, alienated Indian because through the prism of the
beautiful trilogy, India looks simplified, crystalline, almost whole. Still,
it is not the 'real' India.

The second phase in Ray is discernible most clearly in *Devi* (1960)
where embarrassment at the Indian reality is almost camouflaged by
nostalgia and the simple, if beautiful, evocation of the Kali cult is
at variance not only with Ray's Brahmo agnosticism but with the
rationalism of the Mill—Bentham-inspired hero of the film. In
Mahapurush (1965) the nostalgia gives way to a more strident critique,
but perhaps *Charulata* (1964) is the *locus classicus* of this mood. Here
there is no longer the tremulous awe of the first period, and surely
even Charu's lyrical awakening to the possibilities of life is a wholly
different thing. There are certainly more cognitive elements operative
in this phase — and this is the *differentia* from the first phase — and
the rift between Bhupati and Charu is symptomatic of a larger rift
between England and India. Politically it is as if India is beginning
dimly to be conscious of herself but, like Charu's fugitive search for
happiness, the attempt is doomed to failure. But the enigmatic end
of the film on a freeze showing both the imminent reconciliation of
the couple and their essential alienation indicates, I think (if I'm not
being too fanciful here) that, like E.M. Forster's Aziz and Fielding,
there can be no true relationship between England and India till India
is liberated. Doubt and dubiety have entered the relationship and if
nostalgia were not also present, the tone of pessimism might have
been sharper. In *Nayak* (1966), too, there is a vein of nostalgia for
a more immediate past, but the burden of the present is felt more
keenly and remorselessly. Perhaps that little girl Rita whom the hero
briefly befriends is too sentimental and too much of a lyric abstraction,
too much of a residual element from the past, to serve as a critique
of the hero's value system and, by implication, of contemporary life.
Pratidwandi (1970) marks the end of Phase II and the beginning of
Phase III and the accompanying mounting irritation. But here, too,
the bird call that symbolizes for the hero some lost innocence (in
our terms the residue of the child's wonder of the trilogy) is too abstract
and metaphysical a device to throw any light on the dilemma of contemporary India. In *Seemabaddha* (1971) the place of the bird call
is taken by the convent-educated Sudarshana with her Sunday school
pieties, but Ramalingam, that wizened quoter of Conrad and the *Kural,*

is a more authentic guide to conduct in the film. In *Jana Aranya* (1975) the exasperation with the present reaches epic Naipaulian proportions and Ray cannot find an anchor within the existing social structure to lend any perspective on the supervening anomie in the social body. The hero's father is really a spent force and his sister-in-law is too cynical to really afford any stay against the centrifugal force loose in society. Significantly, Ray has gone back in his next film *Shatranj Ke Khiladi* (1977) to Phase II — nostalgia covering embarrassment with Indian reality yet again!

The truth is that the colonial experience is, to quote Naipaul again, an experience 'without a past, without ancestors'. Naipaul himself can find anchorage and meaning in India only in cultural oddments, in a communally eaten meal on a Himalayan journey, in an old half-forgotten film song of the thirties, in a garland placed on his pillow by an unknown admirer of his books and, most poignantly, in the gift of cloth from a casual Delhi acquaintance. But, in spite of all this, India at the end of his book is still to him an enigma, a puzzle, an area of darkness. This is symbolized for him in that extraordinary dream reported in the closing pages, the meaning of which, he says, he 'desires above everything else to find, but which I knew I never would'.

To the Indian film-maker, too, India remains, despite his best efforts, an area of darkness. And so he too enacts the awe—embarrassment—irritation syndrome that we examined in Naipaul. As I said earlier, my categories are not necessarily historical, and any one of these may be found in combination with any of the other two, although perhaps the tremulous awe at the 'Glory that is India' has receded somewhat of late although it held the stage for a long time under the guise of neo-realism, or, should I rather call it neo-Raylism — films which were really the lengthened shadow of Ray. In the 1970s the favourite formula has been a combination of nostalgia and anger because in this way, I suppose, our film-makers can hope to get the best of both worlds. Phase II, I should add, is a very attractive position from every point of view. In the early *Samskara* (1970) made by Pattabhi Rama Reddy, a gentle evocation of Brahmin orthodoxy went alongside a somewhat rationalistic critique of orthodoxy that looks strangely colonial in its belligerence towards the past and could have come straight from the author of the four-volume *History of British India*, the elder Mill. This vein of exasperation at contemporary India has proved award-winning for, apart from *Samskara*, M.T. Vasudevan Nair's *Nirmalayam*

(1973) and Girish Kasarvalli's *Ghatashraddha* (1977) come to mind
with their nice mix of nostalgia and irritation. *Nirmalayam* was nostalgic
about earlier residues of feeling and even paid rich homage to them,
but suddenly turned hostile in the depiction of the Velichapad's act
of desecration. *Ghatashraddha* was altogether more genteel in everything,
including its anger, but ploughed the same furrow and reaped the
same old harvest. John Abraham's *Agraharathil Kazhuthai* (1977), albeit
inspired by Bresson's *Au Hazard Balthazar* (1966), even manages a
bit of stray piety and strangely lards its denunciation of Brahminism
with quotations from the *Upanishads* and choice bits from the Brahmin
poet Bharatiyar! This is fundamentally neo-colonial cinema, and I have
little sympathy with it because of the director's complicity with what
he is attacking.

The other vein with which I am intellectually in greater sympathy
is represented in the films of Shyam Benegal, although emotionally
I feel distant from him. His development from *Ankur* (1973) onwards
has shown a movement towards criticism of contemporary India more
from within than without. The formula is the same — nostalgia al-
ternating with irritation, but the nostalgia is not strictly decor but
more organic and structural. *Nishant* (1975) not only begins with the
priest's morning prayers, but the revolt against the *zamindar* is triggered
off by a *harikatha* rendering of the *Ramayana*, and engineered by no
less a person that the priest himself! The invasion of the *zamindari*
stronghold is not a little like the invasion of Lanka by the monkey
hordes of Lord Hanuman! *Manthan* (1976) makes a reference to the
Vishnupurana in its title; in the film both *devas* (the cooperative run
by Karnad and his men) and *asuras* (Amrish Puri and his henchmen)
churn for the proverbial milk before the Goddess of Wealth, Lakshmi,
can rise from the ocean of India's poverty. In *Kondura* (1977), which
I haven't seen, Benegal, I understand, makes use of mythological themes
to meet tyranny on its own terms so that the social enemy can be
fought with his own moral beliefs.

Benegal's solution to the problem of the Indian film-maker today
underscores the need to come to terms with the culture before changing
or reforming society. In this he is not unlike Glauber Rocha and Nelson
Pereira dos Santos (both of Brazil) whose *Tent of Miracles* (1978) was
an eye-opener. Glauber Rocha has gone on record in an interview
in *Imago* (Feb. '70) that in Latin America, 'the Revolution will not
be made by the University people who are working for Marx and
Mao but by the ignorant people. For the Brazilian revolution there

are the blacks, the priests, the bandits, the peasants and the intellectuals who are all caught in the same thing.' Jansco of Hungary, too, has shown in his *Red Psalm* (1971) that revolution does not lie in the destruction of ritual but in a transformation of ritual into something that unites people instead of oppressing them. The peasant's song in *Red Psalm* is, in effect, a *red* Lord's Prayer and hence the film's title.

If the Indian film is to be truly Indian as well as revolutionary there has to be a return to life as lived by her own people with all the complexities (psychological, cultural, and social) brought about by centuries of foreign rule. Benegal himself, though fundamentally on the right track, is unsatisfactory when it comes to portraying the psychological deformities and fundamental alienation which must needs infect even his agents of social change. He is quite unselfconscious in his portrait of the petty bourgeois schoolteacher in *Nishant* and the veterinary doctor in *Manthan*. Both are played by the Oxford-educated Karnad whose clothes and speech mannerisms, particularly when he breaks out into English ('I will teach the bloody swine if it is the last thing I do', is one of his efforts in *Manthan*) need the ingenuity of a Frantz Fanon to analyse. The life-style, particularly the sexual life-style, of the Karnad wives in both films begs for political analysis in post-colonial terms, but Benegal is strangely unaware. But the constant titillation of the bourgeois sexual nerve in all his films shows that at the level of felt behaviour — if not at the level of idea — his cinema shows an even more intense bourgeoisification than the popular cinema that is violently at odds with his avowed political intentions.

How I wish our revolutionary film-makers would study Turgenev, the nineteenth-century Russian novelist, particularly the Turgenev of the later novels like *Smoke* and *Virgin Soil.* Benegal's portrait of Karnad in *Manthan* could have profited from a study of Turgenev's portrait of the poet-revolutionary Nazhdanev's efforts to make his way among the masses whom he hopes to liberate. He is met with stares of bewilderment when he urges them to 'rise'. Enticed into a tavern where the peasants pour vodka down his throat, Nazhdanev, says Turgenev, 'began talking, talking endlessly, shouting wrathfully, malignantly shaking broad horny hands, kissing slobbery beards'. Turgenev understood it all completely: the liberal's efforts to be what he is not. Benegal shows no such troubled awareness, and his portrait of the liberal bourgeois's discomfiture is confined to the cameo portrait of Karnad's clinging, stupid wife in *Manthan* who sulks when her husband has to be away. Telegram in hand, he announces his transfer to Head

Office in terms of the bitterest irony but ... what about him? In his smart Levis and trendy shirts is he really any different? The way he flings the garland away casually in the beginning of the film tells a lot about him. His portrait, which is crucial to our understanding of the film, is thin and vapid: he is a two-dimensional cardboard figure. The missing dimension — the Turgenev dimension — is the consciousness of his urban background which would have enabled Benegal to give us a rounded portrait. As it stands, *Manthan* is marred by psychological and sociological naïvete. Still, in the scene of the burning of the Harijan huts, it has crossed the Rubicon and the true political cinema of tomorrow seems at last a distinct possibility.

Indian films have to come to terms with the past before they can deal with the present. Irritation or anger at oppression or servility — Naipaul's annoyance at Ramachandra in *An Area of Darkness* — is no substitute for honest analysis. Mrinal Sen's films of late, tending to substitute irritation for objective appraisal, commit this mistake and fail to be credible. The structures of the past have to be carried over into an analysis of the present before the solutions of the future are to be sought. Not contempt for the past but an enlightened use of it to throw light on the present will revitalize the Indian cinema. Such uses of the past alone will bring it out of the doldrums of the colonial period into the drum-beats of the pulsating and pregnant future.

2

Art and Commerce: Is There a Choice?

Anyone who has given the least thought to Indian cinema (and who hasn't except, of course, the government and maybe a few madmen) is aware of the prevailing confusion between the conflicting claims of art and commerce. Of late, it has got a novel twist by being cast in political terms. The champions of art are invariably cosmopolitan intellectuals (who have probably spent their formative years in the capitals of Europe), frightened at the prospect of encroaching indigenization: Shahani's nightmare is of a 'Hindu physics, Buddhist psychology and Muslim sociology reconciled in a new, secular, sovereign way'.

The champions of commerce, on the other hand, translating their box-office anxieties into the new, fashionable language of alienation, talk glibly of 'Indianness' and the need for Indian cinema to have an 'identity'. They cloak their degenerate values by talking, these days, even in terms of Third World cinema. Of course there are quite a few caught in the middle who belong, really, to neither world (Shyam Benegal) or simultaneously to both (Shabana Azmi, the late Smita Patil). The Film Institute boys and girls (particularly the girls) have done little to resolve the dichotomy and even the great hopes pinned on the International Film Festivals have not really materialized. Anyone who witnessed the dismal spectacle of the Indian Panorama at the Delhi Film Festival in 1981, where art and commerce cohabited shamelessly for a continuous fortnight is not likely to forget it easily. The most disturbing aspect of the anthology of essays, *Indian Cinema Superbazaar*, edited by Aruna Vasudev and Philippe Lenglet is that the editors have no perspective either on the direction Indian cinema should take. Lacking an overall view (there is, rather disconcertingly, no comprehensive introductory essay), the editors merely appear — nondescriptly,

innocuously — among the list of contributors, and even here their in-
terventions do little to dispel the general confusion that prevails. The
result is a bewildering display of cinematic exotica ranging from Madan
Gopal Singh — acolyte at the shrines of Marx, Althusser, Lacan and
Rashmi Doraiswamy! — to the octogenarian V. Shantaram who made
his first film in 1932. There is little or no perspective on the growth
and development of Indian cinema except as a meaningless medley
of dates, although we have some pretty high sounding titles. So we
have B.D. Garga's 'diachronic perspective' which tells us nothing which
we did not already know about Raghunath Raina! This is not the
Raina who railed only three years ago against the 'colonial' middle-class
Ray, the Raina who told us that Ray made films without villains,
without anger, and whose attempts 'to present characters in the social
context' were dismal failures 'for exactly two decades'. Instead we are
now told that Ray's 'characters have a recognizable identity and their
relationships are explored within the social context'. Strange, indeed,
are the whirligigs of time! Confusion, then, is rampant.

Let's take a quick look at the hot-shot film merchants represented
here to see the way the cookie crumbles in Bombay. Yash Chopra's
ideas of the 'experimental' low budget film, the new 'parallel cinema',
are symptomatic of a hypocritical ethos. He simply scoffs at it: 'It's
not experimental in saying' [*sic*] our oracle asserts, 'It's experimental
in rupees and paise.' His example of a truly 'experimental' film is
his very own *Silsila* on the making of which we are given some truly
astonishing details. 'For Silsila [*sic*] I needed flowers, so I went overseas.
Within one hour of reaching the location I started shooting. And the
moment I finished, I took a plane back. We spent four days shooting
and two days travelling.' This, then, must be the truly 'experimental'
film, 'experimental' in terms of 'rupees and paise'! The famous director
of *Sholay* (1975) is equally forthright in defending violence in films.
'What do you mean by too much violence in films?' he shoots back,
'A *nation* is *entitled* to *keep its army*. What can you do when com-
municating with ignorant masses? You give one blow, it doesn't register
with them. So you have to give ten blows before it finally registers.'
Feroz Khan, too, sings the same old song. For him 'it's a question
of terminology. If you call action violence, we call violence action.'
He even resorts to dubious scientific evidence to *prove* that violence
in films is not socially harmful: 'It's been proved medically that a
person even under deep hypnosis cannot be made to do anything that
is contrary to his will ... *It's been proved* .' More medical facts follow

in defence of the indefensible. But medicine or no medicine, the fact remains that people in India *are* influenced negatively by violence in films. What does Feroz Khan have to say about that? 'But here with the lack of education, the standard is low, therefore people tend to be a little more influenced,' the Khan grudgingly concedes. No more talk of medical evidence it seems?

We can't honestly blame the film industry tycoons when even our best critics seem blinded by their infamous tryst with Bombay's cinematic destiny. No less a person than Bikram Singh has this to say of realism, Bombay-style. After some token gestures against the lack of 'realism' in Bombay films, Singh proceeds to give us his ideas of 'realism'. Realism is Smita Patil's bathing glory in *Chakra* (1980) (every box-office merchant would heartily concur), *not* Ray's portrait of destitution in *Pather Panchali* which is too obscene a thing for representation ... a kind of pornography'. Please note that it is poverty that is obscene (unless it is properly dressed up as in Mehboob's *Mother India*)and not Smita Patil's fleshy and ample charms! Again the Bombay film merchants would assent wholeheartedly. In the same vein, our apostle of 'realism' offers a spirited defence of the current wave of crime films as 'in some way or other a vehicle of protest against the dehumanizing effects of poverty and the conditions and systems that create and sustain it'. Thus Amitabh in his films, 'acts to set things right ... stopping at nothing ... to plan a victory'. The 'Amitabh persona' is 'the desperate fantasy of a nation wishing for ... a strong, uncomplex, dynamic person who can snap his fingers and set things right ...' By the end of the essay, the *Hamlet* quoting Singh sees *relevance*, after all, in the Bombay commercial film. In a companion piece, Manojit Lahiri, sees in the 'clean commercial' (which surely is a contradiction in terms), 'the dawn of a golden period'. This I take to mean a period where more gold is made — from dawn to dusk.

Just how confused our film-makers are about what constitutes 'art' and 'commerce' comes out in the confused nature of their answers to the question: what is the meaning of commitment in cinema? We have already examined Bikram Singh's extraordinary thesis that the Bombay cinema is 'in some way or other a vehicle of protest' (I like that 'in some way or other'!). The late Sukhdev — the blue-eyed boy of documentary cinema — takes this thesis to the farthest point of absurdity by declaring Hollywood to be 'the most perfect kind of *political* film-making'. Why? Because 'the real political film has got to be seen by the masses'. On this count naturally every kind of Bombay imbecility

— from *Sholay* to *Shalimar* (1978) — qualifies, for these meet the Sukhdev requirement of being 'seen by the masses' — which seems a further watering down of the Bikram Singh requirement of 'acceptance by the mass audience'.

The obverse of this kind of quiet sell-out (not for nothing was Sukhdev one of the very few artists in India who found the Emergency positively bracing) is the pessimism of a man like Karnad who thinks political films can't be made at all. If you make a film on the burning of Harijans, that is 'an exploitation of the subject' and, according to Karnad, 'will in no way solve the problem'. To solve the problem 'you should go there and work for them'. This seems a needless confusion of the purposes of art with those of politics. It leads Karnad to the judgement that Mrinal Sen is not 'a working-class revolutionary' in *Ekdin Pratidin* but a middle-class father, 'and that K.A. Abbas is not 'a communist, a leftist, a revolutionary' at all but just a sentimentalist. But this old venerable game of unmasking pretensions can degenerate into downright cynicism masquerading as forthright moral judgement, and can reduce to a shambles any honest effort, let alone Abbas's. The Oxford-educated Karnad is just suffering from a guilty conscience, a moral hangover from his *Samskara*, *Kaadu* (1973) and *Vamsa Vriksha* (1971) days. Everyone is guilty, he insists, simply because he is guilty. Benegal is far shrewder than this. He simply blames a particular kind of popular political cinema (and we know just who his targets are!) where 'there's no sense of exploring ... no process of articulating'. His simultaneous defence of entertainment 'looks less convincing and more suspect', especially when he claims that it can be 'totally anti-status quo'. Pious hope indeed, unless Benegal can first redefine 'entertainment' suitably. Far, far more 'honest' to reject political films because you don't like them, because you are not 'interested in politics'. This is exactly what Shashi Kapoor tells us, though he goes on, disingenuously, to find fault with K.A. Abbas's theory of political cinema.

'To ridicule the rich and [go] in for the poor' is not just old-fashioned theory as Kapoor imagines but quite, simply bad cinema. But this doesn't dispose of the other varieties of political cinema.

Ultimately we are left with two authentic spokesmen: one for the 'popular' cinema (the psychoanalyst Sudhir Kakar) and one for the unpopular 'political' cinema (Kumar Shahani but, alas, not Mani Kaul whose 'cinematic object' is stranded in the labyrinthine maze somewhere between Kaul's own 'Walking sprout' and 'Invariant deep sleep'!). While Bikram Singh found the *Pather Panchali*an poverty 'pornographic',

Shahani reserves the epithet for the political film *à la* Costa-Gavras: 'I think one of the most reactionary film-makers in the world is Costa-Gavras, and he has probably done more harm to the actual realtionship between politics and cinema than anyone else I can think of. He utilized it for absolutely commercial purposes.' Well and truly said, indeed, especially in India, where Gavras has a cult following (his *Missing* [1982] was awaited more avidly than any other film with the exception of Guney's *Yol* [1980]). Political cinema, for Shahani, has to be made through the form and not through the content. So commercial cinema, however 'revolutionary' its content is 'just madness'. He, however, grudgingly concedes its sociological value: 'Of course, it is a very important sociological force and I see it only as that, but I am not interested in it as cinema at all.' Because commercial cinema goes 'from the known to the known to the known and onwards', and not from the 'known to the unknown'. To go from Shahani to Sudhir Kakar is to go from one intellectual peak to another, with the confusions of art and commerce clearly visible in the valley that divides them. Kakar's defence of the commercial film rests on Bruno Bettelheim's distinctions between the 'unreal' and the 'untrue'. Hindi films, Kakar argues, may be 'unreal' but demonstrate a confident and sure-footed grasp of the topography of human desire and its vicissitudes and hence are not 'untrue'. Their domain is fantasy, the bridge between desire and reality, and they serve as vehicles of hope and healers of trauma. They alone help to keep, for adults, 'the road to childhood open'. And thus does Shahani's 'bazaar realism' transform into 'collective fantasy' in Sudhir Kakar's hands.

The Kakarian psychoanalytical model is basically an *affective* theory which starts with the experience of the audience. The Shahanian model stresses the creativity of the artist and the essential inviolability of his intentions. Between intentionality and affectivity, between the claims of art and its audience, Indian cinema stands petrified at the crossroads.

3

Films from Literature

The relation between Indian literature in English and film in India really begins with the making of R. K. Narayan's *Mr Sampath* (1949) into a film in 1951 (both in Tamil and Hindi) under the celebrated Gemini banner. The milieu of the film is south Indian and the characters basically speak Tamil. Gemini Ganesan, who was to become one of Tamil Nadu's leading stars, played the lead role while another budding star, Padmini, appeared opposite him in the Tamil version. In the Hindi version, Motilal replaced Gemini Ganesan.

Subsequently, several of Narayan's books have been made into films, the best known of them being *Guide* (1965), which was made both in English and Hindi. Pearl S. Buck wrote the screenplay of the English version which was directed by Tad Danielewski. The film was widely publicized since it was made in wide screen and in colour at an enormous cost. The little temple alone, at which Raju's apotheosis takes place, cost Rs 80,000 to build and had to be rebuilt elsewhere as it was washed away by flash floods.

Strangely, Narayan himself took exception to the film in a hilariously satirical essay published in *Life* magazine, entitled 'Misguided Guide' (included in his 1988 Penguin collection, *A Writer's Nightmare*). He was aghast at the extravagance of the locations (Jaipur and Udaipur in Rajasthan instead of tiny, fictitious Malgudi whose topography was known to thousands of Narayan's admirers all over the world) as well as by the constant shift of place. He even quoted Mrs Indira Gandhi as telling him 'Why should they have dragged the story all over as if it were a travelogue, instead of confining themselves to the simple background of your book?'

Also, the 'drastic changes' in the plot (like bringing Rosie back at the end to throw herself at the feet of the dying hero) and in the very conception of the characters themselves (particularly Rosie's archaeologist husband, Marco, who is turned into a drunkard and womanizer in the film) upset him. He quoted the director as justifying the changes by saying, 'We have paid the star three lakhs for her role and that is a lot of money. How can we let her get off midway? She will damn well stick till the end.'

Stick she certainly did, but not without getting her own back on the director. She refused to do a kissing scene as 'unbecoming an Indian woman'. Soon Narayan himself gave up: 'I trained myself to give up all attempts to connect the film with the book of which I happened to be the author.' On the whole, the film is unsatisfactory and the tantalizing ambiguity at the end of the book is wholly lost. Still, *Guide*'s delectable songs — the music director is the redoubtable S.D. Burman — shot mostly outdoors (unlike, say, American musicals which are mostly stylized and set indoors) have remained fresh and green in one's memory.

Where *Guide* departed quite riotously from the original, *Banker Margayya* (1983), made in Kannada and based on Narayan's *The Financial Expert* (1952), was so scrupulously faithful to its source that it has elicited unstinted praise for its maker, T.S. Nagabharana, from the author himself: 'Your presentation of my novel *The Financial Expert* is superb ... the storyline of the original is fully achieved, an unusual experience for me in the film world.' The film, a very moderate success, was included in the Indian Panorama at the Bombay Film Festival in 1984, and Narayan himself came down from Mysore to help the film along. The film has certainly a period charm and minor lapses in the leading lady's wardrobe do not mar its general impact.

More recently, *Swamy* (1988), based on Narayan's earliest book, *Swamy and Friends* (1935), was made initially in Hindi before being dubbed in English and shown at the London Film Festival (LFF) in November 1988. Loosely episodic, the film, directed by the late Shankar Nag, is vintage Narayan in a way that none of the earlier films, even *Banker Margayya*, was. The LFF programme note described it as 'timeless, amusing and thoroughly engrossing'.

Perhaps Narayan's views on the relation between film and literature may strike one today as being unduly biased in favour of the written word. Aesthetically, he clings to a strict bourgeois realism in the portrayal of both persons and places. Violation of the unities of action and place — if not of time — is, to him, a serious matter. His reflections on cinema (scattered throughout his two collections, *A Writer's Nightmare* and *A Story-Teller's World* [1989], also published by Penguin India), reveal a neo-classical outlook wholly at variance with that of most contemporary Indian film-makers.

Only Satyajit Ray shares much of Narayan's strictly orthodox outlook. His own views on cinema collected in *Our Films, Their Films* (1976) reveal a deeply 'classical' outlook, a label he himself has not disclaimed: 'If classical implies an orderly unfolding of events with a beginning, a middle and an end *in that order*; a firm rein applied to emotion; an avoidance of disorientation for its own sake, then I will be only too happy with the label.'

Ray's own adaptations from Indian literary classics are best illustrated by his adaptations from Rabindranath Tagore. *Three Daughters* (1961), a three-part film, is based on three of Tagore's short stories; *Charulata* (1964), again on a short story, and the *The Home and the World* (1984) on Tagore's novel published in 1912.

The first episode in *Three Daughters* is *The Postmaster*, unquestionably one of Ray's very best. His departure from the Tagore original is not merely in the addition of a few peripheral characters but in the marked change at the end. Instead of making the little girl, Ratan, plead with the departing postmaster, begging him to take her with him, Ray masterfully underplays her hurt, opting instead to focus on the hero's dilemma. As she walks past him with a bucket of water, ignoring his tip, she matter-of-factly informs the new incumbent, 'I have brought you water, Sir'.

Monihara, the second episode, is a horror film in a sense the Tagore story was not and Manimalika is certainly unlike any of the women in the Ray canon. The use of a famous Tagore song as a musical motif foreshadows similar employment in *Charulata*.

The last episode, *Samapti*, is more playful than either but is quintessential Ray, gently mocking the institution of marriage. It is not surprising that, in the same year (the Tagore centenary year), Ray made a full-length documentary on Tagore.

Charulata (1964) marks the peak of Ray's cinematic career, and the Tagore short story, *The Broken Nest* (1901), on which it is based, is ironed out to remove some nagging psychological gaps and improbabilities. One is the lack of appropriate build-up for a crucial plot turn (Umapada's treachery) and the other is the husband's 'marathon incomprehension' (the phrase is Ray's own) of his wife's love for her brother-in-law.

But the most serious departure from Tagore is at the end. In the Tagore story, Bhupati leaves his wife forever, but in Ray there is more than a hint of imminent reconciliation (if essential alienation) as the closing frames freeze on Bhupati's outstretched hand. The film is undoubtedly Ray's *chef d'oeuvre*.

Ghare Baire (1984), adapted from the Tagore novel of the same name even before *Pather Panchali* was made, is, ironically, the least satisfying of his films. The Tagore original itself is both florid and in somewhat questionable taste (as E.M. Forster noted in his review) and, worst of all, the characters are mere mouthpieces of the author's philosophy. These weaknesses are insufficiently mitigated in the Ray film, but the chief difficulty lies in the portrayal of the protagonist, Nikhil, himself. In the Tagore original, he comes across as flawed and all too human, but in Ray he is a plaster saint set on an impossibly high pedestal. The film's unremitting 'wordiness' makes it difficult to see or feel anything. If *Charulata* was a perfectly translucent mirror revealing the essentially tragic nature of love, in *Ghare Baire* the mirror is — to adapt Nikhil's own words — 'so broken ... crooked ... dusty' that it tells us very little about human love which, self-confessedly for Ray, the novel is all about.

Ray apart, several Indian film-makers have adapted novels, from various Indian languages, into film. Some of the best films on Indian subjects have been produced by the Merchant—Ivory team, and two of them — *The Householder* (1963) and *Heat and Dust* (1983), which had an international cast including Greta Scacchi and Julie Christie — are entirely based on the novels of the German-born Ruth Prawer Jhabwala, who has lived in India and is married to an Indian. Other writings (though not always by Indians), have provided material for expatriate Indian film-makers like Mira Nair in films like the recent *Mississippi Masala* (1991) and the Toronto-based Deepa Mehta, who is currently making a film on Bharati Mukherjee's *Days and Nights in Calcutta* (1977).

4

Richard Attenborough, *Gandhi* (1982)

A giant hoarding — put out by the United India Insurance Company — caught my eye in Madras. It showed Ben Kingsley as Gandhi at his *charkha* spinning ... yes, gold yarn! All was gold — representing, neatly, the eight Oscars the film bagged in Hollywood. The caption read A STRING OF SUCCESSES and, up above, in the right-hand top corner of the hoarding, a beaming Gandhi safely ensconced in fleecy white clouds — enjoying, no doubt, a well-earned rest from terrestrial exertions — seemed to look down with a good deal of satisfaction at his Hollywood apotheosis. Still the distance between the real Gandhi and the movie Gandhi — as the hoarding unwittingly suggests — is truly astronomical. Whereas Attenborough has concocted his yarn from beaten gold, the real Mahatma wove his from pure *desi* cotton. By trying to turn base cotton into shining bullion, Attenborough's cinematic alchemy has sought to improve the real Gandhi by ridding him of any adventitious imperfections. Forgotten in the process was Nehru's warning: 'Whatever you do, do not deify him — that is what we have done in India — and he was too great a *man* to be deifed.' In the result we have a shining new deity for mass worship, three times a day, at all the cinema palaces of the world, not the frail figure who trod untrodden paths in search of India's freedom.

Let us look at the cold facts first. While making *Gandhi*, Attenborough said, 'I want millions of people to know Gandhi' and so, no doubt, he spent millions of rupees to make sure that they did. Shooting — an average of about one minute 29 seconds of film a day — began on 26 November 1980 on a daily budget of Rs 5.7 lakhs. Multiply that by roughly 24 weeks location shooting and you get an idea of the cost of the film. But Richard is no fool and the returns — thanks to the two million dollars Columbia Pictures allegedly pumped into publicity alone — have been stupendous. US grosses have exceeded 400 million rupees and the rest of the Western overseas market has been a tidy million. All this, mind you, before May. In Bombay's Regal, it far outpaced the 17,000,940 rupee mark set by *The Towering Inferno*. Why even the charity show organized by the Gandhi Peace Foundation in Bangalore grossed Rs 36,650! So now we have another towering inferno belching fumes of non-violence upon a gullible world. For everyone will agree, I'm sure, that non-violence is the central subject of the film. (Significantly the last words of the film spoken in Gandhiji's voice are: 'When I despair I remember that all through history, truth and love have always won. There have been tyrants and murderers and for a time they can seem invincible but in the end they always fall. Think of it. Always.') The defendant is the West with its pitiful belief in violence and the chief witness for the prosecution is Mohandas Karamchand Gandhi. But the trial is rigged in a number of ways, the result a foregone conclusion.

So the film becomes a kind of didactic tract, really, proving in scene after pitiless scene that the West is guilty and wrong while Gandhian India is innocent and right. Nearly all the scenes in the film are con- scripted into the service of this doctrine, but Attenborough, with one eye cocked judiciously in the direction of the American market, is too shrewd a man not to add a bit of 'cheese' to the offering. And hence Candice Bergen's appearance somewhat late in the film when both Gandhi's and the film's energies seem to be virtually exhausted. Still, true to the iconography of the film, Miss Bergen, decked out in Army khaki, is heralded into the film in an army jeep driven by a Major of the US Army. Now, although the original Margaret Bourke- White was something of an intellectual who even wrote a book on India, there is nothing in Miss Bergen's voluptuous unctuousness to even remotely suggest this. 'Sometimes I would set up the camera in a corner of the room, sit some distance away from it with a remote control in my hand, and watch ...', wrote the self-effacing Miss Bourke- White; but Miss Bergen is anything but self-effacing. Of course she has been brought into the film for her sex-cum-box-office appeal (not for nothing is she given top billing with Ben Kingsley in the credits), and although she is made to mouth some pious platitudes, Attenborough is careful to train his camera on all the right angles. There is a particularly idiotic scene with Kasturba (wholly fictitious, of course, since Miss Bourke-White met neither Gandhi nor Kasturba in the Aga Khan palace), who tries to interest the American journalist on Gandhi's views on the injustices to women and untouchables. But the sexy American photographer has her mind on other things. 'Does it rankle being separated in this way?' she beguilingly asks the ageing woman and gets instead a long lecture on the Hindu philosophy of sexual renunciation. Undeterred, she pursues her quarry: 'You mean he gave up married life?' she asks incredulously, to which Kasturba replies with a shocking un-Indian candour: 'Four times he tried and failed but then he took a solemn vow.' 'And he's never broken it?' asks the sex-pot American star, and the pious Kasturba — after a properly respectable pause — says 'No'. Just how much importance Attenborough attaches to Miss Bergen's physical presence can be gauged by the fact that he lets the 'Torturer' (as Gandhi used to call Miss Bourke-White) hog the entire final scene. Turned out this time in figure-hugging clothes, she quizzes the Mahatma obliquely but irrelevantly on his private life, although the real Margaret Bourke-White asked Gandhi — she met him at 2 p.m. on the fateful day but took no photographs — about much graver world issues.[*] The overpowering feminine ambience of this scene — there is Manu, Abha, Bourke-White, besides the ubiquitous Mirabehn — only serves to accentuate Miss Bergen's undoubted charms as Attenborough keeps his camera trained, unremittingly, on her charming *derriere* through the entire course of the scene. 'You are a temptress', blurts out Gandhi as he tries to wrench himself away from the temptation. 'Only an admirer', protests Miss Bergen weakly, and Gandhi's last sentence in the film is addressed to her: 'Nothing is more dangerous especially for an old man.' Towering inferno indeed!

When R. R. Diwakar, the Chairman of the Gandhi Peace Foundation, was shown the completed film he was asked if the omission of certain aspects of Gandhi's life, the treatment of certain episodes in the film or certain personalities involved in the struggle for Independence distressed him. His reply must rank surely among the film's most cloudy trophies: 'What you have done,' he told Attenborough 'is a work of art. One would not dictate the number of feathers Picasso might chance to display on a dove's wing' (Richard Attenborough, *In Search of Gandhi*, p. 219). I am not aware of any doves that Picasso painted but let that pass. In any case, Attenborough is by no stretch of imagination

---

[*] *See* Margaret Bourke-White 'The Last Days with Gandhi' in *Profiles of Gandhi*, Delhi, 1969, pp. 85—92.

a Picasso, which is probably why he ventured to brighten the plumes of this particular dove in order to make it more attractive to the West. I'm not here to blame Attenborough for minor lapses. Indian criticism, for most part, has oscillated between the poles of sentimental adulation (Khushwant Singh was 'in tears most of the time' but then so were many others) or empty, silly complaints. Why does the fasting Gandhi not grow a beard wondered our premier playwright, Tendulkar, and decided it was a 'serious lapse'. How could Nehru wear a rose in his buttonhole when visiting a fasting Gandhi (fast again!) observed the outraged editor of the *Maharashtra Times*. So went the litany of complaints. Of course, Western criticism, too, has tended to blind adulation or to ill-informed (in a few cases ill-tempered too like Richard Grenier of *Commentary* [April 1983] who savages not only Attenborough but also the subject of the film!) criticism. Thus Sir Algernon Rumbold, KCMG, author of *Watershed in India 1914—22* (1979), who had served personally under Lord Irwin besides having worked in the India Office from 1929 to 1947 writes:[*]

Dyer is shown subsequently being asked trick questions by barristers on the Hunter Committee of Enquiry, without the benefit of legal aid. That is correct, although the film is wrong in recording exchanges which imply that women and children were present at the monstrous deed.

There are at least *four* errors concealed in Sir Algernon's observation. Firstly, although there were two Indian barristers on the Hunter Committee, in the film only one of them — Sir Chimanlal Setalwad — is shown actually asking Dyer any questions. Secondly, none of the questions put to Dyer can be termed as 'trick questions' although, often in the film, it is put into the mouth of the wrong member (as we will see later). Also Dyer's most damaging admissions were made to Lord Hunter and not to the Indian barristers, as Lord Sinha pointed out in the House of Lords. Thirdly it is not true historically that Dyer was denied the benefit of legal aid, and clearly Sir Algernon is simply repeating the canard spread by Dyer's adoring biographer, Ian Colvin. But this has been disproved ages ago in Sir George Barrow's *The Life of Sir Charles Monro*. On the contrary, legal aid was pressed on Dyer not only by the Government but also by well-meaning friends who knew his propensity to irritability. But the obstinate Dyer refused, saying he would and could conduct his own defence. Finally, Sir Algernon's assertion that women and children were not present

[*] 'Film, Facts and History', *Encounter*, March 1983, pp. 63—5.

at 'the monstrous deed' flies in the face of all evidence and is contradicted by almost everything we know about the event. (Only Dyer, in his submission to the Army Council, maintained the contrary.) So much for the still lingering apologists of the Raj.

But, the question remains: Has Attenborough remained 'faithful in spirit to the record' and tried, as he promised at the start of his film, to capture 'the heart of the man'? On the contrary, despite the initial disclaimer ('No man's life can be encompassed in one telling. There is no way to give each year its allotted weight, to include each event...', etc) the film tries to do precisely that. Titles periodically announce the period and place of the episode depicted and events *seem* to unroll before us in a stately, well-ordered procession. This looks like history itself, not the attempted recreation of the 'spirit' of any period or individual named Gandhi. But careful examination of any of the episodes in the film reveals that they have been twisted out of shape and distorted to propagate Attenborough's message to the West that there are 'other ways of ultimately solving our problems than blowing the other man's head off' (from the text of his speech to the American Motion Picture Academy on receiving his Oscar). What we have witnessed is not a film on Gandhi but a propaganda tract on the merits of non-violence. Hence the encomium at the start of the film from a Military General of all people, George C. Marshall, General Eisenhower's Secretary of State — about Gandhi being the 'conscience of all mankind'. And hence, too, those words of Gandhi to Mirabehn (East to West, pacifist to an Admiral's daughter) heard again at the end of the film as Gandhi's ashes are being immersed. We feel no grief, nor are we meant to.

In order to establish my claim I shall choose just three major episodes with which the film deals (Jallianwala Bagh, Chauri Chaura, and the Salt Satyagraha), although any of the South African episodes would have served just as well. Jallianwala Bagh, for instance, is so burnt into the national memory, so well documented by historians that one would expect Attenborough to tread warily here, for he treads on the single most ignominious act of the British Raj. The British still haven't forgotten it and only a few years ago an Englishman published a book on it. I daresay that there isn't a single Indian anywhere in the world who entirely retained his composure during this chilling scene. To this extent it must be admitted that Attenborough has achieved a measure of success. Also the casting of Edward Fox (remember the cold-blooded assassin of *The Day of the Jackal* [1973]?) as Dyer added just that

element of infernal callousness to this episode which made, let us remind
ourselves, not only Lenin write a letter of sympathy to all Indians
in the *Amrita Bazar Patrika* but even that imperialist diehard, Churchill,
explode in the House of Commons. Undeterred by his position as
Secretary of State of War, Churchill roundly condemned Dyer's action
as 'without precedent or parallel in the modern history of the British
Empire ... an extraordinary event, an event which stands in singular
isolation'. In fact it was at Churchill's insistence that Dyer was dismissed
from the Army. Still, we must respectfully observe that in a town
rent asunder by arson, firing, and fearsome rioting only three days
ago, it is difficult to believe that large queues of people (mostly women)
would have so quietly congregated in the Golden Temple for worship
just before the massacre at the Bagh without betraying the least alarm
or hurry. Also, it does seem unlikely that that militant-looking Sikh
speaker inside the Bagh would have preached (or be allowed to preach)
Gandhian non-violence on the thirteenth as he does in the film. This
is stacking the cards needlessly. Also, although the crowd in the Bagh
has been variously estimated as between fifteen and fifty thousand,
the crowd in the film — despite Attenborough's boast — is surely in
the region of some two or three thousand. (Costume designer Bhanu
Athaiya told *Indian Express* after her Hollywood triumph: 'In the Amritsar scene we had to prepare 3000 people in one hour to face the
cameras'.) So the shooting looks more gratuitous, a sheer slaughter
of innocents. The dramatic slam cut from the child crying besides
its dead mother to the cross-examination of General Dyer by the Hunter
Committee makes it almost look like a court martial (no wonder poor
Rushdie was misled) which it wasn't. Attenborough's one-sided presentation of events gives the impression that all the members were u-
nanimous in their condemnation of the General, but Lord Hunter
himself was an arrogant man whose heart didn't exactly bleed for the
victims of the massacre as his questions to Dyer imply. It was left
to the Indian members (who fell out with the Chairman, Lord Hunter)
to probe Dyer's actions searchingly. They entered a Minute of Dissent
from the Majority Report which was to cost the patriotic Chimanlal
Setalwad his appointment to the Viceroy's Executive Council. By subtly
glossing over these differences, the film insinuates that the indictment
of Dyer was unanimous which it emphatically was not.

Controversy has since raged round the action of the General. The
House of Commons and the Army Council censured his action but
the House of Lords approved of it by a majority of 121 to 86. A

public subscription raised in his honour by loyal Englishmen, both here and in England, netted the princely sum of £ 26,317 in just a month. But it is well to remind ourselves, occasionally, of the merchants and shopkeepers of Amritsar who thanked Dyer for rescuing their city from mob violence. Why, the guardians of the Golden Temple even enrolled the General into the Brotherhood of Sikhs and built a shrine for him at their holy place at Guru Sat Sultani! Even the great Annie Besant defended Dyer. Such, indeed, are the ironies of history. The fact however remains that Dyer was deprived of his commission. But back home in Bristol the ageing General — struck down by paralysis in November 1921, followed by thrombosis — spent his last years haunted by the ghosts of Amritsar. He went into a state of permanent depression and once admitted to *The Morning Post* that 'the act I was called upon to perform filled me with horror'. 'I don't want to get better,' he told his daughter-in-law before his death, 'I only want to die and to know from my Maker whether I did right or wrong.'* Certainly Gandhi would have pitied the man, but Attenborough with his black-and-white morality presents him as a psychopathic killer who can tell his firing troops, 'Take your time.' Yet as a boy the same Dyer had turned his back on a career in medicine because he was 'sickened by the atmosphere of the dissecting room.'†

In fact Attenborough's entire presentation of the Amritsar tragedy makes it appear to be the decisive turning point in Indo—British relations. And this is surely why Gandhi is shown telling the Viceroy: 'Things have gone beyond legislation ... General Dyer is but an extreme example of the principle. It is time you left.' But Jallianwala Bagh did not induce Gandhi to speak in this fashion even at the Amritsar Congress in December 1919, let alone to the Viceroy. Indeed, it was the wholly dubious issue of the Khilafat that made Gandhi launch his famous Non-Cooperation movement. This has been avidly seized upon not only by right-wing historians like Savarkar and R.C. Majumdar but even leftist historians like Hiren Mukherji have been compelled to concede it. But Attenborough merrily distorts history and foregrounds Amritsar to suit his book.

Chauri Chaura is too 'cinematic' a subject to have escaped Attenborough's hawk-like attention. The scene is staged, quite gratuitously, at night with a pitifully small group of processionists shouting the

---

* James Morris, *Farewell The Trumpets*, London, 1978, p. 298.
† Draper, *Amritsar*, 1981, p. 22.

Mahatma's name and carrying flaming torches as if they already knew
that they would be called upon to burn a police station later that
night. The sheer savagery of both the policemen who opened fire and
the bloodthirsty mob (numbering nearly 2000) who mercilessly hacked
to death 21 policemen and one sub-inspector before throwing the
mangled remains into the raging flames is toned down in the film
to just one ruthless axing.* It is Gandhiji's own reaction to the butchery
that interests Attenborough, and this slant is understandable in a film
which is after all about Gandhiji. But there are limits to which an
artist, even if he be a Picasso, can go in rearranging or altering history
to suit his interests. Gandhiji goes on a fast, agreed, but Attenborough
cannot have Gandhiji fasting in the film without an assortment of
females, both Indian and foreign, bedecking his bedside. So for this
fast he conveniently prepones Mirabehn's arrival in India by roughly
three years and stations her at his bedside for much of the rest of
the film. (Actually Mirabehn — whose clinging importunity annoyed
the Mahatma — was present in none of the episodes the film chronicles
except the incarceration at the Aga Khan Palace. But at least she was
physically present in India, which you can't say for Kallenbach who
never set foot in India at all!) She had to be here — this spiritual
refugee from the West — as the sole recipient and official custodian
of that Gandhian wisdom (about the eventful downfall of tyrants and
murderers) meant exclusively for the West. (Incidentally, the reasons
Attenborough assigns to Gandhiji for undertaking the fast in his *In
Search of Gandhi* are quite preposterous and reveal his fundamentally
shallow grasp of the Gandhian *Weltanschauung.* 'He undertook a fast
unto death,' writes Attenborough, 'until all cooperation with the British
was restored and there was an end to any form of protest' (pp. 95—6).
The fast was for five days, not 'unto death' as Attenborough imagines.
Further, one has only to glance at the articles in *Young India* that
Gandhi wrote during this period, particularly the magnificently defiant
'Shaking the Manes' (23. 2. '22) — a bare fortnight before his arrest
for sedition — to see how wide off the mark Attenborough is. To
compound his errors, Attenborough has a starry-eyed Nehru (who was
actually in prison at the time) tell a fasting Gandhi that Patel, Jinnah,
and all Congressmen have agreed to suspend the movement. This not
only ignored the fact that Jinnah had already left the Congress fold but

* Gandhiji's own account of it in *Young India,* 16 Feb. 1922 cited in Fischer 1950,
p. 219.

Richard Attenborough, Gandhi *(1982)*   103

gravely distorts the record by unfairly playing down the opposition
to Gandhi on this score. Actually Nehru received the news with
'astonishment and consternation.'* In fact Sardar Patel alone, among
the leaders, stood behind Gandhi's decision. But all this doesn't suit
Attenborough who wants a Mahatma whose every whim is law, whose
every bidding a Commandment.

The start of the famous march to Dandi is somewhat marred by
Kingsley's un-Indian gestures — he puts up his left hand to *namastay*ing
villagers who have lined his path and wags his chin from left to right
in a wry, amused way. (Kingsley is really half-Indian — his real name
is Krishna Ranji — but he's never been to India before and his gestures
here tell their own story.) The actual *satyagraha* itself at Dharasana
doesn't go down too well with Indian audiences who find the proceedings
unaccountably funny. That Attenborough doesn't attempt the actual
historical scale (there were actually 2500 Congress volunteers under
Sarojini Naidu — Maulana Azad wasn't there at all nor was Mirabehn
who merely visited the wounded in prison at Bulsar on 6 June 1930
— facing 400 Indian police under the command of six British officers)
probably doesn't matter here. Less pardonable, however, is the failure
of direction — just look at the blank and passive way these so-called
Gandhian *satyagrahis* offer themselves meekly, like lambs to the slaughter,
to the police *lathis* without betraying the least emotion on their faces.
One has only to compare this scene to the all too human behaviour
of the reformed criminals under similar circumstances in Shantaram's
magnificent *Do Aankhen Barah Haath* (1957) to see the difference
between the ersatz and the authentic. But Attenborough doesn't stop
here. He editorializes blatantly. This is apparent in the text of the
despatch that the American reporter (based surely on on the famous
Webb Miller whose report made world headlines, appearing in more
than 1000 newspapers at home and abroad) sends soon after. Miller
was a veteran reporter with 18 years of reporting experience in 22
countries, unlike the dimwit in the film who can't even bear to see
what is going on in front of him (as Pauline Kael has acutely observed).
Miller himself wrote a book on his experiences† and I don't think
he would ever have written — while the struggle was still on —
'Whatever moral ascendancy the West held was lost today. India is
free.' Ironically, these words are heard as we see Gandhi climbing the

* *An Autobiography*, London, 1942, p. 81.
† *I Found No Peace*, New York, 1936.

steps of the Viceregal Lodge to parley with the representative of the King Emperor!

Blatant changes are sometimes less annoying than minor ones, but both are to be preferred to the tourist postcard pictures of an 'eternal' India that fairly litter the film. Even an outright racist like Enoch Powell has testified recently to 'falling helplessly and hopelessly in love with India at first sight', but there is nothing in Attenborough's film (or in his life for that matter) to suggest even remotely any redeeming emotion for the land that gave birth to the Mahatma. There was, of course, that bust of Nehru by Epstein purchased at a Christie auction for £220 that led to the meeting with Kothari, then Mountbatten, then Nehru and then.... to the making of the film. Instead of any strong emotion we have exotica: fake bucolic types who engage clergymen in conversation on the roof of trains; the woman washing in the river (whom Gandhi pities) with her natty nose-ring and inviting knees (which suggest dieting rather than starvation); Gandhiji's preposterous elephant-back rides through Champaran (we have it on the authority of no less a person than Judith Brown that Gandhi toured the Champaran countryside on foot or by bullock cart;* the picturesque camels that the American journalists pass on their way to Porbander, a seaport town mind you; the parody of the sacred *saptapati* (with a bullock cart crawling in the foreground and buffaloes bathing in the background) that Gandhi enacts for the benefit of the visiting worthies; the bearded mentor of Godse (of course the real Karkare had no beard and so Attenborough shuffles history as usual and borrows this facial appendage from Digambar Badge) seated always inside some contraption (even inside Birla Mandir?); the huge Austin pulled by a bullock cart with the cartman riding the fender; and of course, piquant conversations between an ageing Kasturba and a simmering young Hollywood starlet on the ordeals of sexual abstinence. Even the choice of locations seems to have been governed not by considerations of authenticity but by the need to exhibit exotic Indian faces to Western audiences. Thus the unit was made to undertake 'the very considerable journey upto the North—East since I was very anxious to film the very different facial structures and skin colour indigenous to that part of the country'.†
Yet when it came to the vastly more important Jallianwala Bagh, it was felt that 'the journey to the North—West of India would have

* Judith Brown, *Gandhi's Rise to Power* (Cambridge, 1972, p. 68)
† *In Search of Gandhi*, p. 216.

been completely impractical in terms of time required for the whole unit to travel' (ibid., p. 206). Since Amritsar is closer to Delhi — where the unit camped — than Bihar we can only assume that 'the facial structures and skin colour' there were not alluring enough. With this fixation on externals like 'skin colour', etc. it is not surprising that Attenborough shows the least sensitivity to Indian culture. The early scenes between Gandhi and Kasturba are nothing short of a travesty of husband—wife relationships in India in the nineteenth century (Indira Gandhi seems herself to have objected to their absurdly contemporary dialogue) and mercifully a clearly intended scene of lovemaking between the two in South Africa has been left out. But not quite, as traces of it still remain in Hattangadi's suggestive pout before slithering into bed (ostensibly to remove Gandhi's bandages). The South African sequences, generally, oscillate between the sublime and the ridiculous, and often the two are indistinguishable. 'We are from an ancient civilization. Why can't we walk on the pavement?' asks the young Gandhi in what must surely be the film's most memorable line. This then is Attenborough's picture of pre-Partition India: both quaintly antique and absurdly modern. And yet such is apparently his reverence for the Mahatma that he always visits the *samadhi* (which twice in his book he misspells as *samardhi*) at Rajghat, not as a 'rhetorical gesture' he tells the reader but because 'of the phenomenal responsibility I feel in having undertaken this particular film'.[*]

But in fact there is nothing in Attenborough's career to indicate that he was equipped to take on this 'phenomenal responsibility' in the first place. A combat pilot in the RAF during World War II, Attenborough was never exactly a pacifist. Nearly all his films have been about war. There was, to begin with, Noel Coward's *In Which We Serve* (1942) (based on Lord Mountbatten's exploits on HMS *Kelly* during World War II for which he was awarded the DSO); there was *Guns at Batasi* (1964) (in which Attenborough plays Sergeant Lauderdale); there was *The Sand Pebbles* (1966), co-starring Candice Bergen whom Attenborough found 'as beautiful as any woman I think I have ever met'[†] there was *Oh! What a Lovely War* (1969), *Young Winston* (1972), and, of course, the film just prior to *Gandhi*, the monumental *A Bridge Too Far* (1977) on the abortive Arnhem campaign. I am not aware that any of these films was specifically pacifist or anti-war.

---

[*] *In Search of Gandhi,* p. 61.
[†] Ibid., p. 133.

Indeed, Attenborough seems to have undertaken *Gandhi* precisely because of the logistical hurdles involved in shooting it. Equipped with the 5000 litres of diesel per week that the Petroleum Ministry had sanctioned the shooting unit, he seems to have gone about the task with the thoroughness of Rommel in North Africa. In fact he himself has likened filming to military manoevres: 'I have already compared filming with military manoevres and would further the analogy by agreeing with Napoleon that an army marches on its stomach'.* What with an estimated 350,000 mourners at Gandhi's funeral (98,000 of whom were transported into Delhi 'by bus and by lorry and by every conceivable form of transport',† not to speak of the vast hordes at Champaran, it must have been quite an army. Small wonder if the central message of the film gets a little submerged in all the brouhaha.

The film presents a very flattering picture of the British in India. They merely issue orders but are never shown firing on crowds or wielding lathis — all this is left to the poor Indian sepoy. But even the poor Indian sepoy had his own sense of honour and compassion. Witnesses told the Hunter Committee that the Gurkhas initially fired into the air, despite Dyer's orders, and even the Government advocate, Herbert, asked Dyer about the bullet marks on the second and third storeys of buildings surrounding the Bagh. But Attenborough presents them as lifeless creatures, almost automatons, who come into the Bagh at a rhythmic, almost equestrian, trot. Likewise, the lathi-wielding sepoys at Dharasana show little diffidence or hesitation in carrying out orders. And yet history records that during the *same* year the Gurkhas of the Second Battalion of the 18th Royal Garhwali Rifles mutinied and refused to fire on Muslim crowds at Peshawar. The British, of course, are endowed with scepticism, irony, and tolerance. 'We are too damned liberal,' says that wizened old indigo planter before affixing his signature to the Indian charter of demands at Champaran. The Lieutenant-Governor, too, seems a paragon of virtue with his open admiration of Gandhi ('At home children are writing essays about him,' he reminds the planter). Even Lord Hunter is presented as a compassionate man, deeply distressed over the presence of women and children in the Bagh. Against all this, one has to admit that Broomfield (who tried Gandhi in 1922) was the shining exception with his careful yet courteous judgment, but even here Attenborough goes too far by exaggerating the deference

* Ibid., p. 217.
† *Society*, May 1983.

shown to Gandhi at the commencement of the trial. Surely, the trial judge at Champaran with his blend of grudging respect and mounting exasperation is nearer the true British norm, and his English clerk is even shown motioning Gandhi to rise in a shockingly disrespectful way. Was this an unconscious (if revealing) slip on Attenborough's part because it certainly doesn't fit the rest of the picture he paints? Even Lord Chelmsford (now why on earth is he listed in the credits as 'The Viceroy?) is deferential to a fault, circling the Mahatma and almost apologetic about the Reforms he has himself authored. His advisers are presented as harmless buffoons doodling away caricatures of the Mahatma as the Empire is quietly slipping from their grasp. Lord Irwin, alas, was a great opportunity lost because Gielgud hopelessly misreads him (unless the mischief is Attenborough's) and Sir Reginald Rumbold (who was briefly Lord Irwin's amanuensis) is for once absolutely right in complaining. Obviously Attenborough needed a stiff Irwin to dramatically highlight the Gandhian victory, and so truth is once again sacrificed at the altar of the overall thesis. But Richard is careful to balance the picture. An early scene shows British troops enjoying a game of cricket (synonymous with fair play), but at other times I'm afraid they were busy with their 303 Lee Enfields keeping the Pax Britannica. Jallianwala Bagh was only one of their many atrocities at Amritsar. There was the notorious 'crawling order' and the flogging of innocent boys by the avenging Dyer. Elsewhere, at Gujranwala, there was even aerial bombing of the civilian population and machine-gunning of helpless villagers. No, the British record is none too bright.

'Independence will fall like a ripe apple,' says Gandhiji after his return from the Round Table Conference to disappointed fellow Congressmen. In putting this picturesque metaphor into Gandhi's mouth, Attenborough clearly implies that *Swaraj* was a natural, organic process which could not have been unduly hastened. And, indeed, by altogether omitting the turbulent course of the 30s and the explosive 40s with its 'Quit India' movement, Attenborough has rendered the coming of freedom wholly effortless — more like the fall of a ripe apple. True, the struggle may not have been epic or momentous (as in, say, Russia or China or Vietnam), and a historian like Anil Seal can even mock it by likening it to the struggle 'between two hollow statues locked in motionless and simulated combat.' Thus both the Right and the Left join hands unexpectedly by running down the freedom struggle:

* Anil Seal, *The Emergence of Indian Nationalism,* Cambridge, 1968, p. 351.

the former by saying that it came naturally in course of time (like
the fall of an apple) and the latter by saying that it was no struggle
at all (like the combat between motionless statues). A more judicious
approach would see that the apple began to ripen from the earliest
days of the freedom struggle, in the early 1920s, to be exact, when
the terms of trade turned against India. The collapse of India's foreign
currency earnings (from the export of primary produce) in the late
20s and early 30s hastened the process, and by 1943 (with the domestic
economy largely 'closed') the apple was ready to fall. Certainly Gandhi's
'Quit India' movement could not have been better timed. But Attenborough tells a different story. For him Gandhi's Salt March in
1930 (undoubtedly the *locus classicus* of non-violent satyagraha) is the
Austerlitz of the whole freedom campaign. This is the grand climax.
No wonder Gandhi is told by Lord Irwin to attend the Round Table
Conference in London 'to discuss the possible independence of India'.
So the Mahatma goes to England and, on his return, enunciates his
famous 'apple theory'. And then in 1947 India is mysteriously free.
Not surprisingly, Attenborough stages this important event not at midnight but in broad, unmitigated daylight. That is why I said at the
beginning of this essay that the film is inhospitable to truth, the colour
of which, I suspect, is a modest, unspectacular grey. The British Picasso
has given us, then, not a dove but a shrieking parrot whose sole message
would appear to be 'Richard the Great'.

5

Aparna Sen, *36 Chowringhee Lane* (1981)

36 Chowringhee Lane (like its Calcutta stablemate, Victor Banerjee's *An August Requiem*) is a film by English-speaking people, of English-speaking people but, alas, not necessarily *for* all English-speaking people.

Most of the English critics I spoke to in Calcutta didn't like it (with the exception of that withered priestess of cinema, Adrienne Mircea, and she is American!) and I learnt that the film was not invited for the London Film Festival. Derek Malcolm of *The Guardian* must have surely had it in mind when he observed at the symposium on 'Cinema 2000', 'My hope is that Indian cinema, or rather Indian films, will find an identity of their own which successfully expresses something unique and powerful in world cinema. It has always been a mistake to think that only by aping the West can Indian film-makers conquer it.' Much the same point has been subsequently made by that old warhorse, John Warrington, who has charged *36 Chowringhee Lane* with being 'remote from Indian Experience' and obviously made 'with an eye on the West'. May I humbly propose, as an alternative theory, that it is Ms Aparna Sen who has had an overdose of Victorian morality.

36 Chowringhee Lane is generously bestowed with souvenirs of the Victorian era. Victoria Memorial, for instance, is the site of the film's gayest sequence and also its saddest one. The film ends appropriately, if quite gratuitously, since Miss Stoneham lives nowhere near it, opposite the Victoria Memorial at night. Queen Victoria is truly the patron saint of the film, breathing heavily through every single frame. The film sets the starved and unsexed loneliness of Violet Stoneham against the burgeoning carnality of the young lovers, Samaresh and Nandita. But the resulting equation is skewed because, as Satyajit Ray told me, the lovers do not act as a proper foil for the Victorian Violet. Only once when Violet winces at the hot *phuchka* while Nandita enjoys hers in true *desi* style is the opposition of cultures apparent. But otherwise, the behaviour of the lovers, issuing intermittently from an anachronistic Victorian code, is shot through and through with contradictions. Let me illustrate. The first time that Miss Stoneham permits the lovers the use of her apartment, she is about to leave when she remembers something. She goes to the bathroom to pick off her wet bra and panties from the clothesline and puts them away into a dirty clothes bag. Very propah, you see! (Needless to say, Aparna won't leave it at that. She has Samaresh, on a subsequent afternoon, dip his hands into the selfsame bag for the missing Sir Toby, and the Violets in the audience have their little *frisson*). From the prim and spinsterly Miss Stoneham this is, I suppose, to be expected but what about our classy Nandita? Her affair with Samaresh is surely founded on those well distributed lies at home and her youthful hunger, we will grant, is solely for those stolen kisses and not for 'champagne and caviar', of which, metaphorically, there is plenty at home. Still, to have her necking, however reluctantly, in the back seat of a taxi in broad daylight! (A young veteran, who has had his fair share of these things, informs me that an upper middle-class girl will not be caught dead necking in a taxi by day). And then we are asked to believe that the same Nandita will baulk and act coy just because of an intrusive cat! Still, I must admit that I find the whole sequence of her sudden 'scream' following Sir Toby's magnificent leap from the cistern (which suddenly 'flushes' to the feet of the still naked lovers) witty and quite simply sensational. Actually it is doubtful if a girl like Nandita would have gone all the way all at once without the intervening middle-class hassles. Remember she is still staying with her folks. An interesting sidelight on the mores of cinematic love-making — let alone the real thing — is to be found in Debashree Roy's *Super* (Feb. '82) interview:

Well, my mother used to accompany me for shootings, but for a few days she could not go with me and that was the time when the scenes were shot. I reached the location with Reeta — a good family friend — and was asked to do the scenes. Aparna assured me that they would be done artistically. She told me, 'Debashree if you don't do the scenes my film won't run.' So after a lot of persuasion I agreed. There was no time to prepare myself for the scenes. They were just thrust onto me.

Now unless you are going to dismiss all this as outright hypocrisy — which I am not willing to — you really begin to wonder just how much of a 'glimmering' our modern Indian directors have of 'what it is like to be Indian' and female. So even Samaresh and Nandita's wedding is arrived at without any hitches. Samaresh gets a job (resulting in a nocturnal celebration at Miss Stoneham's apartment with gin and sherry to the strains of 'Auld Lang Syne' and the next thing you know he and Nandita are married. Didn't her parents kick up a shindy before consenting? We are not told of any Liccnps and we don't see any 'parents' at the wedding either. If Nandita gets a fabulous house as a wedding present from her parents, it is only to enable Miss Stoneham to be brought there for her tragic finale. Yet Pritish Nandy has found the film 'simple, quiet and honest' (*Sunday,* 14 Feb.'82) and has even ventured an extended comparison with *Pather Panchali*! First Ray and now 'Calcutta's beautiful Aparna Sen'. India, most certainly, is progressing!

'The British Raj is over,' says Violet Stoneham to her brother Eddie. 'India has been independent now for over thirty years.' But judging from the film you wouldn't think so. Eddie himself doesn't think so. He's going to petition the King for an extension 'tonight'. The film itself is so replete with departures (first Rosemary, then Wendy McGowen, and there is a hint at the end that even Miss Stoneham might leave), that there is a sense of something having just ended. Mrs Ainsley, the old Principal, has just retired (although she still keeps in touch with her old colleagues) and Mrs Swaminathan, the brassy Tamilian, has stepped in. Just once, in the scene where Mrs McGowen complains that a Santhal boy has got the job in place of her son, Tony, a consciousness of social change breaks in, but the theme is not developed further. For the most part we inhabit an unchanging world, rather like Miss Stoneham's apartment where everything is still as it used to be in Nandita's time. Even the period songs, 'Lipstick on Your Collar', 'House of Bamboo', and 'Yellow Polka Dot Bikini' (which is used as a bridging device during the film's sole montage sequence) don't evoke just the early 60s but a much earlier era. They belong with Violet's New Year Eve parties at the Railway Club at Asansol, with Eddie on horseback — he was in the Mounted Police — during the march-past on the King's birthday (now, when was *that*, please?) and with those fading snapshots of Davie and Violet of a bygone era. (Actually Aparna should have used the songs of, say, The Andrew Sisters, but seems to have settled for the more popular songs of a *much* later period.)

36 *Chowringhee Lane* depicts a very colonial world divided strictly

into masters and servants. At the very bottom of the heap are those beyond the pale, the shivering pavement-dwellers, who are the object of a merely sentimental Christmas pity — we see them, in passing, to the lovely strains of 'Silent Night, Holy Night'. Above them is the vast anonymous, faceless lumpen mass of India — the *rickshawallahs*, the *phuchkawallahs*, the hawkers on the street and, saddest of all, that unseen sweeper boy who is the object of a swift rebuke from Miss Stoneham in her broken Hindusthani: 'Jaldi karo, jaldi karo! Kitna time lagata!' The middle class (which includes people like Miss Stoneham) is blatantly condescended to: while Samaresh — clearly an author surrogate — speaks contemptuously of a 1200-a-month job, Nandita wrinkles her nose at the mere mention of an Indian Principal. I found almost *all* their scenes with Miss Stoneham intolerable on this account and this is why I cannot believe that Aparna has any genuine compassion for her Anglo-Indian teacher. The upper class goes scot-free, of course. Nandita herself is dowered with her creator's own fruity—sexy wine-dark voice which successfully papers over all the moral cracks in her character. After all, the forces that produce the Nanditas of India are twofold. Firstly, the moneyed background leads to a thick-skinned callousness that makes lying come easy. Secondly, the 'posh-school' background engenders sexual hypocrisy which, in turn, breeds coyness (hence Nandita's reaction to Sir Toby). Is it any wonder if that girl in Miss Stoneham's class nudges her gum-chewing neighbour to look at erotica? Similarly, is it surprising to find in the composition notebooks of these girls lines like, 'The monk had a hungry abbess on his knee'? But Aparna, who has no politics, does not establish any connections and plays all these scenes strictly for laughs. The whole treatment of the upper class is slipshod and lackadaisical. I found the crowd at the Samaresh—Nandita Christmas 'do' (to employ Samaresh's own trendy lingo) quite scruffy and positively unwashed. Nandita's parents, I'm sure, would have had a fit if they had got within a mile of it. Its chief spokesman is that oaf who rolls his eyes heavenwards and interjects, 'Man! It's beautiful' on hearing 'Silent Night' on Stoneham's splendid Thoren. 'An interjection', we may remember from Stoneham's class-room instruction, 'is a word or a sound which is thrown into a sentence to express some state of mind'. Some state of mind indeed!

The whole package is set in motion by three characters — two ostensibly Indian and one Anglo-Indian, but they are all Anglo-Indians really. Samaresh — played with a near-permanent smirk by Dhritiman

Chatterjee — is supposed to be some kind of writer — 'James Joyce in the making' — and actually produces a slim volume of poems with the predictable title, 'Calcutta: If You Must Exile Me' (in a no doubt conscious pun on Joyce's play *Exiles*)! But he does not look as if he has strayed beyond his north Calcutta home except to meet his south Calcutta sweetheart. In any case, what Miss Stoneham would make of Samaresh's book — dedicated in contemporary style 'to Nandita' — is anybody's guess. Our schoolmarm, apart from her daylight murder of *Twelfth Night* has not ventured beyond that classic for morons, Barbara Cartland (whom she is seen reading at night), matching in this regard her brother, Eddie, who is an Archie-comic fiend. Not a family, you might say, distinguished for its literary taste! Not surprisingly, Miss Stoneham's English is laboriously Anglo-Indian (so entirely suffixed by 'and alls' that the strain produced its 'own dying fall'!), and I even began to wonder in her scenes with Nandita just who taught whom. Eddie's language didn't seem cut from the same cloth as his sister's and sounded almost painfully English.

At the end of it all, when that crumpled and tawdry mediocrity, Violet Stoneham, alights from her taxi in front of Victoria Memorial and proceeds to quote those extraordinary lines from *King Lear*, the film achieves, not sublimity, but a splendid bathos. Miss Stoneham's sudden elevation to the status of a tragic heroine is wholly unmerited, for Violet has not passed through the valley of the shadow of death. She has probably gone to sleep every night of her life with a hot water bottle. The towering Lear, in his purgatory of madness, has had his vision of those 'poor naked wretches' as well as the terrifying one of 'unaccommodated man' before reaching the plateau of his great 'Pray, do not mock me' speech. Stoneham has been so intolerably sane all her life that she and her ilk deserve to be quietly forgotten. They belong rightly to the dustbin of history. Still, perhaps, Samaresh's epitaph for her is well chosen. History will certainly remember her role in the film. For, as Malvalio realizes, while some are born great and some achieve greatness, some, like Violet Stoneham and her creator Aparna Sen, have greatness thrust upon them.

6

Aparna Sen, *Paroma* (1985)

Expectations ran so high about Aparna Sen's *Paroma* that the film was inevitably headed for a letdown. Still one hoped for a great deal from the maker of *36 Chowringhee Lane* (a good, certainly not a great film, by any standards, despite its Manila award) and the ensuing disappointment has been comprehensive. The film can only be described (as an English friend of mine put it) as 'a Hindi film sensitively made'. To make a film these days where one of your chief characters is a photographer is, I think, asking for trouble. After Susan Sontag's notorious book on photography you simply cannot pretend to be oblivious to the moral implications of photography, particularly fashion photography. Here, I'm afraid, Aparna Sen does not show any such awareness. It all began in films, at any rate, with Antonioni's *Blow-Up* (1966) where a high fashion photographer has his moral come-uppance.

Kieslowski's *Camera Buff* (1979) went even more deeply into the moral implications of photography because its chief character is an insignificant employee in a factory. Mrinal Sen's *Khandhar* (1984), too, has a photographer in the central position but seemed unaware and uninterested in the moral problems that it poses to the film-maker (who is so heavily reliant on photography). For the photographer is basically a figure who stands at a remove from reality, observing rather than participating in it. Only in Aravindan's *Chidambaram* (1985) does the photographer (Shankaran, who is the cause of all the upheavals in Sivakami's life leading to Muniyandi's suicide) move from the position of spectator to that of active participant, forsaking, in the process, his camera. But Aparna Sen seems wholly indifferent to the moral stature of her photographer, Rahul, who is, for her, merely a catalyst in the awakening and liberation of Mrs Paroma Chaudhury. If this is indeed the case, why was Rahul ushered into the film at the beginning, where his formidable US reputation even upstages the Puja celebrations in the conversations of women in the Chaudhury household? He is the man who, Othello-like, has braved the dangers of Lebanon and Beirut, living dangerously (he quotes, approvingly, the Nietzschean maxim to a frightened Paroma negotiating a tricky pathway to the terrace), and at the end of the film he is reported to be — in Chad! In his brief Calcutta sojourn, alas, none of this is really visible. On his list of places to be photographed are Marble Palace and Kalighat Temple, but for a political photo-journalist he seems strangely uninterested in this side of Calcutta. He talks, dresses, whistles (that out-of-date old English song), and behaves very much like a tourist from the First World. 'Just look at those eyes,' he drawls in his best Yankee twang, projecting a slide of a tribal for the assembled guests at Paroma's house. Is one to believe that this nitwit lived dangerously enough to be 'reported missing' (the ultimate accolade for a journalist)?

Paroma, herself is far, far more credible and, as played by an aging Rakhee, has all the *gravitas* that is so much a part of the appeal of upper-class Bengali women. She is neither ambitious beyond that humble desire for a flat in Ballygunge, nor is she in any way, particularly unsatisfied. Surrounded by her children to whom she is particularly close (except her college-going daughter, the burgeoning feminist, with whom she doesn't seem to have any real relationship), her life with her husband, the marketing executive on the make, is singularly untroubled, if unexciting (they simply live together, each in their own world). It is into the clear blue sky of such a life that Aparna introduces Rahul with his Nikon and his American razzmatazz, and we are asked to believe that Paroma's world is completely overturned. And, like a true Hindi movie, Aparna stages Paroma's sexual awakening with the aid of blustery weather which gives way to a veritable downpour, if you get my meaning! Paroma recalls to Rahul — to press home my point — the hailstones of childhood and the long summer vacations at Mussoorie. All metaphors of wetness! Meanwhile — punctuating the daily afternoon copulation — Paroma resumes playing the sitar which she was taught by Soumenbabu on those tranquil Sunday afternoons at her north Calcutta home. Poetry, too, makes a humble appearance (preludial to the sexual intoxication) when Paroma, slowly awakening from her marital slumber, declaims Premandra Mitra on the terrace with a view of the Kidderpore Docks in the far distance. But will such a woman casually ask her driver to collect Rahul's letters from the US (from Sheila's place) after picking up the kids from school. She even asks Rahul to write home directly when we see that letters in that upper-class house are dropped into a mailbox downstairs. We see no eagerness or impatience in Paroma for her lover's letter (think of Charulata avidly devouring Amal's letter before his departure to England), only a suicidal tendency to get into trouble; and so when that issue of *Life Magazine* comes with her photographs (there was little in them *per se* to cause all the brouhaha except Rahul's 'Remember! Love, Rahul') and all hell breaks loose in Calcutta upper-class circles, we don't feel any particular sympathy for her. We only feel annoyed at her carelessness. We feel that her suicide attempt and hospitalization are not organic developments of her character, but merely imposed on the plot to elicit our sympathy. The film is edited badly (sequences go on long after they are really over; a good example would be the last scene which really concluded much earlier when she leans out of the window and we hear the muezzin's call) and has faulty subtitles (the Bengali *boudi* for the Hindi *bahu* and so on). However, one or two scenes do come off. One is that early scene with the *dhobi* who keeps staring at Rahul and his camera before Paroma sharply asks him to get on with the job. Yet another scene at Paroma's own north Calcutta is truly hilarious with its Alla Rakha joke. So, too, is the scene where her husband promises to take her to New York — he waxes eloquent about the great shops on Fifth Avenue — while Paroma is lost (and Rahul's characteristic whistle is heard at this point) in memories of the America that Rahul has evoked for her: Wyoming, Nebraska, the plains of the Omaha Indians, and so on.

The hoot of the siren on Bhasker's shouted 'whore' to her later is also quite effective. Unfortunately for a film that celebrates adultery, the love scenes are a pain in the neck. Indians look far more convincing when they are not making love. When they are, the whole business looks forced, contrived, and bloodless. In fact Aparna herself has so much trouble convincing us that her lovers are actually unclothed and making love that she does a slow pan across the room to show the various items of clothing and underclothing of the parties concerned strewn decorously on the floor.

The only portrait of working women we have is also far from convincing. One of them has the look of independence, although we are told that one is a painter, another is a writer and Sheila — played with a quiet dignity by Aparna herself — runs a school for spastic children. Paroma — and Rakhee's 'traditional Indian beauty' (Rahul's words) don't help at all here — doesn't in the least look as if she belonged with these people or went to school with them. Even Paroma's friends don't talk like liberated women: nobody — except Paroma — is having an affair or an abortion. And so the liberation of Mrs Paroma Chaudhury staged at the end with such symbolism (the potted plant associated with the innocence of her childhood) and care, looks wholly unreal. In their last confrontation alone, before her hospitalization, Paroma asks her husband imploringly: 'Is a single incident enough to destroy an entire relationship?' But it was not a 'single incident' where she impulsively yielded to another man, but one planned and programmed over a period of time. Paroma does not have the moral right to offer such excuses, and by her own exacting Brahmin standards (she is offended with Rahul in the car when he eats the *prasad* without touching it to his forehead) her action is, quite simply, unpardonable (symbolically Aparna has her heroine nearly shaved!). Aparna stages a scene in Bombay where Bhaskar makes a pass at his young secretary (but was it necessary to have the girl so improbably, so invitingly and so happily stretched out on the sofa before Bhaskar gets ideas), and this may point to our double standards of morality. This is entirely correct but it does not and cannot exonerate Paroma. Little wonder then, if Paroma is shown racked by guilt (although she denies it improbably at the end) and even goes to the point of suicide. That incredible potted plant is simply no stay against the strains of a confused identity, and it is not at all clear why she doesn't discard this gift of Rahul's when she can tear up the news item about his whereabouts that Sheila has brought her at the clinic. Despite its tell-tale name — *euphoria* or *Krishnapallabi* — which she recalls at the end in a clearly epiphanic moment, this flowerless plant is as dead and uninspiring as Paroma herself. Still staying at her posh Elgin Road residence, with numerous servants to do various jobs, it is no big deal to be a salesgirl at Khadi Bhavan. What will she do when her upper-class relatives and friends come there for Puja shopping? Sulk, take leave, run to her potted plant, or take another lover? Since the answer to this crucial question is not clear, it is hard to agree with Aparna who presents Paroma's paltry decision to work as a giant step for Indian womanhood.

7

Shyam Benegal, *Junoon* (1978)

'Revolutions are not made with grease,' thundered Disraeli in his three-hour peroration to the British Parliament on 27 July 1857 in support of his belief that the rising was not a military mutiny but a national revolt. But whatever revolutions are made of, 1857 is not a year to be easily forgotten even if you don't go all the way with Savarkar and call the uprising, the Indian War of Independence. A subsequent generation of Indian historians of the period (S.N. Sen, Tara Chand, R. C. Majumdar, Praful Chandra Gupta) have been, on the whole, sensible and haven't always played up to patriotic expectations. Surendranath Sen, the official historian of the period, is scrupulously objective in his magisterial book on the rising, starkly titled *Eighteen Fifty-Seven.* And while neither the business of the *chapatis* (supporting the theory of prior preparation, propaganda, and conspiracy) nor the affair of the greased cartridges (that lends weight to the theory of religious persecution) holds centre stage any longer; other tendencies have been noticeable of late among chroniclers of those turbulent years. There has been a shift of interest from causes to debates about who committed more atrocities and which side initiated them.

In the post-colonial period, it is understandable that Benegal's film, almost wholly indifferent to causes, dwells rather pointedly and almost lovingly on British atrocities: Sarfraz, a former sepoy of the notorious 34th Regiment, refers movingly to native soldiers blasted from the mouth of cannon and breast-feeding infants mercilessly slaughtered. But there is much evidence, argues Alexander Llewellyn in his *Seige of Delhi* (1977) that 'the practice of "blowing away" from guns was learnt by the British from the Indians'. (curiously, it was not the ethical but the religious aspect of the practice — the shattering of the body jeopardizing the soul's immortality — that was widely deplored by the British!) All this, however, is not to suggest that the English merely followed in the footsteps of the Indians. They probably gave as much as they got, but as shining knight exemplars of proud Britannia their misdeeds don't go easily with the song of the White Man's Burden. This probably explains Benegal's emphases and, certainly, he misses few opportunities to drive them home. There are repeated shots in *Junoon* of Indians hanging from trees, and Benegal further reinforces his point by letting his pretty heroine Ruth (played by the delectable, if dumb, Nafisa) even have nightmares of these cruelties. Oddly, though, two of her nightmares are instances of English cruelty, which is a little disturbing to say the least, considering that she is half English. It is a good index of how far Benegal will go to present his case.

Clearly Benegal is weighting the scales against the British, fairly reversing Ray's procedures in *Shatranj Ke Khiladi.* The solitary instance of 'Indian cruelty' in the film (if we except one of Ruth's lurid nightmares which shows even the politically inactive Javed at the slaughtering game) is the massacre in the church, but even here women and children are spared. But women and children were not spared elsewhere, and this is what lends the Revolt its special poignance. Even Marx, virulent critic of British rule in India, admitted, while reporting on the Revolt for the *New York Daily Tribune*: 'The atrocities committed by the revolted sepoy in India are indeed appalling, hideous, ineffable ...' And, what is more, writing a hundred years later, the Indian historians, R.C. Majumdar concedes in his *History of the Freedom Movement, Vol .I*: 'The first act of cruelty animated by racial hatred, was the indiscriminate massacre of Englishmen at Mirat [*sic*] ... It is alleged that helpless women were butchered without mercy and children were slaughtered under the very eyes of their mothers. When the sepoys of Mirat reached Delhi the murder scenes were repeated there ...' In Nana Saheb's infamous massacre at Bibighar in Kanpur, women and children were mercilessly hacked to death by four butchers summoned from the local bazaar to perform a task which even the sepoys refused to undertake. When Forbes Mitchell of the 93rd Highlanders saw the floor of the slaughterhouse at Bibighar it was 'littered with torn dresses of women, shoes, slippers and locks of long hair'. Most horrible of all, he saw a hook in the wall from which a child had been hung: ' ... all round the hook or on a level with it was covered the hand prints and below the hook the foot prints, in blood, of a little child'*.

Major North, in his memoirs, has testified that 'in the dreary house
of martyrdom ... clotted gore lay ankle deep on the polluted floor
... also long tresses of silken hair, fragments of female wearing apparel,
hats, books, children's toys were scattered about in terrible confusion'.
Swanston found the 'floor of the yard and the verandah and some
of the rooms ... bespattered with blood and bare blood marks of children's
hands and feet, women's dresses, hats, Bibles, marriage certificates lay
scattered about the place' (*My Journal* [1890]). As against all this we
have Surendranath Sen citing the testimony of Sherer who was 'one
of the first few to visit Bibighar'. Writes Sherer: '.. the whole story
was so unspeakably horrible that it would be wrong in any sort of
way to increase the distressing circumstances that really existed. And
I may say once for all that the accounts were exaggerated ... The whole
of the pavement was thickly caked with blood. Surely, this is enough,
without saying "the clotted gore lay ankle deep", which besides being
most distressing, is absolutely incorrect .... Of mutilation, in that house
at least, there were no signs, nor at that time was there any writing
on the walls."* Whichever account we choose to accept, there is no
denying the fact that the Indian massacre of women and children at
Bibighar is one of the blackest chapters in Indian history and it is
certainly the one that angered the English most. Their retaliation was
swift and terrible. Col. Neil, in his relief of Kanpur, saw to it (and
this we have on his own testimony) that Indians were made to lick
the caked blood at Bibighar — with suitable encouragement from the
lash — before being hanged.

Benegal does make a passing reference to the Kanpur massacre in
his film. A poor relation of Chachijaan's says, with obvious relish,
that the English were taught a good lesson at Kanpur where 'their
livers and intestines were ripped out'. Hafiz chides her for her grossness
(she has a fascinating list of English shortcomings), but when he is
thanked by Mariam for this, he declines it curtly saying that there
is such a thing as *sharafat*. Clearly Benegal is uneasy about it all, and
here and elsewhere, too, we sense his unresolved dilemma: the need
to be fair to the English is at war with his even greater need to be
wholly on the Indian side. He cannot be seriously blamed if the latter,
wins out for the most part. When, for instance, in one of the film's
most moving scenes, Sarfraz returns from battle to report the loss of

‡ (Llewellyn, op. cit.)
*Sen, *op cit.*

Delhi, he says that the British were more savage than Nadir Shah himself. (Benegal's source for the comparison with Nadir Shah is probably Majumdar who quotes from the Bombay correspondent of *The Times*.) And indeed Nicholson and Hodson at Delhi were quite terrible: Nicholson, who wanted flaying alive, impalement or burning the mutineering sepoys because 'the idea of hanging the perpetrators of such atrocities is simply maddening', and Hodson, who in cold blood, shot the royal princes in Delhi with his own hand before a dumb-struck crowd. No, the English — despite 'Clemency' Canning — have much to answer for in the Mutiny. Still, Benegal does appear to be playing down somewhat our own misdeeds during those dark and terrible months. The English never forgot Kanpur and the massacre of women and children there. The severities after the Kuki rebellion and Dyer's ruthlessness at Amritsar are to be traced back to Kanpur.

All this in no way detracts from the excellence of Benegal's film which presents the Revolt almost entirely from the Indian point of view. For the most part we follow the fluctuating fortunes of the rebels and the result is a certain unity of effect. Even the continued presence of the captive Labadoors does not in any way affect the emotional balance of the film, for we are allowed to see them, for the most part, only through the eyes of their successive hosts. Only briefly at the beginning, in the domestic scene of the Labadoor family at dinner followed by the Sunday morning service at church, are we allowed to glimpse a different ethos and a more self-contained world. But even this is done with tact and a certain dry wit without the least trace of prejudice. The *pankawallah* presiding, like some pagan deity, over the former and, in the latter, Geoffrey Kendall, as minister, invoking, in his most stentorian tone, the thunder of God on the erring heathen — why, these are the very pulse and breath of life in the nineteenth-century cantonments of British India. The off-white European bungalows lazing like lizards in the stifling up-country heat, the darling little memsahib clutching her bunch of chrysanthemums, the *mali* tending the pathetic little garden, the *burrasahib* properly accoutered for church — tail coat, boiled shirt, white waistcoat, cravat, tacky white gloves, peaked cap et al. — the red brick church (in the early Indian ecclesiastical style piquantly known as Disappointed Gothic) with its maladorous parishoners. All these cameos of social history are the more effective for coming on the heels of the film's epic start — surely the longest (approximately eight minutes and a little over) and, arguably, the most sustained opening in Indian cinema. The sheer pacing of the scene, with the camera first a discreet spectator and then as the *maulvi* howls his grim prophecies of doom — blazing eyes, sweating jugular, soaring index-finger — a bewitched participant, is one of the masterpieces of direction in recent years.

The script is cunning and well-knit beyond compare. Initially I thought that the central love story did not have the same wrought-from-within quality of some of the peripheral triumphs. But repeated viewing (and discussion with my incomparable young friends, Mahesh and Akumal) has convinced me that this is not, in fact, the case. What I had regarded as a certain want of passion in Javed Khan has turned out to be something else. We see him at the very beginning of the film, quite phlegmatic and unmoved by the maulvi's rivers-of-blood speech and indeed a man quite simply obsessed with his inamorata — he virtually haunts her home like a resident spectre — for whom the Revolt is a huge and hopeless irrelevance. The political upheaval merely gives him an opportunity to lend respectability to his obsession and bring his beloved home, ostensibly as a hostage of the Nawab. After the fall of Kanpur — and before the crucial seige and fall of Delhi — we see him for the first time troubled by events outside. He doesn't stay behind in the mosque to pray for the success of the rebels with Sarfraz and the others. But as he rides away clearly vexed with himself, he rudely breaks up a wayside group of merry-making Hindus (they are slyly mocking his obsession with Ruth) and even berates the chief singer soundly. Returning home he barely notices even Ruth and goes on to have a bitter quarrel with his wife whom he taunts cruelly about her childlessness. Even his beloved pigeons give him little solace as he hoarsely calls them home in a voice bitter and without the least tenderness. In the ensuing scene of love-making he is violent and distracted with his wife, clutching and tearing her hair in a wild frenzy. His sudden animal cry of pain, as she renews her caresses, is followed by shells exploding on the battlefield, and we suddenly realize that all along he has been thinking of Delhi. Sarfraz's rage and explosion at Javed after his mournful return from a lost Delhi — marvellously intercut with the sad gaiety of the Moharram processionists — proves crucial in Javed's political development. Although even now the change in him is slow and imperceptible (and Shashi Kapoor's unrelenting braggadaccio is not a little to blame here), it is there nonetheless. It finally arrives with the tragic death of Hafizullah in battle and suddenly we remember Sarfraz's early remark that even Javed will join the rebels when the going gets really hot. His subsequent behaviour, first in the battlefield — even if this appears a touch histrionic — and then at the church in the film's finale, even if his anguished desire to see his beloved one last time sounds a bit forced — deserve to be looked at from the perspective of his sudden radicalization. He has at last crossed the Rubicon. The metamorphosis from lotus-eater to firebrand partisan, from lover to warrior is complete. Perhaps this is why at the end, with the prize finally within his grasp and Ruth returning his hitherto unrequited love, he rides away to die in battle.

Ruth's own metamorphosis is also skilfully plotted. She moves through initial fear (albeit faintly touched, as her dreams reveal, with a certain fascination), through virginal fantasies of rape at the prospect of being married to him, to anxiety about his return from battlefield, to a final surrender of the heart so complete that she dies unwed, we are told, fifty-five years later in London. The turning point for her is reached in that hastily improvised nocturnal funeral for Mrs James. Ruth, lamp in hand and standing beside Javed, looks yearningly at his face (as he does too) while her mother intones the Lord's Prayer. Her eyes brim with tears at the words 'They will be done in earth, as it is in heaven', which suggests an acquiescence in love as if it were divinely ordained. And by the close of the service her face is irradiated with a beatific glow, a token no doubt of the heart's final surrender against the dictates of cold Victorian propriety. From this point onwards she is the lover, the one with the *junoon* (literally madness or obsession) and Javed gradually secedes from love's haloed kingdom as the political imbroglio claims him. It is one of the many sombre ironies of the film that Javed's love for Ruth is at its meridian at the start of the film while Ruth reaches this point only at the very end when it is too late. Their looping and opposed parabolas of love limn the surrounding darkness and touch briefly in the funeral scene only to swing away to different and tragically different destinies at the end: his to a sudden lonely death on the battlefield and hers to a long spinsterly isolation in far-off London.

The film is replete with observations which function both at the micro-psychological and at the macro-social/political levels. There are marvellous vignettes in Ramjimull's house set off against the mumbling monochrome of his mother's never-ending prayers. Her reading from the *Sunderakandam* in the beginning is not in the least accidental: not only does this serve initially to liken Ruth's captivity to Sita's but has the further purpose of furnishing, through the gloss provided by Ramjimull's sister, a reason for the English presence in India. The gloss comes artlessly in that richly comic scene of the letter writing. Here a wholly bemused Ruth is told that the *rakshasas* looked after Sita so well in Lanka that she blessed them and prophesied that they would be born again as the English and rule over India for a hundred years. (Incidentally this generalizes the maulvi's prophecy in the beginning and thus does Benegal provide a kind of psychological justification for the Revolt). This tolerant Hindu attitude to life in general reappears in many cunning guises. It is there, for instance, in Ramjimull's tender solicitude for the English ladies. It is there again, touchingly if comically, in the offer to the English ladies of ladles in lieu of spoons by Ramjimull's sister who, in an earlier scene, had even undertaken to wash their clothes! Mariam's relationship with Ramjimull, in particular, is masterfully sketched. There are even faint erotic overtones, with Ruth and later Firdaus acting as barometers. But these are, however, buried in the deeps of Ramjimull's anxious solicitousness and Mariam's understandable gratitude.

Muslim attitudes to the English, too, are finely calibrated all the way, from Sarfraz's bitter rage at them, through Javed's ambivalence to Hafizullah's tepid concern for the safety of the English ladies. The women's attitudes don't fall into any set patterns and are more varied. While Firdaus (Shabana's most convincing portrait yet of female bitchery — all bared fangs one moment and soft womanly surrender the next) looks askance at Mariam's holding Ramjimull's hands while taking leave of him, that poor relation of Chachijaan's (played by Pearl Padamsee in one of those scene-stealing roles) finds the *firangi* ladies in need of aquatic and religious purification. She is positively malicious about English toilet etiquette, but reserves her choicest venom for the wife of the English resident at Lucknow. In marked contrast, the childlike Dulhan is all sweetness to Ruth (whom she dolls up and plays with) while the incomparable Chachijaan (played to the very life by the marvellous Sushma Seth) is uniformly considerate and hospitable in the best Nawabi tradition. She plays host to them, relieving the pressure on Javed's household, and in that languidly beautiful garden scene she and the pregnant Dulhan (her daughter-in-law strike the most harmonious chords with the English ladies. The general amity here mocks the Revolt outside and is clearly intended by Benegal to do so. Mariam, too, in this scene, is splendid, *mubarrak*ing Chachijaan graciously on the prospect of a grandchild and herself singing a song on the happiness of lovers. (Jennifer Kendall plays Mariam with a truly marvellous inward understanding of the character, but why was the camera trained so unremittingly on her enormous bosom?) But, elsewhere with Javed, she is forced into defensive postures, rather like a lioness jealously guarding her prize cub. Her attitude to Ramjimull's family, in striking contrast, free as it is of the spin-offs of the Revolt, is much warmer because less guarded. There is no menacing Sarfraz here or rashly importuning Javed, and the scenes have a lightness and even a certain unforced gaiety. Still, the most tranquil scenes are at Chachijaan's. Gentle, soft rain, breaking the humid heat, marks the arrival of the English women here in *dolis* and the soothing, liquid notes of the spring song speak of a happiness that can never die. For the first time we see Ruth happy as she lets the cool showers bathe her face. This scene and its immediate successor — the garden scene — are oases of love in the surrounding desert of human feuds.

I reserve my final accolade for Benegal's marvellous handling of death in the film. All deaths, in this most murderous of all tales, are treated with dignity and respect. This acquires a special poignance in a context in which human lives are robbed of grandeur by the indignities of both sides and the senseless butchery. Mrs James's death (the only *natural* one in the film) is treated gravely. Even Firdaus looks pityingly through the bamboo curtains at the weeping Ruth, and the following day her tone with Mariam is subdued and kind. At the funeral itself Mariam indicates to Javed that he should remove his *pugree* which he promptly does. Graves are ceremoniously dug, not only for Charles Labadoor but also for that marauding sepoy from Sitapare whom Mariam kills. And then there is the moving and heroic death of Sarfraz (Naseeruddin Shah's playing of him is simply peerless and surely one of the outstanding performances in the film) suddenly swordless in battle, as he roars for a *talwar*. He is killed at the exact moment he acquires one and is gruesomely dragged away by his horse.

But Benegal reserves his most sombre treatment for Hafizullah's death in battle. Anil Dharkar of *Debonair,* like most of our Anglicized critics with stiff Victorian notions about the role of emotion in art, finds the whole sequence 'clumsily handled' and marred by the use of that 'cliché of clichés — the breaking of bangles by the young bride'. Why 'bride', one may ask? After all, she has been married long enough to him to be pregnant. He omits, in his exasperation, to mention that cliché of cliché of clichés — the heartbreakingly lovely song about spring which Dulhan first sings in that tranquil scene in the womb-like garden. We hear it again as Hafizullah leaves for battle flanked by his tearful mother (who ties the talisman on his arm) and his mutely sorrowing wife. And now, as Hafizullah is slain in battle, Benegal cuts to pigeons in the sky and the lovely strains of the song are heard yet again. Ruth looks at the pigeons and she, in turn, is anxiously watched by Mariam. A game of checkers is in progress. Mariam has just tossed the dice and things are going the English way in more senses than one.

Hafizullah's young wife is treating herself to a feast of new bangles and offers her *mehndi*-decorated hand to be kissed by her mother-in-law, Chachijaan. Benegal now cuts to the grim silhouette of a mosque and we hear again (alas!) that now tiresome maulvi at his game of prophecies. Luckily the break in tone is redeemed by the silence that follows as the dead Hafizullah is brought on a *charpoy* and placed on the shaded verandah barely kissed by the afternoon sun. We see Chachijaan, in long shot, move towards her dead son, but her grief is too profound to show itself at once. When it does, it is monumental, but Benegal wisely leaves her alone with her sorrow as he cuts to shots of the desolate Dulhan and (even) Mariam's choking grief. The song of spring, poignantly heard again, has turned now to a plaintive anthem of the winter of discontent. Benegal now cuts to the widowed Dulhan, overwhelmed by grief, smashing those new bangles (the jingling of which the song had celebrated) — only to be comforted by Ruth. The irony of the whole situation is complete. It is into this charged situation that Javed now arrives. Solemnly he takes up the dead man's sword as we hear not only the plaintive notes of the song but also Chachijaan's dying sobs. Thus does Benegal redeem this 'cliché of clichés' and endow it with renewed life. The scene is surely fit to rank with Ray's best efforts in the imperishable Apu trilogy.

Everything considered (just once does Benegal bow in the direction of the imperious box-office in that *filmi* Rafi *ghazal* set off visually with incredible romantic triangles!), Benegal's *Junoon* is a towering achievement in Indian cinema. The screenplay (by Benegal again) is as finely spun as a spider's web and Govind Nihalani's work in the film deserves to rank with the best in the world. The lighting in the interiors is most imaginative (Ruth before the mirror in that early scene surely recalls the Dutch masters), and the battle scenes in their pacing, detail, colour verve, must surely be the best of their kind to have come from an Indian director. Is it any wonder, then, that Benegal takes his place besides Herzog, Meszaros, Rademakers and Scorcese as one of the five directors of the year in Peter Cowie's *International Film Guide*? At long last Ray has, I think, found a worthy successor.

8

Shyam Benegal, *Trikaal* (1985)

Shyam Benegal has yet to make a truly distinguished film. *Nishant* (1975) and *Junoon* (1978) were nearly there but somehow failed in the final assault on the summit. Increasingly, it would seem, he seems to have become too obsessed with a milieu, a way of life of a small group or collective, to convey the sense of an 'extended reality'. He has himself recently confessed, 'I started to get tired with single individual's stories. I think that they don't express reality.' Maybe they don't express the reality of life in India where people have not so much the hard-edged subjective self of Western man as a much softer, blurry, amorphous self (as Sudhir Kakar, the psychoanalyst, has shown). But the danger with a generalized group as subject-matter is that the film-maker may — especially if he is blessed with a solid budget turn from the role of artist or psychologist to that of an anthropologist or, even worse, a tourist. This is what happened to Attenborough's *Gandhi* (1982) where the camera seemed more engrossed in 'the skin colour indigenous to that part of the country [Bihar]' (Attenborough, *In Search of Gandhi*) than in the political dilemmas of the peasants. This nearly ruined Benegal's *Mandi* (1983) which seemed an exercise in campy aestheticism. In *Junoon* this never happened and we witnessed a most fruitful union between history and aesthetics without the one outweighing the other. *Kalyug* (1980) was too claustrophobic, both spatially and emotionally, to achieve any real balance and the *Mahabharata* theme was too schematically imposed to allow either the characters or the audience to breathe freely.

In *Trikaal* the sense of milieu and the sense of people (often conceived broadly, comically) are never heterogenously yoked together by violence and, for most part, the two are in a state of dynamic harmony.

Its most perfect expression is the party following Ana's wedding engagement to Erasmo. This sequence is surely the most sustained single
segment of its kind in Indian cinema: the soothing strains of waltz,
the languidly beautiful Ana herself (played with a Madonna-like charm
by Sushma Prakash who is as stunningly beautiful as Claudia Cardinale
was in Visconti's *The Leopard* [1963]) and the general mood of un-
complicated gaiety — before doom strikes both in the personal and
political sense, for the period is just before the Indian Army occupation
— captures old Goa in a transient moment of colonial splendour. Ana's
romantic escape to Portugal with Leon is the last flicker of the dying
flame — the 'noble ethos' in the Hegelian sense. This high key and
florid romanticism is the true foil of all the buffoonery and low comedy
of the rest of the film. Not surprisingly, it is the only action that
Dona Maria (played with a sense of decaying grandeur by Leela Naidu
in a role that would have fitted the late Jennifer Kendall like a glove),
otherwise sunk in historic stupor with her endless seances, reacts to
with a sense of calm excitement.

As long as Benegal deals with the past, his hold is firm and secure.
It is when he turns explicitly political as in the portrait of Vijay Singh
Rane — whose grandfather was imprisoned by the Portuguese —
(material paraphrased second-hand in the seances with Milagrinha) that
Benegal's grip falters. The political comment is too intrusive, the point
of view too erratic and the harmony, referred to earlier, lost. The
portrait of Milagrinha, however (a bastard child of Ernesto) — played
carefully and intelligently by Neena Gupta, although she shouldn't
have tried swaying her none too ample hips so often — makes the
same political point far, far more subtly. Milagrinha's quietly envious
look at the dancers at the engagement party before being dragged off
to the floor by the drunken Francis speaks volumes more than the
staid didacticism of the Rane scenes. Appropriately the film ends with
the birth of her own illegitimate child, clearly with the blessings of
Dona Maria. The film consciously avoids the tragic or even the elegiac
mode for the richly comic vein of Shakespeare's late comedies where
injuries are healed and enmities forgotten. 'Happiness is a desire for
repetition,' says Dona Maria at the end. I must confess to a strong
desire to see *Trikaal* again if it were not for the aesthetically jarring
and often obstrusive Hindi used throughout the film.

Satyajit Ray: Artist and Craftsman

1

The Humanism of Ray

Artists have been described as the conscience of the race, but it is only given to one or two in an entire generation to speak with the voice of a whole people. Tagore was the spokesman of renascent India, speaking in the twentieth century in the accent and with all the fervour of the nineteenth. But his yeasty romanticism has since expired and is only to be found in the crevices of Raja Rao's highly Sanskritized prose or the sickly-sweet sentimentality of Kamala Markandaya's early novels.

Had Tagore been born in the twentieth century (why is it so difficult even to conceive of this?), he might have, like Cocteau, turned to the motion picture as the most ideally suited medium, for, did not the Frenchman say that 'the film is the poet's weapon'? Tagore didn't make any films but his pupil at Santiniketan, Satyajit Ray, did and, in doing so, emulated his master. For he is today one of the world's greatest film-makers, taking his place beside Antonioni, Godard, Bergman, Kurosawa, Renoir, and the man who has probably influenced Ray most, Vittorio De Sica.

Looking back on a career that has spanned nearly two decades and been uniformly productive, one is struck by the consistency and evenness of Ray's work. From the earliest of his films, *Pather Panchali* (1955), to *Ashani Sanket* (1973), one discerns in his work an underlying moral sensibility that has largely contributed to the unity of his work and to its universal appeal. If one seeks to define the hallmarks of a Ray film one does not do so in terms of the currently fashionable or of the merely innovatory. One is driven to the employment of old hallowed notions that belong essentially to a bygone age as if 'the clear stream of reason' of the classic liberal dream of Tagore had somehow survived in the midst of all the dreary desert sands of the modern scene. And, indeed, in the leisured spaces of Ray's sparsely crowded canvasses one discerns the workings of a finely honed sensibility, surprisingly whole despite the iterated interruption of wars, pogroms, revolutions, and recording quietly the progress of man in one small corner of this planet during, say, the last one hundred years. Ray's is essentially an optimistic and yea-saying imagination: he believes in the human spirit, chiefly its capacity to endure but, also, by implication, its capacity to change and renew itself. This is what the Marxist critic, John Howard Lawson, has called the 'Promethean theme' of Ray's films. And it is a matter of common consent by now that this theme has found its deepest and truest articulation in the great trilogy with which he began his career.

Pather Panchali is certainly one of the most humane films ever made. Yet it has had its detractors: Francois Truffaut walked out of it in annoyance, stating that he was not interested in a movie about Indian peasants. Ray himself has recorded that another Western critic was 'so upset at the spectacle of Indians eating with their fingers that he had to leave as soon as the second dinner episode commenced'. These reactions merely reveal the many cultural and ethno-geographical barriers to human understanding that have to be surmounted before the true proportions of a film like *Pather Panchali* can be correctly perceived. Fortunately, not many found the barriers insurmountable. For, in portraying rural Bengal, Ray had not merely revealed the dark underside of India with its dormant villages tormented by an age-old want, but had distilled history and forged (to paraphrase Joyce) in the smithy of his art the uncreated conscience of the Indian cinema. Hitherto the latter had got along with the techniques of the stage barely adapted to the needs of the new medium. The advent of sound, which had first alarmed and then challenged the giants of the silent cinema (particularly Chaplin) to their greatest heights, was used by the Indian film-maker to introduce song and music not as adjuncts to the visual but as its lord and master. But sound in Ray's films is always the willing handmaiden of the total aesthetic design, illuminating the work's dramatic or lyrical structure by leading the spectator to an inward and more complete participation. This is why, perhaps, his films teem with more sounds than those of almost any other contemporary film-maker. The sounds in his films (except deliberate speech and background music which is always minimal) are usually the sounds of workaday reality: the humming of telegraph poles, the music from an adjoining house, the delicate melody of bamboo pines rubbing against one another, the barking of dogs or the passing of lorries. It is this emphasis upon the ordinary that characterizes Ray as a film-maker and that is why he has been labelled a neo-realist.

But Ray is something more than a neo-realist. He is a humanist in the truest sense of that word. Yet his humanism is by no means a Christian humanism, although no one has imbibed more from the West than Ray. It is a specifically Indian humanism; one might even describe it as a truly Hindu humanism (although I do not happen to know what Ray's religious beliefs were). However one might describe it, it avoids simplistic extremes and schematic ideal types. Thus there are no 'heroes' in his films and, as a corollary to this, no villains either. The only heroism he permits in his films is the heroism of brave endurance and, as for villainy, it is almost completely absent in the early films. I cannot remember a single villain anywhere, the only candidate for this title being the potential seducer in *Aparajita* (1956) but even he is not of the true stuff of villainy because, after a solitary try he loses heart! Instead of heroes and villains, Ray gives us ordinary human beings. He has himself said,'I feel that a common person, an ordinary person is a more challenging subject for cinematic exploration than persons in heroic moulds, either good or bad. It is the half-shades, the hardly audible notes that I want to explore and capture.' So his films are packed with 'failed poets, unpublished writers, perpetual students' (Kael) and he has devoted a whole film, *Abhijan* (1962), to a taxi driver. And then there are the old men and women (the eighty-year old crone in *Pather Panchali* being the most memorable of all) bent with age and patiently awaiting their death. But Ray's films are also full of young people eager for toys or amusements, delightfully and perennially mischievous, and full of a choking beauty. Then there are the immature and the unlucky and the wealthy who all suffer, each in his own way. It is this suffering, and Ray's almost feminine understanding of it, that give his films their characteristic tonality. There are no contrastive moral whites against evil blacks, but only suffering, infinitely suffering human beings. There is no anger, no indignation or tiresome nostrums as the panaceas for the world's or India's ills, but merely a benign and gentle objectivity. These are the hallmarks of Ray's unobtrusive humanism.

Ray's compassion and understanding are not only reserved for men but seem to extend also to Nature. Consider the animals that throng his films. There are cats and dogs in nearly every one: geese and the solitary cow in the ruined shed towards the elegiac close of *Pather Panchali*; birds and monkeys who have a temple all to themselves in *Aparajita*; there is the pig which is tragically run over in *Apur Sansar* (1959); there is a beautiful horse (Toofan) in *Jalsaghar* (1958) and also a magnificent elephant which has the run of Biswambhar Roy's estate in the same film; mules in *Kanchenjunga* (1962) which effectively disrupt the unlucky Banerjee's imminent proposal; a caged parrot in *Charulata* (1964) and in resplendent technicolour in *Ashani Sanket* (1973) where, too, an ordinary garden lizard and two fluttering butterflies have a scene all to themselves; a lonely heron, again, in *Charulata* ; a squirrel in *Samapti* (the tail piece of *Teen Kanya* [1961]); a snake at the end of *Pather Panchali*; and, finally, there is even a ghost (which I choose to regard as a species of animal!) in *Monihara* (the centre-piece of *Teen Kanya*). Ray shows none of these creatures as harmful to men and always presents them as in every way indubitably linked with the life of Homo sapiens. None of the animals is shown as dying or killed, with the exception of the pig in *Apur Sansar* whose death is linked with the death of Apu's bride in childbirth. This pervasive sympathy for the entire order of animal creation is found, I suggest, in none of the artists of the modern world and, for parallels, one will have to go to the Kalidasa of *Shakuntalam* or the Pallava sculptors of the gigantic rock-cut at Mahabalipuram depicting the penance of Arjuna. In this colossal piece of sculpture there are, among other well known features, a monkey family, set a little apart from the rest on a raised platform, absorbed in the venerable occupation of picking lice and a cat doing penance — inspired no doubt by Arjuna's example — entirely oblivious to the numerous mice scampering round its feet. To this great tradition of Indian humanism Ray is the true heir.

Ray's work, like that of any great artist, has revealed remarkable range and development. He has not confined himself to the rural scene as a lesser artist may have done. He has accepted the challenge of the present, and in *Jalsaghar* (1958), *Mahanagar* (1963), and *Charulata* (1964), we get a record of the struggle — always a painful one — of the passage from the old to the new. These are the 'transition' films with their intensely Chekhovian flavour (particularly *Jalsaghar*) which leave the pastoral simplicities of the great trilogy behind to explore the margins of insecurity which widen and constantly expand under the pressures of the present. *Charulata* is the truest and most abiding crystallization of Ray's humanism: the best traditions of nineteenth-century English liberalism distilled from a Tagorean romanticism to give us the imperishable face of one important phase of Indian woman-hood. Charu is probably Ray's greatest creation and the film undoubtedly his *magnum opus*. The purely urban films (*Nayak* [1966], *Aranyer Din Ratri* [1969], *Pratidwandi* [1970, and *Seemabaddha* [1971]) are relatively less successful, partly because of a greater technical preoccupation on Ray's part and partly because their protagonists do not provoke that immediate sympathy with their moral predicaments which gave the trilogy its contours of universality. It is indeed singularly heartening to note that Ray, after a long absence from his chosen domain, returned to it magisterially in his *Ashani Sanket* ('Distant Thunder'). The subject is the terrible Bengal famine of 1943 and Ray conveys his great theme of human endurance amidst adversity with all his customary restraint and subdued pathos.

But whatever he turns to, his works bear the stamp of his intensely personal vision. He appears today as the one true star on the firmament of India's tawdry heavens, and the poverty he depicts seems more resplendent than all the bejewelled vulgarity of filmdom's great moghuls. He has engineered the recrudescence of neo-realism when that movement seemed to falter after the blazing triumph of *Bicycle Thief* (1948). If the new-realists looked where the others ruminated, Ray looks and looks again. He came, he *saw* and he conquered. What he saw and has made us see is nothing less than a whole history of our times.

He gave us eyes to see the truth, a truth which later generations will come to live by. Above all he has earned the lasting gratitude of the nation for he has taught us the most elementary and yet most difficult of truths that to be a true Indian it is first necessary to be a citizen of the world.

2

Pather Panchali (1955)

The story of Western reactions to *Pather Panchali* (from an Indian point of view, that is) is an unwritten chapter in the history of Indian cinema. Such an account would be a valuable footnote not only to the history of the image of India in the West but will also provide a useful clue to the ways in which Western perception of India has been sensitive to the disappearance of colonial rule from India.

When we look at Western reactions to *Pather Panchali* down the years, we find a bewildering swing from early exasperation to uncritical celebration. Kingsley Amis, the British novelist, in his *Esquire* review said that the film was just 'pad, pad, pad through the paddy fields'. Francois Truffaut said he was not interested in a film about peasants, while another critic, Ray records, was 'so upset at the spectacle of Indians eating with their fingers that he had to leave as soon as the second dinner episode commenced'. Bosley Crowther of the *New York Times* patronizingly called it an 'exotic import' and found it so 'listless in tempo' that he declared that no editor in Hollywood would pass it even as a 'rough cut'.

In Boston the film opened to a select audience who had been, prior to viewing the film, wined and dined at the Hotel Vendôme where the waiters wore Indian turbans and the guests were treated to Indian curry and Indian sweets! All this probably ensured the good reviews the film received, but at the earlier New York premiere things didn't begin too well. A critic told Harrison who had put up the guarantee money, 'I'll need a second head to understand this film'. Another 'sympathizer' suggested that the film should be shown to the staff of various embassies to persuade them to do something for these 'poor people'.

Even the usually perceptive Stanley Kauffmann of the *New Republic* thought the film could use 'condensation by about a fifth'. The story to him looked 'simple to the point of banality': it could at best be taken as 'dramatized documentary'. Baffled cinematically, Kauffmann resorted to an etiolated aestheticism: 'In the most commonplace daily actions these people move beautifully, in the poorest home the bowls and the platters, the windings of the ragged shawls have some beauty.' Still Kauffman's heart was not wholly in this palaver, for in his review of *Aparajita* (1956) he reverted to *Pather Panchali*:

... the story was so freighted with catastrophe that one began to baulk. It is doubtless a regrettable human frailty that when excessive woe descends on one house, the spectator's sympathy fails. He suspects either that compassion is wasted on people so hopeless or that the gods, if not the scriptwriters, have a slight addiction to soap opera.

A serious consideration of *Pather Panchali* today must begin elsewhere than such aesthetic bric-à-brac or such moral callousness. The poverty depicted in the film is not just decor and it is sheer evasion to talk as Kauffmann does about the bowls and the platters and the windings of the ragged shawls as if this were all the film was about. This strange emphasis on *inanimate* objects rather than on the *people* in the film is characteristic of Western criticism of *Pather Panchali*. One finds much the same kind of thing in Eric Rhode's *Tower of Babel* (1966).

In spite of death and destruction, what we mainly remember from this film are its glowing images of passing bands and rickshaws, of children running through sunlit glades and of trains — especially trains — with their hope of work in Benares and the promise of a new and better society. The English translation for *Pather Panchali* is aptly *On the Road*. It is above all else, the activity of life that counts. As one of the villagers sagely remarks, 'It's staying in one place that makes you mean.'

Apart from the mystery of where Rhode found those phantom 'rickshaws' in *Pather Panchali*, the passage is noteworthy for the same strained and positively gory aestheticism that results in a complete failure to engage seriously with the moral intentions of the film. Possibly misled by a facile and glib translation of the title ('On the Road', unusual even for those days) Rhode assumes that, like Kerouac's novel of the same name published in the late 50s, *Pather Panchali* is a freewheeling road odyssey loosely strung together. With the film thus totally out of focus, it is not surprising that he completely misses the irony in Shejbou's remark to Sarbojaya about staying in the same place making

you mean. There is surely nothing 'sage' about the snivelling and pes-
tilential Shejbou who, if anything, merely couches her secret relief
at Sarbojaya's departure in the hypocritical remark about the value
of change.

Many of the difficulties of the film have their source in the hopelessly
inadequate English rendering of the Bengali title of the film. One
of the English translators of the Bibhutibhushan book has frankly confessed in his 'Introduction' to the book that 'the title is untranslatable'.

The first word 'Pather' is the genitive case of a noun which means road,
but the second word has no equivalent in English ... *Song of the Road* has
been used as a sub-title to Pather Panchali, because the Bengalis who have
been consulted tend to feel that, in spite of its manifest inadequacy, it is
the nearest one can get by way of translation: but were I free to ignore the
exigencies of translation and choose an English title more in keeping with
the content and spirit of Banerji's novel, I should prefer *Bends in the Road*,
a phrase which occurs in several places in the text. It retains, as the original
does, the symbolism of the road broken into a series of stretches divided
from one another by bends which conceal what lies ahead. This symbolism
of a road viewed in segments conforms also with the episodic structure of
the book.

It would also have equally conformed to the apparently episodic
structure of the film. Unfortunately, as it turned out, *Song of the Road*
won out as title with disastrous consequences for criticism. Clearly
the 'lyrical' title led to the many 'lyrical' interpretations of the film.

Ray's film has only a loose relation to the tenor of the Bibhutibhushan
book where the death of old Indir (Pishi in the film) occurs in the
first section of the book, called 'Old Aunt', in a pretty straightforward
way. Whereas Ray has enmeshed this death with the celebrated jaunt
of the children to view the railway in ways so opaque that critics
even fail to sense a difficulty here. (For most critics the train sequence
is emblematic of the whole film: the progressive discovery by Apu
of the outer world, which will eventually take him away from the
narrow confines of Nischindipur.) Further, in spite of the book's immense popularity with the public (in the Bengali original, I mean)
it has a certain rhetoric wholly absent in Ray's film. Here, for instance,
is Bibhutibhushan Banerjee on the death of Durga:

From time to time the hand of eternity breaks through the blue veil of the
heavens and beckons to a child, and the little one, no longer willing to wait,
tears itself away from the breast of Mother Earth and is lost forever down
a road that knows no returning. In that dark evening hour of her sick and

restless life Durga had heard that summons and leaving the paths she loved so well, she commenced her new journey down a highway her feet had not trodden before.

With how much more restraint does Ray handle Durga's death in the film! There is no wailing or beating of the breast, and the sequence is memorable chiefly for 'the hysterical death music' of Ravi Shankar's soaring *sarangi*, as Saul Bellow has described it in his *Herzog*. But otherwise in Ray's handling of it there is not the slightest rhetoric or false note. Ray, of course, took many liberties with the novel which was originally set in the nineteenth century (more exactly: old Indir is described as young in 1833). Ray brings the action forward to the early decades of the twentieth, reorders the two sections of the book, and subjects the material to a decidedly cinematic treatment. There is also a greater compression (the novel deals with Durga's illness and death in a rather protracted way) and also a surprising elasticity of treatment.

The film is well beyond any merely pictorial beauty or any equally pictorial poverty that the West finds in it. There have been no serious considerations here in India of the film but the efforts in the offing seem equally embroiled in the 'wonder-syndrome' of the West. The film is falsely broken up into episodes ('the guava-stealing episode', the necklace stealing episode', 'the chaddar-begging episode', and of course the master episode, 'the children discovering the train') in Professor Satish Bahadur's handy film appreciation course material[*] so that the critic can conveniently propel himself forward at a leisurely pace savouring 'episode' after 'episode' like so many courses at a multi-course dinner. That all the episodes may be manifestation of the same underlying truth can hardly be inferred from this 'instant' breakdown of the film.

The truth is that the film is an unrelenting study of poverty, but in a wholly different vein from De Sica's *Bicycle Thief* (1948) which, incidentally, Ray had called 'the ideal film for the Indian film maker to study' in an early essay. Ray is reported to have told Georges Sadoul in 1965 that 'after having seen *The Bicycle Thief* in London, I decided to film *Pather Panchali* according to neo-realistic methods'. Still if he is close to De Sica at all, it is to the De Sica of Andre Bazin (Bazin, incidentally, was indirectly responsible for directing the jurors' attention to *Pather Panchali* at Cannes), Bazin who invoked the name

[*] *The World of* Pather Panchali; Study Material Series No. 10/A, National Film Archive of India.

of St Francis of Assisi and his celebrated Canticle to describe the spirit
of love animating the De Sica film. In Ray, too, there is something
of the same pervasive sympathy towards all animal creation that one
finds in the Kalidasa of *Shakuntalam* or in the Pallava sculptors of
the gigantic rock-cut at Mahabalipuram showing the penance of Arjuna.
In this piece of sculpture there is a whole galaxy of animal creation
coexisting in serene and unequalled harmony (one at once thinks of
that scene in *Pather Panchali* where Durga's kitten is shown frolicking
with the dog). To this great tradition of an Indian, as opposed to
a strictly Christian humanism, Ray is the true heir.

If humanistically and cinematically, De Sica and *Bicycle Thief* provide
one component (and we might include here Renoir in his respect for
physical space and Cartier-Bresson for a certain compositional rigour),
the years at Shantiniketan provide the other. Ray himself has admitted,
'I do not think my *Pather Panchali* would have been possible if I
had not my years of apprenticeship at Shantiniketan. It was there that
sitting at the feet of "master-*moshai*" I learnt how to look at nature,
how to respond to nature, and how to feel the rhythm inherent in
nature.' He describes in his essay 'Calm Without, Fire Within', students
being made to learn the rudiments of Chinese calligraphy at Shantiniketan. 'Draw a tree,' Professor Bose told his students, 'but not
in the Western fashion. Not from the top downwards. A tree grows
up, not down. The strokes must be from the base upwards.'

Still Ray's sensibility is a very complex affair and very difficult to
pin down. We know, for instance, that, like Eisenstein, Ray was a
great admirer of Leonardo Da Vinci's *Notebooks*, and clearly his eye
for graphic design is remarkably acute, as witness his sketches of projected
sequences for his film. He admired the frescoes of Ajanta which he
found very different from European frescoes. The blend of the Indian
— or should one say Eastern? — and the Western produced one of
the extraordinary sensibilities of our time.

It is likely that Western critics, encountering for the first time this
unusually eclectic sensibility, reacted to the Eastern component more
and failed altogether to do justice to the Western component (I know
of only one critic, Vernon Young, who has found *Pather Panchali*
somewhat un-Indian due to Ray's 'conscious attempt to stand outside
his material, in the manner of Western sociology'. I must add that
Young 'found *The Music Room* and *Charulata* more Indian (more Eastern, let me say) than the *Pather Panchali* trilogy'.) But the elements
are so marvellously mixed in *Pather Panchali* that a consideration of

the one without the other would be to falsify the spirit of the man and his extraordinary film.

What is attempted below is an attempt to work from 'the base upwards' in the spirit of Professor Bose's recommendation, because the poetry stems from the poverty depicted in the film. It cannot and should not be relished separately. And the poverty is not simply a matter of 'the guava-stealing episode', 'the necklace-stealing episode', 'the chaddar-begging episode', *à la* Professor Bahadur, but the way the whole narrative is woven, the build-up of each scene leading to the same underlying theme of poverty, so that no one scene read in isolation makes sense. The poetry is therefore not a matter of sunlit glades, or trains, or phantom rickshaws. Not in the least! The poetry is in the pity, nowhere else. It is in the encompassing compassion that envelops the build of each scene, each speech, each episode that make this film (a truly neo-Raylistic masterpiece), the most searing exposé of the moral and physical degradations of poverty in India at the turn of the century.

Take the very opening of the film — the so-called 'guava-stealing episode'. We see Shejbou on the terrace shouting at Durga for stealing from the orchard. Sarbojaya is down at the well in the Mukherji courtyard drawing water with difficulty (she is expecting) and is abused by Shejbou for Durga's thefts. In between these separate scenes we see Durga dropping the stolen guavas into old Pishi's pot and then feeding the kittens. From the scene at the well we move to a scene showing Pishi eating and licking her fingers, only to see Durga at her elbow sitting unnoticed by her. She apologizes to Durga for not leaving anything for her. Durga smiles and Pishi discovers the guavas beneath the bananas, and at this point Sarbojaya enters to chide Durga for stealing from Shejo Khuro's orchard. This is followed by a long scene between Pishi and Sarbojaya, in which the old woman is accused not only of spoiling Durga but also of generally pilfering things from the kitchen. This leads to Pishi's leaving the house in a huff.

The scene establishes several things at once, the least of which is the stealing of the guavas. It shows the relationship between Harihar Ray's family and the neighbouring rich Mukherji family very economically. In Nilmoni's solicitousness to Sarbojaya at the well and her offer of help is anticipated the later development of the relationship, Nilmoni being Sarbojaya's mainstay in the village. The sequence also establishes the deep bonds of the Durga—Pishi relationship, a relationship based on love but also on mutual deprivation. Like Durga, Pishi too steals from the Harihar household. It is interesting that in the opening sequence Harihar is absent.

This is not really his story but that of the women and of the interweaving relationships between them. This, too, is something of a major shift from the run-of-the-mill Indian film where women play insignificant parts, and certainly the story is not told from their point of view. They are either mothers or objects of love or lust of the men but seldom central to the action. Women, like servants in the classic British mystery story, are rarely perceivers but merely the perceived. They are part of the furniture of the setting through which the plot majestically moves forward, essential to the set but inessential to the action. They are simply 'there'. But Ray, with the true artist's sympathy for the truly oppressed in this peasant society, unfolds his plot expressly from their viewpoint.

Technically, too, the opening establishes the style of the film. The sequence has 55 separate shots most of which are in long shot (21), some in extreme long shot (5), others in medium long shot (4), or medium shot (20). There are only three close shots and one medium close shot, and just one close up of old Pishi's hand digging into the bowl of rice gruel. This style determines the emotional distance Ray keeps throughout the action, though this by no means implies any coldness but rather a non-partisan love for his characters. Clearly he has no 'viewpoint character', although all Western critics have put up the candidature of Apu for this role just because they seem incapable of understanding the film except as the story of someone's growing up. Apart from all this, several important musical 'motifs' are introduced in this opening sequence which are to recur at important points in the film. The first and principal musical motif is the lovely signature tune of the film heard during the Durga—Auntie interlude, binding them together irrevocably. The second musical motif is the all too brief (if tantalizingly so) candy-seller music, here associated with Granny during the scene of her first quarrel with Sarbojaya (it is heard again, importantly, just before Auntie's and Durga's respective deaths). The cymbal music leading up to the 'Death theme' is also heard here, as Auntie goes out of the house in a huff at the end of the sequence. (This will be heard again during the final death throes of Auntie which begin as the children are having their little adventure in the fields.) Only the music at the beginning of the film, as Durga runs past the bamboo grove, can be described as incidental or illustrative. But all the other motifs serve a valuable structural function. Such is the severity of Ray's economy.

The opening sequence, then, contains all the *leitmotifs* of the whole film. The 'necklace-stealing episode' on which critics (particularly Robin Wood) wax eloquent is really a full-scale reprise of the opening in all its features, down to the absence of Harihar during the entire proceedings. The sequence starts with Sarbojaya feeding Apu who is playing with a makeshift bow and arrow. Into this placid scene erupts Shejbou with her charge that Durga has stolen Tunu's glass bead necklace. Durga's box is cruelly ransacked for the missing necklace and hot exchanges between the women ensue, with Sarbojaya understandably on the defensive throughout. Durga has meanwhile emerged with more stolen fruit and Sarbojaya just manages to stave off a thrashing for Durga from Shejbou. Pishi, who steals on the scene, as it were, dragging a palm leaf, pathetically intervenes but is ignored all round. Shejbou now abruptly departs after demanding instant repayment of the loan of five rupees. This is the signal for Durga's flogging with a birch. Once again Pishi intercedes but in vain as Durga is dragged, beaten, and pushed out to the accompaniment of some of the harshest music in Ray (drums) — the staging, pacing, and music of this scene in many ways like early Elia Kazan. The scene closes with Sarbojaya's anguished collapse on the side of the door with the humiliated Durga outside. Pishi tenderly gathers up the scattered oddments into Durga's box while a somewhat shaken Apu rinses his mouth in a youthful gesture of bravado at the end of the courtyard.

Looked at closely, this sequence is merely a repeat at a higher voltage of all the features of the opening sequence. It is yet another 'bend in the road' traversed by the principal characters, but no more momentous than any earlier or later 'bend'. But Western critics hyped and hung-up on the notion of linear development cannot see it this way. They have to read 'meanings' into it willy-nilly. Thus Robin Wood, in his woefully wrongheaded book, *The Apu Trilogy*, has seen the simple action of Apu rinsing his mouth as 'albeit unconsciously — expressing his repudiation of her decisions and her influence'. For Wood this action of Apu's — first rinsing his mouth and then reading his arithmetic lessons with his father — is nothing less than 'a moral judgement' on Sarbojaya, a 'turning — and not without ostentation — from his mother's to his father's influence and to the education that will separate him from Sarbojaya'. It is of course nothing of the kind! The whole of *Aparajita* is there to prove it, particularly the sequence when the now grown-up Apu deliberately misses the train in order to placate his mother. This merely goes to show that most Westerners (except professional sociologists these days) have simply no clue whatsoever to the intensity of mother— son relationships in India.

The 'necklace-stealing episode' merely underlines the precarious social position of the Harihar family due to their financial bankruptcy. The return of the five rupees is going to take precedence over other more pressing domestic requirements — like repairs to the house. Shejbou's parting shot — 'Like mother, like daughter' — points not only forward to the scene, just as the rains start, leading to Durga's illness, when Sarbojaya is shown stealing a fallen coconut, but also backward to the first protracted conversation between Harihar and his wife (while Pishi rocks the infant Apu to sleep in the background) when they dream of better times to come. But this conversation — on which most critics are strangely silent because it is 'talky' and so lacks plastic values, you see — holds the clue to the repeated 'bends in the road' that the characters precariously navigate. Harihar has been driven by dire economic need to more or less abandon his traditional vocation of priesthood for a dubious salaried job (Rs 8 per month) in the accounts office of Ray Khuro, the very landlord who, in fact, appropriated his ancestral orchard. Harihar's father had borrowed Rs 300 from Ray Khuro and, unable to repay it, had surrendered the precious orchard. The dual irony of Durga's stealing fruit from the very orchard that was once theirs is now apparent. And so the guava-and necklace-stealing episodes reinforce the economic plight of Harihar Ray's family. But Satyajit Ray's focus is not on the plight of individuals merely, nor is he interested in patiently charting Apu's so-called growth. His aim is epic, wider than the constricting arena of customary bourgeois drama.

It is not for nothing that we are told that Ray Khuro is a moneylender. This is a drama, then, of peasant impoverishment and destitution through the greed and rapacity of landlords. It is a measure of Ray's historico-social view of the impoverished peasant that Harihar repeatedly, in this early conversation with his wife, refers to Ray Khuro as 'a gentleman'. When his wife wants to know if he is going to be paid regularly, Harihar's naïvete is revealing: it is perfectly in keeping with his 'nobility' for such blind 'trust' is enjoined by feudal relationships. Ray is charting the course of socio-historical change with barometric accuracy. For we learn in the course of the next conversation between Harihar and Sarbojaya that he has not been paid by Ray Khuro for the last three months. Still, Harihar is afraid of bringing up the subject of salary for fear of losing his job! (It is true that we learn subsequently that he is eventually paid, but Rs 24 for three months is hardly enough to meet Harihar's pressing requirements. He now sets his hopes on rich Mahesh Biswas whom he meets in Khuro's place, but by the end of the film even this hope sputters out with the untimely death of Biswas's two children). In the same conversation between Harihar and his wife we also get a hint of Durga's declining health due to malnutrition. 'The girl is running a fever without medicine and a proper diet,' Sarbojaya tells her husband. 'For God's sake, do find some way out,' she implores. The film demonstrates, quietly, that under the prevailing social and economic relations between people there is really no way out.

The train sequence is the *locus classicus* of all Western (and Western-inspired) misreadings of Ray. Let me straightaway confess that it is one of the loveliest sequences in the whole of Ray and there was a time, some 20 years ago, when I made the weekly pilgrimage from Warangal to Hyderabad (a distance of some 90 miles) every Sunday with my wife for several months running just to see the Apu films and rejoice in their imperishable 'beauty'. But then, in my newborn euphoria over the Ray magic, I saw through a glass darkly and saw only 'beauty'. That time is past and all its 'aching joys and giddy raptures', I have to confess with some regret. But the sequence is not, as I see it now, 'the discovery of India *à la* Nehru' or of trains, that Western critics have made it out to be. This reading is common to all Western admirers of Ray. For Eric Rhode, 'There is a pivotal moment ... when Apu sees a train for the first time and begins to understand the extent of man's powers... All quite usual for us perhaps; but for Apu a Mechanical Messiah is born.' (I like that 'All quite usual for us perhaps'). For Robin Wood it is 'a moment of decisive transition from the primitive world of the past to an advanced world of the future'. For John Russell Taylor the train is a symbol of progress as against the static pond. 'The train moves, and suggests travel, progress... The pond is static, stagnant, a place to sit aimlessly by.' Still, by a mysterious power, we are informed, Ray integrates the train with diverse other things in the film — 'the actors ... the grasses, death' (but why leave the pond out after having stepped so far?) into the 'unity' of 'Apu's developing consciousness'.

But all this is to wholly misread the sequence cinematically, for Ray has not shown the train sequence in isolation but has carefully intercut it with old Pishi's death. The sequence is too well-known

for me to dwell on it here, but suffice it to say that Ray cuts from
the visual premonition of death on the old woman's face (also we
hear again the 'Death theme' we heard at the end of the opening
sequence of the film, so well does Ray prepare us) straight to Durga
with her ears to the humming pylon and the aural continuity between
the 'Death theme' and the humming pylon would seem to point more
to Durga's approaching death than to the birth of any Mechanical
Messiahs for the benefit of young Apu. This reading is reinforced by
Durga's fall as she runs towards the embankment to see the train
(significantly, during her last fatal illness she asks Apu whether they
can go to see the train when she is well again) and by the disturbing
and somewhat sinister closing frame of this particular sequence with
the gyrating and inky black smoke stark against the sunless sky with
the telegraph pole on the far left of the frame and signal on the near
right. And during all this we have the certain knowledge that Pishi
is in her last moments elsewhere, and surely this must govern our
reading of the whole sequence.

Trains in the trilogy are, in fact, the Angels of Death. In *Aparajita*,
as Sarbojaya sits under the tree waiting for Apu's return, we see and
hear a train in the distance billowing smoke. She is to die soon after.
In *Apur Sansar* the train symbolism is even more insistent. We hear
the screech of train whistles as Apu and Aparna are about to enter
their Calcutta homestead after their wedding. Again, as Aparna leaves
for her confinement, there is an ominous low angle shot of the engine
just before the train leaves. And then Aparna's death in childbirth,
as also Apu's suicide attempt, are dramatized unforgettably through
the symbolism of an approaching train and at the end of the sequence
(during which a pig dies), smoke from a factory chimney trails the
sky. And so the train sequence in *Pather Panchali* must be read *backwards*
from the perspective of the completed trilogy so that its true import
can be grasped. It simply won't do to talk of Mechanical Messiahs
in a dumb, allegorical way. But then Western critics, struggling with
the stereotype of a primitive India, easily slip into the error of seeing
the trilogy as 'the development of the boy Apu's consciousness from
the primitive medieval village life of *Pather Panchali* through the modern
city streets and schools of Benares to the University of Calcutta in
Aparajita ' (Pauline Kael) and misread the scene entirely as having
to do with Apu's initiation. Only Robin Wood, among all Ray's critics,
appears to make some kind of allowance for a more complex reading

of the train symbolism in *Pather Panchali.* But this, too, turns out to be deceptive.

He adds, just after the passage cited from his book on the trilogy: 'Against the "negative" of the useless old woman's meaningless death, the train is not the only positive. There is also the life in nature, the calf, the stream, the seeded grass, the play of sunlight and shadow among the trees: a serene harmonious world the train temporarily blotted out.' 'The "*negative*" of the *useless* old woman's *meaningless* death' is not the remark of a man who has the least understanding of either India or Ray whose whole approach to old Pishi's death is informed by love and understanding. Otherwise, would he have identified her in so many sequences with Durga (in Bibhutibhushan's novel Durga clearly takes the place of the daughter old Indir lost)? Would he have dowered her with the lovely candy-seller music whose strains are mysteriously heard as she dies, to be followed by the heartbreaking lament of her own boatman song? (Incidentally John Russell Taylor, in his preoccupation with the aesthetics of the long shot, mistakes this song for the singing of the children! Perhaps this, too, for him is part of the mysterious 'unity' achieved by Ray in this sequence). But gerontology aside, Wood seems divided between his two irreconcilable 'positives'. Does he want the train or 'the serene harmonious world the train temporarily blotted out'? Our Leavesian Luddite seems on the horns of a familiar dilemma. Ray is indeed, quite ambiguous about progress in the Western sense. His is neither the thermodynamic world of the progressivists nor the static, crystalline one of the anthropologists, and any facile pigeon-holing is fatal to an understanding of his work. Certainly he is no 'primitive', but a highly sophisticated artist, as the earlier part of this essay attempted to show.

Stripped of the Western metaphysics about the train, we see it simply as a device to render more poignant the death of old Pishi. But the real burden of her death is conveyed in that boatman song she first sang on that moon-washed night, and which is heard again as the funeral pyre bears her corpse away. The song is about her not having the fare to pay the boatman to row her to the other shore! 'I have done my day's work! I have no means to pay the fare,' she wails in her last lament. Money, money, money, the lack of it, is the real theme of *Pather Panchali.* Even Pishi's lullaby to the infant Apu touches on money: 'Bulbul, the bird has flown away! How to pay the dues now?' Never for one single moment are we allowed any respite from the 'determinations' of money and the degradation of poverty. But

Kauffmann, who delighted in bowls and platters and the windings of the ragged shawls, found that when it came to the *people* in *Pather Panchali* 'compassion is wasted on people so hopeless', and this led him to speculate whether 'the gods, if not the scriptwriters, have a slight addiction for soap opera'. Ray it is, and not the Gods, as might be supposed, who wrote the script and directed *Pather Panchali*, Ray with his 'slight addiction' to the truth. Is this addiction soap opera, Mr Kauffmann?

There is absolutely nothing in *Pather Panchali* that does not have a bearing on money and the consequences — both social and psychological — that its possession or its lack entails. Even in the soft 'humorous' portraits, sketched with a touch of Daumier, there is the same nagging mediation of simple economics. The apparently humorous scene of Apu's education at Prosanna's makeshift grocery-cum-school looks bright and cheerful at first inspection, but even here there are dark shadows. Majumdar (who, half playfully, refers to Prosanna's wards as so many 'catches' who will, in good time, do their turn at the plough), at the termination of the scene himself fails to 'catch' (it is an outstanding and much used verb of poor societies) angler Chakravarty for the obligatory, if painful, Puja subscription. Chakravarty eludes Majumdar who himself had cajoled Prosanna into giving him the oil. He also hints that 'from time to time I would look for little favours from you'. And these are the people of whom Harihar says, as he is preparing to leave, 'Had I wanted help from you, perhaps I would have got it'! In this world poverty alone is the reality. Its effects are sometimes comic (as in the scene just examined), but elsewhere, as in Harihar's household, tragic. But comic or tragic, the art, the poetry, derives from the same underlying reality.

Examples of this are so numerous that I will have to quote the entire screenplay. There is one particularly harrowing scene when the virtually destitute Sarbojaya refuses help and money from the compassionate Nilmoni, just after Durga's death. Pride struggles with need in the tormented and wretched woman, but it is really no contest. For everything in the house — including Sarbojaya's precious 'dowry' vessels — has already been sold and it is clear from all this that Durga's death has really been the result of malnutrition (during Durga's final illness Sarbojaya has to even borrow *sago* from the loyal Nilmoni), and the lack of the wherewithal to buy medicine. The following morning Nilmoni's daughter, Bini, comes with a basket of vegetables. It is a brief, artless little scene, for we notice that Bini is wearing four braids and sickeningly we remember Durga asking her mother to plait her hair into four braids and Sarbojaya's answer to that simple request. This is how time and time again Ray fuses art and economics.

The famous death of Durga is really of a piece with the destruction of the 'ancestral house', the upkeep of which was the burden of Harihar's pathetic efforts. As he returns to Nischindipur for the last time (shortly after Durga's death), and reaching home finds the cowshed in ruins, he mutters to himself one of the film's truly melancholy lines: 'Well, wouldn't you wait for a few more days?' Now at the end, with his manuscripts eaten up by white ants, Harihar is faced with the prospect of having to sell all his belongings — simply to meet his debts. The final note is struck when Apu discovers the stolen necklace and throws it into the pond.

Stolen necklace! Stolen guavas and stolen tamarind seeds! Stolen chillies and salt and oil! Stolen sweets for Durga from friend Ranu! Stolen oil for Durga's pickle from brother Apu! Stolen coconuts from Sarbojaya! Stolen orchard, too, I suppose, though the iron laws of moneylending that Ray Khuro practises probably give it a different and more respectable name. It is out of these ordinary and prosaic materials, *not in spite of them*, that Ray has fashioned his incomparable film that will haunt men beyond the reaches of their souls. Two paise eagerly sought for the marvels of the bioscopewallah, two paise, too, to buy the necessary *gur* for Apu's *payash* — these are the moments of respite and grace in the life of a people steeped in the numbing chills of penury. Other chills need shawls, but poor Pishi doesn't live long enough to enjoy the warmth of Raju's generous gift.

In this bleak and forbidding world, even marriage is not of true minds but reduced to two mouthfuls of rice a day and two sarees a year. As Sarbojaya, with some justification puts it, 'What more is necessary?' Still, for some, it's a long, long way to Tipperary. For vain is Harihar's windfall at the end. He unpacks a rolling pin, a saree for Durga, and a framed picture of the Goddess Lakshmi that Sarbojaya wanted so much. The picture of the Goddess Lakshmi! That is about as far as these miserable people will ever get. Not to wealth itself, but to the framed picture, to the word for 'wealth'. It is the word 'wealth' that Harihar once asks the young Apu to write on his slate, the same night that Apu first asked Durga about the train.

3

Death in the Apu Trilogy

Death is an important ingredient of all art and literature, and the cinema makes use of death sometimes indifferently, sometimes violently, sometimes sombrely, depending not only on the kind of material presented but also on the kind of presentation intended. In a run-of-the-mill Western, death is treated indifferently and this is not contradicted by the fact that death is often the motive for subsequent action usually taking the form of revenge. But death itself is neither glorified nor sentimentalized (this possibility being precluded by the immunity of the principals from death), and, being confined to subordinate players, it is shown as merely the inevitable consequence of wrong actions or merely rashness. Violent death leads us to entirely different considerations altogether. This kind of death (which is significantly absent from Westerns) is often found in the intermediate category of films which, while dealing with some primitive emotions of life like horror, often employ a somewhat simplistic psychology to act as an explanatory façade for the violent action in the plot. *Psycho*, for instance, deals with violent death, and much of its impact as a film depends on the use of violence to portray death. We are dealing here with the pornography of death (to borrow a phrase from Geoffrey Gorer) for violence here, and death along with it, are offered much justification but merely act as drugs to heighten sensation. But here, too, as in Westerns, death is used instrumentally to further the action of the plot by providing a motive for further activity in the form of more deaths or looking for the murderer, etc. Death as used sombrely differs markedly both from its use in Westerns and its use in the horror film in that, here, death is not a means to any other end but is the end itself. Its occurrence is felt as irreparable loss, and often it operates as a yardstick to measure the value of the surviving life (or lives). Death in this category of film sometimes imparts and often clarifies the meaning of life.

The indiscriminate and widespread use of death in Indian films has somewhat obscured its basic functions. There is something very ritualistic and obligatory about death in our films. Usually it is an ailing father or mother, and the death of such a person is often used to bind the survivor(s) to some impossibly idealistic code of conduct (such as marriage to an undesired person), and the film is a working out of the grim consequences of following out such a commandment. Sometimes it is not a father or mother but the inconvenient and obtrusive third person of the eternal triangle who is victimized to resolve the dilemma of the romantic pair. Thus, for instance, in *Sangam* (1964) the death of Gopal is entirely to be explained as a necessity of the plot, as is the death of the doctor in *Dil Ek Mandir* (1963). These deaths are often the most wanton and the crudest since they are inflicted by the plot and not by nature. Such a death is truly a *deus ex machina* , and is often resented by the sensitive film-goer, although the resentment is often smothered under the tidal waves of masochism released in the process. But outside the mother, the father or the inconvenient lover, the Indian film does not seem interested in death *per se*. The death of a wife or a brother or a sister is seldom witnessed in our films because these seem to carry an insufficient charge for the machinery of the plot, which has to be kept constantly in motion to appease the impatient spectator. The indifference to death *per se* in our films is ultimately an indifference to life, for a life where death has lost its significance is ultimately life in which everything has lost its significance.

Death in the films of Satyajit Ray mark a point of departure for a consideration of his art. I shall confine myself to some remarks about the treatment of death in his celebrated Apu trilogy because it is only here that the subject of death receives its most extended treatment. In *Pather Panchali* (1955) an old woman, and a young girl die, in *Aparajita* (1956) it is both the parents of Apu, and in *Apur Sansar* (1959) it is Apu's young wife. Significantly the only omission is the death of a friend. But this apart, the treatment of death is comprehensive but the manner of it is always varied and individualized. Death is deprivation of life, but this deprivation is shown to be of different kinds, depending upon the kind and quality of life that has been lost.

Before investigating further, a few preliminary remarks seem to be appropriate. Ray never hastens his deaths in these films, nor does he seem anxious to forget them after they have occurred. The deaths are both *paced* and *spaced* on either end of the continuum of life and thus thrown into clear perspective. If death can be described as an event in space—time (not in the Einsteinian sense), Ray takes care to present a number of preceding events in space—time contiguous with the event of death, and death itself appears as the last event in the remorseless causal chain. In this way he seems anxious to rob it of its quality of indeterminateness or chanciness, and instead emphasizes its natural character and thus presents it as a natural event, like the coming of spring or the growing up of children. After thus endowing it with a quality of determinates or necessity, he unleashes a different chain that equally shows the human impact of death. This chain runs contrary to the first and usually emphasizes the chance element in death, its indifference to the human condition, its character of callousness and its ultimate mockery. This replaying of death reversing the effect of the first presentation, this reconstruction in entirely human terms, is what gives Ray his uniqueness as a cinematic interpreter of death and imparts to his art, particularly to his trilogy, its character of permanence.

Let us examine these contrary chains that lead first to the occurrence of death and then back from the fact of death to its human import. The old woman's death-chain in *Pather Panchali* begins when she feels thirsty. It is water she needs, water that sustains life, but after she has quenched her thirst, her face darkens in the sharp sunlight, a visual paradox that propels the plot dialectically forward into the domain of death. Apu and Durga, we may recall, have quarrelled and their reconciliation is paced with the last remaining moments of the old woman's life. At significant stages, the two sequences are intercut and, little wonder, for in this way death is naturalized, domesticated, and shorn of its terror: it is shown as little more momentous than juvenile quarrels and youthful reconciliations. For just as Apu and Durga are back from their first glimpses of the railway and are now playfully wrestling, where only a little while ago they did so in earnest, the old woman is visibly sinking. The nostalgic strains of the pedlar's jingle is heard as if to emphasize the unutterable sweetness of the life from which the old lady is about to depart. The presence of Durga by her side moves the dying woman to her final effort, but already death has overtaken her. And it is here that Ray employs the most skilful devices both to suggest death and to maintain that equilibrium needed for aesthetic contemplation. A common fly, which in its sinister and abundant life stands for the privation of life, hovers over the body of the dead woman. Here, probably for the first time in the history of the film, we have one of those great conversions of image, of which hitherto only literature at its highest and best seemed capable: life (the fly) stands for death (the dead woman), but the fly belongs to an altogether despicable order of life and enters the human order only on sufferance in its capacity of scavenger. The presence of the fly, I suggest, converts the death of the individual into a more generalized statement of death. The other device Ray employs is the metal pot that tumbles from the side of the old woman into the pond below and balances immaculately on the still waters. I am unable to explain the presence of the pot except as a strategy for achieving that aesthetic distance which Bullough declared in a famous essay some fifty years ago as a precondition of all aesthetic enjoyment. The fly and the pot are necessary complements of Ray's art here: the fly accentuating the facticity and generality of death, and the balancing pot providing a point of aesthetic stasis from which to contemplate it.

The death of Durga is of a very different order. We may recall Ray's marvellously lyrical ballet dramatizing the coming of spring. It is Durga's drenching in the rain here that leads to her fatal illness. Again Ray has achieved the nexus between life and death, further emphasized by Durga's *puja* (soon after her drenching) which is after all the ritual preparation of a young maiden's coming of age for marriage. The marriage of a friend is interposed hereabouts and there is nothing to suggest that there has been any disruption in the natural order of events. This is in sharp contrast to the superstitious treatment of death in most Indian films where an *unnatural* event like a cow not milking or the milk not turning sour is often a prelude to death. Ray will have none of this superstition and his treatment of the subject is more straightforward and natural. Some might object that there is a certain amount of melodrama on the night of Durga's death with all its accompanying lightning and thunder. But these are used naturalistically and even the image of the God is placed against the door only as a bulwark against the raging winds outside. The rain, as happens with most of our films when the crisis is over, is not forgotten in the morning when a sympathetic neighbour wades across the waterlogged courtyard to commiserate with Durga's mother, nor when Durga's father returns home with the wherewithal for Durga's marriage. The fact of death is first played down when the neighbour pays her call and one might think that the episode is over. But Ray has not yet played all his cards. He uses the technique of *deliberately delayed reaction*, and just when we feel that the film has moved to a different situation, he hammers home the fact of death once again unexpectedly and draws from us a reaction that is doubled due both to the element of un-expectedness and the poignancy of the presentation. Durga's father is shown as returning slowly past the solitary cow in its ruined shed and through the bleak and sullen courtyard, and his homecoming is treated with a quiet deference by his wife. She brings him water to wash his feet as also his sandals, and there is no hint as yet of any return to Durga's death. Then Ray plays his trump card. For when Durga's father displays the various items he has brought and comes eventually to Durga's wedding clothes the blow is struck squarely and savagely. For we are helpless against this muted disclosure of a premature death that takes the place of a wedding. When Durga's father breaks down into convulsive sobs and Ravi Shankar's music rises to a sustained wail of anguish (what Saul Bellow in *Herzog* has called 'the hysterical death music'*), it is really we whose reactions have been dramatized. Still thanks to the magic of Ray's art, the fact of death has been brought home to us *after its actual occurrence.* And it is in this that Ray's achieve-ment consists, that he should make its *post facto* artistic rendering more unbearable than the fact of death itself.

In *Aparajita* the death of Apu's father precedes that of his mother, but it is not merely in the order of time that these two deaths are distinguished. They encompass different worlds of experience: the death of the father is presented objectively and dramatically and that of the mother subjectively and lyrically. Once again the technique is involved and subtle. The daily routine of Apu's father in Benares, particularly the early morning ablutions, is established through a series of splendid shots that capture the antique charm of this ageless city. The onset of sickness in Apu's father is first revealed through his absent-mindedness and then through visible signs of physical degeneration. The technique now employed is a return to the technique employed in portraying

---

* "'Recently I saw *Pather Panchali.* I assume you know it, since the subject is rural India. Two things affected me greatly — the old crone scooping the mush with her fingers and later going into the weeds to die; and the death of the young girl in the rains." Herzog, almost alone in the Fifth Avenue Playhouse, cried with the child's mother when the hysterical death music started. Some musician with a native brass horn, imitating sobs, playing a death noise. It was raining in New York as in rural India.'

the death of the old woman in *Pather Panchali*. Scenes of impending death are intercut with the daily business of life, only here the festival of Diwali is chosen as the symbol of continuing life. Apu's father has a long conversation with his young son about his programme of studies and gradually the night deepens. Outside there is the noise of fireworks and youthful merriment, while inside are a dying man and the oil lamps burning uncertainly in the darkness. We move into the still, unquiet night, and in the small hours Apu's mother wakes up her small son to procure the sacred water of the Ganges for the dying man. And once again Ray plays his hand. The sleepy boy moves uncertainly through the narrow street and down the steps to fill his lota with the sacred water. Behind us is a dying man, but there is no melodrama, no queering the pitch. Instead the pace is slackened perceptibly. For just as he dips his *lota* in the river, Apu's eye catches a gymnast rhythmically exercising in the shrouded and melancholy dawn. It is a great moment. Once again the abundance and vigour of life are played against the fact of death, but a new dimension has been added. For this moment of pause in the action at such a crucial stage points at an aspect of Ray's art that deserves examination. For the intrusion of the gymnast is an irrelevance, irrelevant to the tragic emotion that is sought to be communicated no doubt, but a necessary reminder of the life outside the ambience of death. Once again the effect is to domesticate death, to suggest its essential continuity with life. But Ray must also indicate the fact of death as a severance from life, as irreparable loss and as absolute. And this he does with a memorable image. For just as the dying man takes the first gulp of the sacred water, the camera leaves the room and focuses on a temple top from where, all at once, hundreds of birds take their flight. The effect is that of sudden release. It is almost as if the flight of the soul from the body were being rendered for us in all its stark immediacy.

Apu's mother's death, towards the close of *Aparajita*, is rendered less objectively, more through the viewpoint of the dying woman herself. This is new in Ray, and he employs correspondingly different techniques. Death is shown as isolation, as separation from loved objects. With Apu away in Calcutta, his mother is shown as longing for her son's return. In one memorable sequence, after a passing train has given her conviction of her son's return, she makes her way agonizingly towards the entrance opening on the pathway leading to the house. Her expectation is keyed to fever pitch (and the effort is considerable for it draws upon the last ounces of energy in the ailing woman),

and as she opens the door a void opens before her, a void relieved
(or accentuated?) by the innumerable fireflies that are like so many
terrestial constellations of light. Proud Orion himself (and this is a
searing reminder of Apu who was shown the famous constellation by
his headmaster earlier in the film) is reflected in the waters of the
pond below, and the visible and audible emptiness is dense with the
reminders of the absent Apu. This is a high point in Ray's achievement,
an eternal moment of stillness that carries all the anguish of separation
and loss. The formal death of Sarbojaya ensues, but again it is communicated to us through the withered old man standing motionless
in front of the bewildered Apu.

The last death essayed in the Apu trilogy is the death of Apu's
wife in *Apur Sansar*. The nuances of connubial bliss conveyed in this
film are too well-known to need comment. And yet it must be borne
in mind that these nuances, these peaks of happiness, are the symphonic
overtures to the shattering finale, and, as such, must be understood
as a prelude to the catastrophe. The fact of death itself is announced
brusquely, and Ray appears even to depart from his usual practice
when he introduces an element of gratuitous violence, as if emphasizing
the abruptness of the intrusion of death into Apu's tranquil happiness.
For when his brother-in-law brings him the news, Apu slaps him in
a fit of helpless anguish and the scene terminates with a sense of gnawing
incompleteness. But Ray has not finished yet with this death and he
reserves some of his finest art for its artistic revelation. For as Apu
is preparing to leave and crosses the railway tracks, he notices a white
pig while simultaneously discerning the approach of a train. The train
emits a long whistle as it approaches, and as it nears Apu the camera
veers skywards, and the blankness of the empty sky envelops us as
the long deepening screech of the whistle takes the train past Apu.
The white pig is almost certainly run over and this fact is with us
as we hear the shriek of the whistle and stare at the blankness of
the sky. Is it too much to suggest that the death of Apu's wife in
childbirth is dramatized here in that long moment and that it is her
cry of pain and anguish that we hear in the whistle that wails its
long and almost endless lament? Or that it is her feeling of blankness
we experience as we stare at the white sky while life hangs in the
balance, and death eventually tips the scales in its favour? The sight
of the dead pig and the trail of black smoke, almost like a scar across
the face of the sky after the passage of the train, constitute a coda
to the eternal moment that has gone before, but the knowledge of

death has already been communicated through the medium of a perfect objective correlative. For we move to the dead woman from the pig, just as we move from the whistle to the pain. This is the crowning point in the treatment of death in the Apu trilogy and, significantly, Ray has not enlarged on the subject in his subsequent films.

It is a pity that none of the world's great film-makers seem interested in the subject of individual death in their films. Obsession with God or with sex or with the alienation of men in the modern world have usurped the stage, and death itself is treated perfunctorily. When it is treated at all, as it is with disquieting readiness in our own films, it is treated melodramatically as if it were a convulsion of Nature, instead of a natural fact of life. Hollywood has banished the subject from its films and even *The Longest Day* (1962) was managed (as Dwight Macdonald has pointed out) without a single casualty on either side. It would seem that universal death through the agency of the Bomb has permeated the consciousness of people to such a degree that individual death has ceased to matter. It is the destruction of mankind rather than the destruction of the individual that obsesses film-makers, and the impact of a film like *Dr Strangelove* (1964) testifies to this fact. But the death or destruction of the solitary individual has always been the basis of humanistic art. Aristotle based his *Poetics* on such a conception of tragedy. The disappearance of a concern with individual death portends an era of collectivism and the rise of a type of art where personal values will cease to matter. There remain, meanwhile, the dreary alternatives of the violent death of the horror films and the cold, mechanical death of the Westerns. We may well ask with the poet, 'O death, where is thy sting?'

4

Nayak (1966)

Ray's first essay on contemporary life was *Mahanagar* made in 1963, but it was insufficiently penetrative. Its use of external events was more in the nature of a *deus ex machina* to help the sagging plot along in its unsteady march to the dubious, if somewhat predestined, denouement. But Calcutta itself (from which the film derives its name) so tantalizingly suggested in the credit titles — in the towering grey skyscrapers, in the giant hoarding advertising Capstan cigarettes, and the moving semaphore of a tram — remained a promise largely unfulfilled. *Mahanagar* did not do for Calcutta what *Aparajita* (1956) did for Benares in the early passages, and with this goes a parallel failure on Ray's part to suggest the miasmas of urban monotony. True, the atmosphere of upper middle-class vacuity does for once come through in that *ersatz* home in Alipore Road where Arati essays her first canvassing but the highly domestic drama that is being remorselessly played out elsewhere does not, by and large, permit such excursions. At the end there is a feeling that a number of problems have been simply dodged. As Arati and her husband stride out sturdily into the Calcutta dusk and Ray gives us that near-Antonioni close-up of the naked street bulb, we are aware that many of the essential problems of life in a city remain unexplored. It is time to go home and listen to the 9 o'clock news, but is it enough merely to be brave in a big city? The margins of insecurity widen and constantly expand under the pressures of the present, but Ray simply cannot accommodate them in his pretty domestic canvas. The great value of *Nayak*, made three years later, lies in the extraordinary scope of its canvas and its satisfyingly inclusive portrait of life in contemporary India.

Here in *Nayak*, at last, is a film free from the constricting shackles of plot in the much maligned Forsterian sense. Arindam Mukherjee is simply a matinee idol (played superbly by Uttam Kumar with a lazy, throwaway grace) who goes to Delhi to receive an award. He travels in the air-conditioned vestibule train from Howrah to Delhi and the film is a record of his encounters in the train. *Nayak* is therefore necessarily episodic, but there is a compensating aesthetic gain as the film naturally acquires a complex structure and incidentally picks up a wealth of sociological detail. Mostly we are with Arindam and with him too in his conscious reminiscences and the privileged glimpses we are given into the workings of his subconscious. What emerges is a near-complete biography. Commencing with his early days of struggle on the stage and the break with his mentor, Shankerda, we travel via his friend Brijesh (the radically committed man) past the early screen days with the terrible Lahiri (whose collapse is treated in one of the most touching episodes in the film). The order of these sequences, though, is subtly (sometimes confusingly) jumbled, and at the beginning of the film we are ironically almost at the beginning of the end of Arindam's career. He is going to receive a prize at Delhi, yet, he has already begun to slip at the box-office: his latest film *Heart's Desire*, has not been bringing in the crowds.

Technically *Nayak* is superb. There is Arindam's early nightmare where he wades through a sea of banknotes. His slow and almost balletic movements suggest happiness for a while, but suddenly he is enveloped in an atmosphere of gloom (the light visibly darkens), those ominous skeleton hands thrust out from everywhere and he recoils. As he is sinking in the midst of all that money, literally, as in a bag, he espies in the distance the resplendent figure of Shankerda who now begins to approach him. But even his old guru cannot save him now as his hand vainly strives to reach out to Shankerda's. But the *piece de resistance* of the film is that final dream sequence when Arindam wanders, apparently on the set (or is it the forest?) of his latest film, calling out for his co-star (and mistress), the Promilla of easy virtue. It is night and at first we hear her promiscuous and slightly hysterical laughter. She runs away from Arindam through a great white doorway that looms glitteringly, if strangely, in the midst of all the shrubbery. It is a luxury hotel *à la* Marienbad, but here the guests wear dark glasses and sit about in little groups like cardboard figures. Visually and cinematically — if not thematically — it is the high point of the film. The fight that ensues is probably an echo of that nightclub brawl reported in the newspapers, with which the story began and in which

Arindam was involved. Jerked out of the dream, Arindam is a somewhat
shaken man and now drunkenly (he is actually drunk) he sends the
conductor for Miss Sengupta. Thrashing about for a momentary identity,
he mocks the venerable octogenarian (whom he had treated with the
utmost deference as he first entered the compartment at Howrah) with
a crude and obscene song. This is followed by a highly enigmatic
scene. He espies Rita (the little redemptive angel to whom he had
introduced himself earlier simply as Arindam Mukherjee) and beckons
to her in a gesture full of the largest hope. But the little angel makes
a small gesture of her hand and scurries into the compartment. The
expression on Arindam's face is one of a choking grief; his defences
have crumbled. He has been judged silently by standards he has not
yet learned to repudiate and found wanting. Leaning out of the open
door of the compartment, he stares at the icy glint of the rails (his
deeply troubled face is intercut with shots of the remorseless rails seven
times) and there is a smell of death hereabouts, but then the other
angel in the train, the charming Miss Aditi Sengupta arrives in time
to avert a possible catastrophe. Their brief relationship proceeds to
its predictable anticlimax in this predictably anti-heroic film by the
resolutely anti-heroic Satyajit Ray. Down at the platform in Delhi,
while Arindam is mobbed by his numerous admirers, Aditi walks away
with her father(?) barely noticing her companion of the last two days.
A supremely ironic ending to a supremely ironic film!

Besides this there are other minor glories. Ray is merciless in his
unmasking of contemporary shams. The make-believe world of cinema
is matched by the even more make-believe world of advertising represented by the balding Sarkar and his bored and pretty wife, Molly.
An expertly sketched sub-plot shows Sarkar's relentless pursuit of the
globe-trotting Bose (the rich client with a five-lakh budget) whose
domestic puritanism (he disapproves Arindam's mention of 'family
planning' in front of his wife and daughter!) is matched by his impotent
lechery ('Molly, jolly, by golly! — your mate's great,' he tells the cringing
Sarkar during a chess game). There is the enormous Swamiji with
his atomizer, his filthy eating habits, and his ridiculous vanity. Ironically
it is he who, towards the end of the film, dangles a 30,000 rupee
budget to an astonished Sarkar to advertise WWWW ('World Wide
Will Works'). The film is superbly atmospheric. The raw country feel
of the wayside station at which Arindam has his only quiet moment
— he has a cup of tea in an earthen vessel — is evoked beautifully
and economically, and elsewhere, at one of the busier junctions his

fans swarm in front of the dining car where he is chatting with Aditi
— whom they mistake for his latest co-star! In a film so full of fine
moments and subtly etched characterizations, the only disappointment
is that Ray has so little to say. *What* he wants to say — that upper
middle-class lives are sterile and vacuous, that screen gods have feet
of clay, that money has unseated all other values, that marriages which
used to be made in heaven are being gradually unmade here below
— lags far behind *how* he wants to say it. For all the booze and the
high jinks, Arindam has a heart of gold. It is Apu in the latest guise
(without a beard!) and the tender sensitivity beneath the dark-glassed
exterior simply underscores the underlying similarities. Arindam is no
more a film-star than my sainted aunt. Whatever, then, did Ray set
out to say in *Nayak*?

5

Seemabaddha (1971)

Seemabaddha belongs among the lesser works of Ray (it is as good as *Nayak* perhaps) and is most certainly a disappointment after the heroics of *Pratidwandi* (1970). Ray had in these years become such a meticulous documenter of social reality that he had little left to say, and the saying of even that little was so forced and contrived that one wished he hadn't made the attempt. John Grierson once remarked, 'When a director dies, he becomes a photographer,' and that is more or less what was happening to Ray. He was so much on a level with the material he was portraying that he was unable to rise above it; certainly he saw what we all don't necessarily see but, often, he was unable to make up his mind what it all meant. The seeing became all. *Seemabaddha* is a case in point. Ray's social detailing has seldom been so acute. The camera catches the exact appearances of metropolitan Calcutta; the orderly, if dour, comfort of an upper middle-class apartment, the imprisoning hardness of the firm for which the hero works, the mean, frenzied look of beauty parlours on Saturday afternoons, and, at a more sophisticated level in the club scene, the mid-Victorian morality of Anglicized India set off against the alfresco gaiety of the Continent. All these and others receive a peculiarly docile treatment simply as if they were there be photographed with the minimum of editorial comment from the director. The same avarice to catch the 'essential' Calcutta is there in the treatment of the characters.

There is the indefatigable Sir Boren Roy with his fund of anecdotes from the immediate British past (hence the one about Field Marshal Auchinleck); there is the snuff-taking, Conrad-quoting Ramalingam who reads out to the hero a 40-year old letter from his father on

how to get on with the English (again the immediate British past!);
the balding and resourceful Talukdar (who engineers the lock-out)
— an insomniac with an inferiority complex; the worldly and superstitious Runu Sanyal (whom Tutul refers to as Shyamalendu's 'rival
jockey') who is probably the least sympathetic character in the film;
and, of course, Dolon (Mrs Shyamalendu Chatterji), perpetually smiling,
perpetually chattering and — perpetually pregnant!

One recognizes everyone in this gallery of portraits all too easily
but, alas, the recognition is all. Indeed, the characters — as in *Nayak*
— are almost the plot itself and, inevitably, one remembers them more
than anything else in the film, frozen in characteristic attitudes: Sir
Boren convulsed with laughter, pipe in hand, shoulders hunched, or
Sir Boren dozing blissfully at the Board meeting but raising his hand
to vote, nonchalantly, when barely prodded; Mr Ramalingam with
his rolling gait, the secretary, Miss Palit, flashing her toothy Binaca
smile or bobbing and weaving her head with the practised ease of
a model; Sudarshana's middle-aged admirer at the party exclaiming
'*eksho baar*'; Dolon, with languidly drooping index finger, showing
Tutul how a geyser works.

The limitations of such an approach are at once obvious. Since
the chief pleasure the film affords is the pleasure of instant recognition,
instant recognition is all there is to it. It is all surface with the least
recognition of depth. Each character announces himself fully on first
appearance and, after that, there is no development or surprise, only
an elegant variation. If Sir Boren, on his final appearance, does not
doze in the car he will be shown, almost immediately afterwards, dozing
at the Board of Directors' meeting. That is all there is to him and
also the others. Similarly with situations. They are immediately and
completely understood all at once. This does not mean that everything
is explicit, Ray being too clever for that. It however means that the
unstated meaning of every scene is always just below the surface and
is always one thing and one thing only. There is no room for any
ambiguity of meaning or interpretation. The consequence of all such
disciplined clarity is too often an unwitting falsehood, and the falsehood
in Ray's film takes the form not so much in a denial of politics but
a subtle evasion of it. The world outside the streamlined office rooms
and the air-conditioned apartment of Shyamalendu is no doubt constantly kept present in conversations but its reality is never made oppressive except in the party scene and in the brief opening shot of
young men milling around hopelessly in front of the Employment

Exchange. The reality of the horrors of capitalism (the real, if un-acknowledged subject of the film) are evaded by reducing it all to the dimensions of a petty personal problem, to the problem of the personal morality of the hero.

The consequence of such evasion is felt in the disproportionate burden that the hero of the film is made to bear. And so it happens that it is the hero alone (played undoubtedly with a certain elegant *savoir-faire* by Barun Chanda) who becomes (especially towards the end) almost inscrutable, invested as he is with moral paradoxes. And yet it is with the moral evaluation of his character that the film is chiefly concerned. He is on the surface, the very image of the well-adjusted man. He is on excellent terms with himself (the opening credits show him in the back seat of the company car, supremely pleased with himself) and with everybody else in the firm. He is on excellent terms with his wife and, when his sister-in-law arrives, he is soon on excellent terms with her. But that is the whole trouble. If this man is so 'good', how then can he also be 'bad', 'bad' enough, let us be clear about this, to deserve Sudarshana's silent, but nonetheless crushing rebuke at the end? And yet Ray goes on piling up the evidence in his hero's favour in this cinema of appearances. Early on in the film, in the scene with the office boy and the brief ones with the delectable Miss Palit and the odd one with Mr Ferris's Anglo-Indian typist, it is true that there are faint hints of a hardness, a certain frayed goodness beneath the bland and creamy exterior.

But these hints are not developed till much, much later in the scenes with Talukdar, the Personnel Officer. And even here, Ray does his best to absolve his hero of any nastiness, moral or otherwise. Shyamalendu is shown as very tense during the development of the crisis (that he himself has contrived!), and when the watchman is injured in the bomb explosion, Ray is careful to insert a shot of the hero visiting him in hospital (all by himself at night and looking distinctly worried). This visit is clearly intended to give some substance to Shyamalendu's remark to Talukdar (when the crisis is well past) that he didn't sleep two nights because of anxiety. And yet the shared com-plicity of his laughter at Talukdar's facetious remark — that if the watchman had died he would have sent a fine big wreath and a condolence note — undercuts Shyamalendu's earlier concern and suggests a moral equivalence between the two men which the film has been at pains, earlier on, to explicitly repudiate. This has the effect of dislocating our moral attitudes towards the hero and so the business of evaluating him becomes increasingly problematic.

This is the case especially when we are confronted, at the denouement, with Shyamalendu's ignominy before Sudarshana, the pretty one from Patna. It is never made clear whether it is her shapely body (his silent lechery of her is unmistakable from countless innuendoes directed at her right from the start) or her pristine moral self that stirs him. Ray wants us to believe at the end that it is the latter, but it has been the former all along and it is difficult, if not impossible, to make the switch at the end. Consequently, Shyamalendu's belated acknow-ledgement of the imperatives of the moral life strike us as rather forced at the end, and certainly not in keeping with the character of the man who could make that 'package deal' with Talukdar. After all, it is not possible to create a character who can contain and reconcile in himself both the worldliness of a Talukdar and the unworldliness of a Sudarshana! The attempt to do so produces some of the most awkward moments for Barun Chanda who is forced to make some bizarre emotional transitions in the closing minutes of the film.

Sudarshana is the chief vehicle of all the film's positive values and pivotally important to the judgement we are encouraged to make of the hero's actions. She, alone, of all the characters in the film is allowed to show any real awareness of the world outside. The word 'Naxalite' is never so much as mentioned in the film, although thrice the movement comes up in conversations in which Sudarshana is a participant. The only major scene in which the movement is more immediately present is during the party scene where a bomb explosion is heard off-stage. Sudarshana alone registers shock while the others go on with their idle chatter (classical south Indian Carnatic music on the veena is heard throughout the party underlining, perhaps, the alienation of culture from politics). Ray brilliantly punctuates the scene for further effect by making Shyamalendu's parents pay a visit at this point. But, even here, more important than the confused reactions of the assembled guests and their momentary unease is the sound of firing heard outside (four distinct shots are heard, the last two distinctly as Shyamalendu's parents are in full view of the guests).

Once again it is Sudarshana who registers pain, but the others go on talking of revolution and the generation gap. The party continues long into the night. The following morning Sudarshana gives expression to her disapproval of Shyamalendu's sterile life: 'You disappointed me last night.' But given her own prolonged discomfiture before the *sundari pujari's* unabashed lechery, what, one might reasonably ask, was she disappointed about? It is of a piece with her remark in the conference room (much later in the film) when confronted by Shyamalendu's soaring ambition: 'It is dangerous.'

The innocuousness of these remarks, their lack of any real moral urgency is only underlined in the latter instance by Sharmila Tagore's clipped, convent-school English accent which is at the farthest remove from any moral dilemmas. Probably that aging dispenser of other people's stock of wisdom — the God-fearing Ramalingam — represents the true human norms, with his qualified endorsement of the pursuit of *artha,* in his quiet warning about the limits of human ambition through the quotation from Joseph Conrad that he recalls: 'All ambitions are lawful except those which climb upwards on the miseries and credulities of mankind.' This is the yardstick in terms of which Shyamalendu's actions are to be assessed, and not surely by Sudarshana's naive and convent-school idealism.

The real weakness of the film comes, then, through the casting of Sharmila Tagore as Sudarshana (Tutul), the hero's sister-in-law. Sharmila ceased to be an actress years ago (if ever she was one) and her dimpled Bombay glamour here (as in *Aranyer Din Ratri*, 1970) is nothing less than a disaster. Except in the incredible final scene where she somehow manages to limp through the paces of a contrived moral crisis, there is not a single scene which she does not ruin with her archness and oh-ever-so-cute lip biting. Her sophistication and poise at the race-track are that of a hardened socialite: just look at the way she asks for the race book with a one—two of a calculated and a practised nod. So her mind-blowing naivetes about MD and FD fool nobody, and even the apparent concern about a bomb exploding in the overcrowded enclosures appears, as uttered in Sharmila's offhand, throwaway style, a piece of shocking callousness instead of the very reverse.

So what emerges despite all the Sharmila-ing is quite garbled and difficult to pin down. One discerns, behind the dimples and beneath the eye-shadow, the faint outlines of an unspoilt darling from the Patna backwoods(!), fond of dogs (remember her Silkie Sidney, Whisky, died of hepatitis — what a false touch this on Ray's part!) and Rabindranath Tagore (because he won the Nobel Prize!) but scared of leering old knights of the British Empire, given to sententious moralizing but not at all averse to some quiet flirting on the side with the all too susceptible Shyamalendu (note in particular her long, lingering 'Good

Night' to him). But behold the quality of her wonder at golf, at the races, at the salaries of convenanted officials, at hairdressers, at neon-ads, at geysers, at cabarets, and what have you! She struggles on womanfully through the 'nightmare' of Calcutta propped up by her psychology (she is a post-graduate student in the subject) and by those ten-page letters from That Boy Back Home.

There is a scene laid in that sanctum sanctorum of Hindustan Peters Ltd., viz. the conference room of the Board of Directors, where the hero explains to Sudarshana — who has dropped in for the obligatory visit — how he is drawn to that room like a jockey to the winning post. And the dainty Sharmila (who by now has become all too familiar with the world of racing despite her losing debut on the 7 to 1 Chrysanthemum) almost nods sympathetically. But the scene is going wrong for India's No. 1 director. So he hastily stuffs some lines into the now dimpling Sharmila who, in a poorly focused two-shot with her face at caressing distance from the camera (Soumendu Roy by the way), recalls the hero's first sojourn to their Patna home, clad in a brown *khaddar* shirt and pyjamas with a cycle, too, to match, to complete the picture of innocence which now   she implies — is irretrievably lost. The hero tries his best to look confused and the little scene terminates on yet another false note with more Sharmila-ing by Sudarshana in front of a glass pane outside the office room where she pauses to touch up her hair.

However, the scene is important for it is the first time that Ray pointedly attempts to present Sudarshana as she is really intended to be in the film; the moral barometer of the audience and the hero's own touchstone. (It is true that Sudarshana had even earlier been given countless lines showing her to be the Angel that she undoubtedly is, but every time Sharmila Tagore got in the way). The scene at the cabaret confirms this change in the presentation of Sudarshana, for here too Sharmila—Sudarshana, after her usual quota of coyness and coquetry, reverts (fortunately for the moral balance of the film) to her now accredited moral role. And Ray executes a finely controlled semicircular pan to give us the growing anguish on Sudarshana's face (this comes just after Shyamalendu's evasiveness not only with Runu Sanyal but also his own wife about happenings in the factory) even as we see the gyrations of the cabaret artist to the strains of a familiar pop number.

So I suppose the stage is well set for the final scenes. As her sister embraces her in joy at the news of Shyamalendu's promotion in the

company — he has just been made a director — Sudarshana weeps and
there is a glimpse of the yard below where little boys are seen playing
football and a few are seen cycling. The scene is clearly intended to
be evocative of the innocence that now — and this is the whole logic
of the film — has been irrevocably lost. As Shyamalendu returns home,
the lift is out of order — a brilliant touch this — and so he has to
climb the seven flights of stairs to his apartment. As he starts the
climb, the shouts of boys at play are heard, but as he climbs higher
(surely this is intended by Ray as a metaphor for Shyamalendu's entire
career) no voices are heard. Everything is quiet and still. It is the
finest moment in the film. Inside the apartment, Dolon beams with
happiness (she is even seen cooking for once since this is a red-letter
day in her life), but Sudarshana — wherefore art thou, Sudarshana?
— is in the doldrums. When she emerges finally — a rather bedraggled
figure — the soundtrack picks up the tune she once hummed days
ago (the morning after the party as she walked into the living-room)
and the hero looks at her expectantly. But, as she turns, the humming
ceases abruptly and we suddenly realize that Shyamalendu has simply
hallucinated the sounds. Walking towards the single sofa across his,
Sudarshana removes the wrist-watch — the one that Shyamalendu had
given her on arrival — and then — *voila*! — disappears. But the gim-
mick — strongly reminiscent of the end of *Blow-Up* (1966) — has
serious moral repercussions in Ray's film, reducing morality itself (as
personified in Sudarshana) to mere appearance.

This surely is the nemesis of the cinema of appearances! Morality
itself becomes illusory, as indeed it is in the capitalistic ethos on which
the whole world of *Seemabaddha* is built, unquestioned by ideology
and questioned only by a dubious Sunday-school morality. But Ray,
with his evasion of politics, seems unconcerned with this possible implication of his film. Instead he concerns himself with the personal
salvation of his hero, and this is how the divorce between politics
and morality in *Seemabaddha* becomes absolute.

From this altogether limited perspective, the sudden disappearance
of Sudarshana during the final frames betokens the loss of essential
moral values from the hero's life. And so the possibility of salvation
(through the regenerative force that is Sudarshana) has now become
the certainty of damnation (through Shyamalendu's final capitulation
to the lure of personal ambition that Ramalingam warned about). Even
if this were the case, we can surely ask in what way is Sudarshana
different from the rest of the rotten bunch of them? She fits into

their way of life like the proverbial glove and Ray simply wants to have it both ways. His portrayal of her is on par with his portrayal of Shyamalendu: they are in every way morally equivalent. And yet by endowing her suddenly with all the stock insignia of an impossible morality — the fact that all her moral heightening occurs towards the end of the film betrays the essential affinity of *Seemabaddha* with the commercial film — Ray makes it quite impossible for us to accept her as a superior moral being, as the norm against which the hero's moral degradation is to be measured. And by making his hero, too, shed a few crocodile tears at the end (at least he does so in the book by Shankar, in the film he more guiltily covers up his wretched face) the upper middle-class audience is enabled to go home with its guilt for all its shabby and ill-earned millions nicely assuaged.

6

Shatranj Ke Khiladi (1977)

Wound not my bleeding body
Throw flowers gently on my grave
Though mingled with the earth I rose up to the skies
People mistook my rising dust for the Heavens.
Wajid Ali Shah

Truly one of the most inglorious chapters of English rule, the annexation of Oudh in 1856, has drawn fire even from impartial historians. 'The facts furnished by every writer on Oudh affairs all testify to same point,' observes Sir Henry Lawrence who became Chief Commissioner of Oudh just before the Mutiny, that British interference with that province has been as prejudicial to its court and people as it has been disgraceful to the British name.' P.E. Roberts has gone further and described it as a 'gross breach of national faith'. The judgement on the British action has been near unanimous. Satyajit Ray has chosen well one of the most momentous events in Indian history as the subject of his ambitious film, *Shatranji Ke Khiladi.*

In the high noon of the Nawabi raj, Lucknow was the epitome of Muslim aristocratic culture. The period produced, in its extravagance, not only the sublime *Indar Sabha* of the immortal Amanat but the ludicrousness of Saadat Ali Khan's banquets where, in a celebrated incident, Staffordshire chamber-pots were set out as milk jugs! The chief actors in the Oudh drama of Ray's film, the imperious Dalhousie and the magnificent Wajid Ali Shah — both of whose careers opened in 1847 and closed in 1856 — have long departed from the stage of history, but controversy still rages regarding their respective roles. Wajid Ali lived a life of great pomp in Matiya Burj, recreating the Lucknow ethos in Garden beach, Calcutta (he once bought a pair of silk-winged pigeons for 24,000 rupees!), till his death in 1887. As for Dalhousie, he left the Indian arena soon after the annexation, a sick man who went home to die, but history has dealt harshly with this many-sided Governor-General whom K.M. Pannikar has described as the ablest of India's proconsuls. His reign heralded the coming of the railway and the telegraph, it is true, but his role in the annexation of Oudh remains largely ambiguous. Ray deals with him summarily and has presented him as a ravenous, rampaging imperialist, as a gobbler of 'cherries', Oudh being the most succulent of them all. But there is evidence to suggest that he did not himself order the annexation of Oudh. He merely wanted Oudh reduced to the position of Mysore, with formal sovereignty retained by the King and administration alone conducted by the British. But Ray, rather unfairly I thought, makes Dalhousie the whipping boy of the Oudh imbroglio, by insidiously quoting some of his unfortunate remarks on Wajid Ali (who had sent his crown to the Great Exhibition of 1851), and then by introducing a series of hilarious cartoons showing the Governor-General gobbling the provinces of Punjab, Burma, Satara, Nagpur, and Jhansi, presented as so many 'cherries'. Dalhousie is never directly seen in the film, except in one scene where he is just a malevolent hand directing the destinies of the Empire. And then Ray saves the Governor General for a final curtain when the narrator informs us that Dalhousie finally got his 'cherry'. Dalhousie has much to answer for, but certainly Oudh is not one of them. As the saying goes, we must give the devil its due! And this Ray doesn't. Perhaps, as P.E. Roberts has pointed out, the 'home authorities and not Dalhousie, were responsible'. In any case, the groundwork for the annexation was well and truly laid long before Dalhousie.

Surprisingly, the only Englishman presented in some depth in the film, General Outram (played with breathtaking control and a cool-studied insouciance by Richard Attenborough), is let off the hook quite lightly. Outram was gallant in the seige of Lucknow in 1857 and he had his moments there before the going got rough — Sir Colin Campbell had to come to his rescue — but he was strictly a soldier, all 35 years of it. He was no Malcolm or Elphinstone, and had absolutely no comprehension of things Indian, least of all the genius of Wajid Ali Shah. Ray does not leave this out of his portrait, but the Englishman is allowed to vindicate himself in a long scene, a scene, let us note, deliberately placed after Wajid's great swan song on his kingship. Speaking to his personal physician, who is strictly a stand-in for us, the

General makes an absolutely incredible speech about the impropriety
of the violation of the Treaty of 1837 and the pricking — of all things
— of his conscience (a point Ray underlines, with some irony undoubtedly, by making a servant enter the room at this point with
a lighted lamp — lead kindly light amidst the encircling gloom!). This
is the same man, let us remember, who stood by on 7 February 1856
when the Company soldiery plundered the palace at Lucknow and
dishonoured the Begums in a manner which had become traditional
with the armies employed by the Company or officered by the British.
Yes, it was in *this* manner and in *this* high fashion that the annexation
of Oudh became, in the General's terse Latin, a *fait accompli.*

It is a pity that Ray softened the portrait of this wretch and chose,
instead, to play down that prince of poets, that author of 40 books,
that peerless patron of the Lucknow *thumri*, that father of the modern
Urdu stage — Nawab Wajid Ali Shah, the toast of Lucknow and, later,
of Calcutta, at whose fall thousands wept. It is a very British view
of Wajid that we get in the film, and even the editing reinforces this
impression! Scenes showing Wajid Ali are twice followed by Outram's
criticism of him. Ray's sources could well have been the infamous
Sleeman report of 1849 where the king is described as dissolute, depraved,
and much given to wine and women (400 concubines and 29 *muta*
wives, to give the 'exact count').

The very first shot of the king in the film shows him squatting,
somewhat incongruously, on the throne! Next we see him playing Krishna to his *gopis*; the very next shot of him shows him beating a *tasha*
(drum) at the head of a 'tom-tom' procession, but the following sequence,
returning to eroticism, shows him reclining languorously in bed surrounded by his adoring harem — not all 400 of them, of course, mentioned by Outram, whose petulance in this matter suggests why his
own Begum often 'ate the air' by the Gomati. The very picture of
depravity! (In point of fact, the androgynous king was rather more
eclectic in his sexual tastes, as suggested by his famous *Parikhana* palace
housing the *paris* (fairies!) which was heavily guarded by women. Ray
probably missed a trick or two here, considering his vast US market!)
But Ray will not leave it at that. He quickly defuses the mood to
undercut the nawab's pretensions by introducing that business of the
crown alluded to earlier. 'The wretch at Lucknow,' Lord Dalhousie
is quoted as saying, 'who has sent his crown to the Exhibition would
have done us and his people a great service if he had sent his head
in it; and he wouldn't have missed it. That is a cherry that will drop

into our mouths one day.' Irony, no doubt, double-edged at that, directed probably even at the Governor-General, but extremely risky with our audiences here — especially the Anglicized ones — ever ready to laugh at Indian foibles. In the event, we get a wholly gratuitous laugh at the expense of 'the wretch at Lucknow'. And, as if this were not enough, Dalhousie's opinion of Wajid Ali is doubly reinforced by Outram's in a long scene that follows immediately, given over ex- clusively to slandering Wajid Ali.

In any case, Lord Dalhousie was not alone in going for Indian scalps. The British did their best to blacken Wajid Ali's image and even commissioned the famous Sir Edwin Arnold to write disparagingly of the last of the Oudh rulers. Most Indian historians have followed suit and only recently has there been any attempt to do posthumous justice to the great Wajid Ali. Contrary to the portrait in the Ray film, there is reason to believe that Wajid Ali was no wastrel but strove to introduce, as soon as he ascended the throne in 1847, some much needed reforms. He was a very strict disciplinarian who wanted all the troops of the Lucknow durbar at the parade ground at a certain appointed hour to be drilled under his personal supervision. He was meticulously punctual at these parades and, according to the testimony of no less a person than Sir John Metcalfe, he even fined himself publicly for unpunctuality! It was the Company's representatives who forced him to give up his attendance at the drilling of his troops. 'When he went out riding,' writes Abdul Halim Sharar, 'two small silver boxes were borne ahead of him and anyone who had a complaint would write out a petition and put it into one of the boxes. The King kept the keys to the boxes and when he returned to the palace, he took out the petitions and wrote instructions concerning them in his own hand.' Certainly this man was no 'wretch'! It is a measure of his pride that he stubbornly refused to sign the humiliating abdication — forfeiting his personal pension of 12 lakhs a year — and Ray's film does scant justice to this magnificent defiance. Instead, the whole episode is treated near farcically. Wajid Ali Shah (played with a mixture of buffoonery and childish conceit by Amjad Khan) merely looks wistfully at Outram and his aide before taking off his pugree and proffering it to Outram who sneers at it Dalhousie-style. Ray himself seems so embarrassed on behalf of his countrymen that he deals with the whole thing in an ellipsis. And this is the last we see of Wajid Ali Shah in the film.

Earlier, too, Ray gives us, in that cruelly mocking scene of Wajid's obdurate, touching, yet finally ludicrous megalomania — the 'tom-tom', one of the King's favourite pastimes, is heard at the end of the sequence as Wajid seats himself for once imperiously on his now slipping throne — the portrait of an essentially childish king, rather like Richard II (to Outram's embarrassed, if unyielding Bolingbroke!), a mock king of verse who will undo himself shamelessly, undo 'the pride of kingly sway from out my heart'. But this Wajid Ali is a figment of the British imagination conjured out of a hat (or sola topi, perhaps) to justify the seizing of Oudh on grounds of 'misrule'. And so pervasive is this image of Wajid Ali that even Nehru repeats the charge of 'misgovernment' in his *Glimpses of World History.*

Flawed as it is in its portrait of the key historical figures of the Oudh drama, Ray's film is nevertheless a rare work of art. Ray has taken Premchand's little ten-page masterpiece and has fleshed it out on the historical side. Premchand paints a picture of swift decay, of the dissoluteness of the Oudh nobility prostrate with pleasure, and stays for most part within the closet drama of his comic nawabs. Only towards the end of the story, as his tandem team of chess players have adjourned to the countryside for a quiet, uninterrupted game, does he allow the larger political drama of Wajid Ali's abdication and capture to come to the foreground. But he closes his story on the tableau of the slain chess players who have killed themselves senselessly while their erstwhile ruler is being carried away in ignominy, prisoner of the English, to Fort William, Calcutta. Ray does rather more history, especially in the opening passages, and he keeps the tone light and frothy with those devastating cartoons. He handles his chess players with a nicely distanced, gloved irony — wholly justified by their marginality, as the corresponding treatment of Wajid Ali emphatically is not — probing with delicate finesse into the drama of their sharply contrasting private lives. He freely improvises on hints in the Premchand original with some wholly unexpected but quite startling results! Mirza has a young, sexually demanding wife and Ray's vignette of their enforced quickie during a chess game is done with the precision of an executioner. For the most part he weaves the personal theme of his chess players skilfully through the varied tapestry of the political upheaval, and sometimes the political drama itself shimmers with the moisture and sheen of the small, the fragile, the enclosed. Thus Wajid, facing the very extinction of his sovereignty, can still recall the poetic names of his cavalry regiments and can still recite one of his old compositions with a sad finality. The scene, in its expert pacing, its sudden shifts of mood and direction, its liquid tracks against the heavy backdrop of the silent moss-green drapes and the pale stained glass windows, is one of the great moments in the film. This extraordinarily difficult scene, with its almost gargantuan irony, calls for the playing of an Olivier, and poor Amjad, quite submerged by his role, does his brave best in it. But enough is not simply enough, and the tangential lights are sadly missing.

Ray's tone throughout the picture is ironic, occasionally leavened by the intrusion of the tragic. Thus, when the chess players adjourn to the house of the lawyer, Imtiaz Hussain, to borrow a chess-board, the man is obviously dying. While this subtly, if unobtrusively, expands into a metaphor for dying Oudh, it is not permitted to usurp the dominant ironic mood. The ironic mood is brought just once tantalizingly close to the tragic in that masterful scene in the open countryside just after Wajid's mournful farewell to Lucknow against the immense pathos of the dwindling twilight. At Mir's house, a little earlier, Mirza had asked his friend if he had actually seen the abandoned mosque suggested as the unbeatable venue. And now there is no mosque! At Mirza's annoyance, Mir can only expostulate that it is still vivid in his mind's eye. Perhaps, as a child, he had seen it in Cawnpore! Commentary here is an impertinence.

Only towards the very end is the irony allowed to turn inwards and now, suddenly, it begins to scar. Tempers are allowed to fray and the proud noblemen teeter on the brink between anger and violence. Till, in a final explosion of rage — timed metronomically through the magic of Ray's art to coincide with the tragic fall of Wajid Ali who, in a travesty of coronation, has just offered his crown to the boorish Outram — Mir shoots at Mirza, accidentally as it were, and we are momentarily allowed a glimpse of the abyss beneath the comic façade.

For Mir's being brought face to face with the fact of his cuckoldry serves as a metaphor for the true plight of the entire Oudh nobility and, indeed, of Wajid Ali himself, and serves as an analogue for his moment of truth. As he walks back, a forlorn figure with crowshit on his shawl ('Even the crows consider me a wretch,' he says) we sense the end of an epoch in Indian history and the mournful yellow sunsets of Lucknow emphasize this. But Ray draws back from romantic pessimism and whatever his private sympathies for the bygone Lucknow ethos — and one learns, with a certain start, that as a child Ray used to spend his vacations in Lucknow with his uncle — he does not end his film on a note of lament for fallen greatness.

Optimism, or rather a sense of bewildered expectancy, is writ large on the young boy's face as he watches the passing English cavalry with the gaily fluttering Union Jack. But this optimism, too, is modified by a sense of choking pathos visible on the faces of both the noblemen. Mirza's valedictory: 'You need the darkness to hide your shame,' distills sharply the tragic plight of humiliated Oudh, but Ray's Chekhovian art demands a return to the sovereign mode of irony. And so a wholly revived Mirza — Mir's shot had merely brushed his sleeve! — welcomes his comrade to a fresh game of chess, English style. After the initial uninterrupted game in the opening credits, the film has ever so cunningly shown the breakdown of every attempt to play chess, Indian style. An importunate and jealous wife, an adulterous nephew or a lawyer's death: one and all of them have worked towards the same end. And so, at last, the Wazir of Indian chess makes way for the Queen of English chess. The Queen's Gambit! Declined, of course, initially, till Gandhi and his political heirs checkmated the British in 1947 after some of the most absorbing political chess in modern history.

But Ray's art does not look outwards at the shape of things to come. The last scene merely reminds us of that early scene with Munshi Nandalal when the merits of the two systems of chess were discussed. Ray merely closes circles, both large and small ones: his is a classical art. And with this goes a certain dry-eyed acceptance of change, leading to that rather aseptic and which perhaps because of its too formal control, doesn't quite do justice to the heartrending drama of abdication and overthrow we have just witnessed. A whole world of dance and music, of art and poetry — it was the epoch, let us recall, which produced some of the greatest Urdu poetry, including those imperishable tragic elegies commemorating the martyrdom of Hussain — has gone by and Nawab Wajid Ali Shah is their unquestioned epitome. But Ray, constrained not only by the shackles of his ironic method but, more perhaps, by fear of sounding reactionary, has allowed the ethos to pass away relatively unmourned. History records that as Wajid Ali departed from Lucknow, he was accompanied by thousands and the scenes of parting were pathetic to behold. Yet Ray has allowed Wajid Ali to make his exit from the stage of history not with a bang but with a whimper — of which his treatment of the King's abdication is the *locus classicus*. The drama here and in the last sequence is too muted, too intellectualized, for us to feel any large or generous emotion commensurate with the moment. We merely get a copybook sunset with some dazzling silhouettes of Lucknow's great palaces against a dying day. And soon we get to Dalhousie and the business of the gobbled 'cherry' and all emotion is flushed out of us. Too Brechtian, if you like. But did not Visconti — a Gramscian Marxist at that — while chronicling the passing away of another order, the nineteenth-century bourgeois order of Europe, in his adaptation of Thomas Mann's *Death in Venice,* pause to pay tribute to it in his terminal images while being implacably critical of it in his overall narration? Ray, perhaps less secure in his political commitments, adopts the liberal's attitude of being absolutely fair to both sides, while wishing at the same time to be a faithful servant of history. This leads him to present the annexation as simply a slice of history, another event in the remorseless march of history. Not the barest hint of the Mutiny which is to come just a year later! Not even a suggestion that the deposed elements of the Oudh army and the irate *taluqdar*s would rally so magnificently under the banner of Begum Hazrat Mahal and drive the English, at least temporarily, out of Oudh.

Still, *Shatranj Ke Khiladi*, superb in its early evocation of mood, painterly in compositional rigour — the very first shot of Shabana in the film derives from Velasquez's 'The Infanta Margarita in Blue' — in its use of space, light, and texture, fails only at the very end to rise to the greatest heights of which it seemed capable. This is certainly not meant to be a criticism of the film Ray has actually given us which, in its calm splendour, is worthy to rank only a little below his own incomparable *Charulata* (1964). Resolutely anti-heroic in its method, Ray's art cannot accord that epitaph for fallen majesty adumbrated in the king's verses quoted at the head of this essay. But did not Shakespeare himself permit the luxury of grief when contemplating the fall of Richard? So

For God's sake, let us sit upon the ground.
And tell sad stories of the death of kings:
How some have been deposed, some slain in war.
Some haunted by the ghosts they have deposed...

A View of the South

1

Kannada Cinema: An Overview

When the silent cinema turned 'talkie' in 1931, there was a veritable flood of films from that Mecca of Indian films, Bombay — a staggering 820 in the course of the decade! But a paltry seven to the credit of Kannada during the same period. The first Kannada talkie, *Bhakta Dhruva* — or was it *Indrajitu*, as some claim — was released in 1934, but Kannada film-making really got going only after the arrival of Prince Charming on the scene and the release of *Bedara Kannappa* in 1954, a film which won some sort of a National Merit Certificate. And the Prince? Why, of course, Rajkumar — Dr Rajkumar, as he is known to his countless fans.

Rajkumar is an institution in himself: Karnataka's answer to Tamil Nadu's MGR and Andhra's NTR. Kannada cinema owes a great deal to Rajkumar, a man of prodigious and multifaceted talent; he is, one might say, the alpha and omega, the patron saint, and the presiding deity of Kannada cinema, all rolled into one. Rajkumar's role was in energizing the Kannada film industry and very substantially increasing the popularity of the films; but his films have not so far merited any significant critical acclaim, although he featured in Laxminarayan's *Nandi* (1964). The first Kannada film to make an impact nationally was undoubtedly Pattabhi Rama Reddy's *Samskara* (1970), which won the National Award for Best Feature Film in 1971. An odd medley of talents came together in the making of this melancholy masterpiece.

The director — Pattabhi — was a Columbia-trained Andhra, barely familiar with Kannada; the star — Girish Karnad — was an Oxford-educated brown sahib who had turned *desi*; the author of the story — U. R. Ananthamurthy — a college professor with a doctorate in English literature; the music director — Rajiv Taranath — also a professor of English who had spent six years learning sarod from Ali Akbar Khan. The film which faced stiff opposition from the Madhwas (a conservative Brahmin caste of Karnataka) and even stiffer opposition from the censors, triumphed against all odds to win critical and popular favour.

The movie was generally taken as an attack on Brahminical orthodoxy, but its militant content was offset and concealed in the languid folds of its soothing, *Pather Panchali*an lyrical charm. It was, for the deracinated urban intelligentsia, a kind of love—hate rediscovery of Karnataka. The Karnataka that emerges in the film is a kind of timeless and ageless land bathed in ritual and austere Brahmin piety. The verdurous glooms and winding dusty lanes of its countryside, the hectic country fairs, and the tranquil streams and ponds were a balm to jarred city sensibilities. Still, the message looked militant. It was not till Naipaul came along and pointed out in his *India: A Wounded Civilisation* the caste ambience of the book that one realized that the film *Samskara* had taken one for a ride! There was just too much nostalgia.

The Nostalgia Express proved a very popular means of cinematic transport for the art film-maker in Karnataka. *Vamsha Vriksha* came along a year later, with rather more Brahmins than *Samskara* and a lot more sex. The directors were two — Karanth and Karnad in tandem. Further, Karnad himself played one of the Brahmins in a manner that now appeared patented from the earlier film. *Vamsha Vriskha* was based on a novel by S. L. Byrappa (yet another don!) and although it, too, bagged a National Award for best direction, it was clearly not in the same class as *Samskara*. It had too many generations in it, too many adulteries, too many characters. It just didn't jell into a coherent whole. And its manifest critique of Brahminism actually looked, in the manner of *Samskara*, more like an apology. To be Brahmin is sin, but to film him is divine!

Karanth and Karnad soon went their separate ways to make, oddly enough, very un-Brahminical films indeed. Karnad did *Kaadu* (1973), a film which is best forgotten, although its leading actress Nandini (Mrs Bhaktavatsala in private life) went on to claim the Urvashi Award for her role here. Karnad was rather more successful with his Kurosawa-inspired *Ondanondu Kaladalli* (1978) (about mercenary warriors in fourteenth-century Karnataka) and its leading man, Shankar Nag, received the best actor award at the Delhi International Film Festival. But somehow these films don't look like the work of an *auteur* but of a very clever student of films — rather like Peter Bogdanovich — churning them out as it were.

The same cannot be said of Karanth, whose *Chomana Dudi* (1975) belongs to the glory days of Kannada cinema. It not only won the President's Gold Medal in 1975 but catapulted Vasudeva Rao, its leading man, to peaks of glory. Based on Shivram Karanth's slim novella, *Chomana Dudi* is certainly among the most socially conscious films to emerge from modern India. The tragedy of Choma and his family, grim as it is, is never allowed to assume the proportions of melodrama. It is among the major ironies of film-making in India that Karanth hasn't returned to direction after his lone moment of triumph.

An odd kind of anti-ritualism would seem to have fuelled the new wave in Kannada cinema. Its most complete expression is to be found in Girish Kasaravalli's *Ghatashraddha* (1977), based — yet again! — on U.R. Ananthamurthy's short story. Girish is a product of the Film and Television Institute of India (FTII) and an ardent disciple of Kumar Shahani. Now Shahani is a fervent critic of the Satyajit Ray kind of neo-realism which abounds, for him, in pathetic fallacies: Durga's coming of age heralded by the monsoon rains would be an example. Now it is true that Girish rigorously eschews these fallacies in his film, but *Ghatashraddha* has its own special brand of fallacies. Let me label them simply as 'the fallacy of rampant symbolism'. The film, which won the National Award for Best Feature Film, abounds in so many symbols of fertility that you begin to wonder if there is anything at all in the film for its own sake. Still, *Ghatashraddha* is arguably the best film made in Karnataka. Unfortunately, Kasaravalli's subsequent films — *Akramana* (1979) and *Mooru Darigalu* (1981) — haven't lived up to its promise.

The new wave began to develop engine trouble in the late seventies when its pioneers began to graze on the lushier pastures of the commercial cinema. Compromises began to be made and, lo and behold, the middle-brow cinema was born. So Lankesh (after *Pallavi* [1976]) made *Anurupa* (1977), the Karnad—Karanth team made the dismal *Tabbaliyu Neenade Magane* (1977) in both Kannada and Hindi — and even Sathyu compromised with the elephantine *Kanneshwara Rama* (1977), and it looked like it was all over, bar the critical moaning. Nagabharana's *Bangarada Jinke* (1980), and T. S. Ranga's *Savithri* (1980) held aloft the white flag of surrender.

Yet Sathyu's *Bara* (1980), produced by its leading man Anant Nag, could well prove, with its resounding success, the forerunner of new trends in the eighties. Based on yet another Ananthamurthy novella, *Bara* shows both the strengths and weaknesses of recent Kannada cinema. Its protagonist is the young, idealistic Satish Chandra, District Collector in famine-ridden Bidar. Caught in the cross-fire of state politics, where the Chief Minister and the Home Minister are fighting their own battles for supremacy, Satish finds himself impotent and powerless. But as a human being he never comes to life.

The film's best moments occur when Sathyu cross-cuts between a clearly bogus Swami's *yagna* for water and a blind Muslim water diviner's more altruistic efforts towards the same end — the mindless and miracle-mongering upper castes behind the former, and the trusting and the helpless poor behind the latter. It is once again the politics of caste that engages the energies of the Kannada film-maker. But when Sathyu — himself a Brahmin — seeks to go beyond caste and reaches class, he seems wholly out of his depth. The contradictions in Satish's lifestyle, his naïvete and gullibility in dealing with the scheming lawyer, Bhimoji, are never brought out, and the film ends on a note of anguished concern for the enlightened but fettered bureaucracy. 'In this country everything is bloody politics,' are the film's concluding words.

After *Bara* comes Prema Karanth's *Phaniyamma* (1982) which has certainly revived the glory days of Kannada cinema by picking up awards at the Mannheim Film Festival. It begins where *Ghatashraddha* leaves off and takes a tidy, if not a particularly close, look at the changes in the status of Indian women over the past 100 years. The battleground — as in so many recent classics of Indian cinema — is sex, and *Phaniyamma* explores, if a little ambiguously, the devastating effects of a ritual-bound society on the sexuality of women. Phaniyamma herself, widowed before her prime, withdraws more and more into a kind of etiolated piety, busy bringing children into the world she can never have herself. But going by some of her reactions to the 'facts of life', one does get the impression that widowhood for her has been a blessing in disguise. For her martyrdom has inflicted upon her that most dreadful of all human conditions: an aversion to the entire human estate with all its attendant states of 'marriage, initiation, pregnancy, children, family, worship, purity'. I have been deliberately quoting from M. K. Indira's novel on which the film is based, and which is also affected by the same crippling misanthrophy. This aspect of the film has been completely missed by many people (including, I'm afraid, the director herself), in their preoccupation with the Subbi and Dakshayini episodes that appear to celebrate sex in an altogether anarchic fashion. An idealistic, other-worldly ascetic aversion to life — masquerading as social benevolence — is the root emotion of the film, stemming from a wanton disregard of the quotidian — the ordinary materiality of life — that makes human existence possible in the first place. The sole, if dubious, merit of *Phaniyamma* is to have taken (however unwittingly) the critique of tradition launched by its illustrious predecessors — *Samskara, Chomana Dudi, Ghatashraddha,* et al. — to its absurd and patently life-denying extreme, as embodied in the life of its eponymous heroine.

Filmotsav '84 brought to the Indian Panorama two important Kannada films: T.S. Nagabharana's *Banker Margayya* and G.V. Iyer's *Adi Shankaracharya*. R. K. Narayan (author of *The Financial Expert* on which *Banker Margayya* is based) himself seemed quite pleased with Nagabharana's adaptation. But there is little of note in the film which is careless in its costuming and sense of period. The story-material of the film is much too 'fabulous', in the modern sense, for the neo-realist format it adopts. Narayan, I conclude after seeing three of his novels converted into films, is to be read, not seen.

G. V. Iyer, on the other hand, has to be seen to be believed. *Adi Shankaracharya*'s (1983) wholly metaphysical ethos removes it altogether from the realm of the 'real' (I almost said 'cinema'!), but surprisingly some things work rather well in the film. There is a feel for place and locale, and Madhu Ambat's camera captures it marvellously. Iyer, Bergman-like, invented not only the character of Death but, true Indian that he is, has also added one of Wisdom (both, literally, personified). There is, perhaps, too much exposition of the philosophy of *advaita* in the script; certainly, the symbolism tends to get a bit intrusive. But the playing of Shankara by S. D. Banerjee was flawless and the final death in the mountains altogether memorable. It put me in mind of the old woman's death in Shohei Imamura's *The Ballad of Narayama* (1983) (which was also screened at the Bombay Filmotsav). *Adi Shankaracharya* went on to win the President's Gold Medal for 1983 — the fourth Kannada film to achieve this distinction.

Roberto Rossellini once said in an interview in *Film Culture*: 'I try to get inside things. Have you ever seen how a donkey acts, if you put a donkey on a new soil, the first thing it does is fall down and start rolling on the ground because it must get the smell, the fleas, the dirt on it to understand what it is. I am just like a donkey. I want to roll myself all over and have the feel of everything.'

Kannada cinema, if it is to do more than win National Awards, must develop a new sensibility. This sensibility must be urban, its rhythms must be more nervous, more staccato and discontinuous, and the life-styles it portrays must be less conceptually oriented, less intellectual, less dichotomous: tradition versus modernity (*Samskara, Vamsha Vriksha, Phaniyamma*); East versus West (*Bilee Hendti, Tabbaliyu*);forest versus civilization (*Kaadu*); Youth versus the Establishment (*Pallavi*); idealism versus corruption (*Bara*). It must be based less and less on great novels and plays, either of the West (the Ibsen-inspired *Mukti* or the Moliere-inspired *Subba Sastri*) or even on local ones (of Byrappa or Ananthamurthy). It must become less and less a vehicle of stale ideas, moral commonplaces, or glib political homilies. In a word, it must become physical: it must try, in Rossellini's phrase, 'to get inside things'. Like the donkey, it must get 'the smell, the fleas and the dirt' of Karnataka and not merely the culture, the heritage and 'The Wonder that is Karnataka', which can surely take care of themselves.

2

From Commitment to Compassion:
The Cinema of Girish Kasaravalli

Girish Kasaravalli's career, spanning well over a decade now, is quite extraordinary in a number of ways. He is our only authentic film-maker, barring perhaps the late lamented Laxminarayan, who has hung on tenaciously and heroically to the original vision first kindled at the Film Institute at Pune where he underwent his formal apprenticeship as a film-maker during the years 1972—75. There he made his diploma film, *Avashesh*, which contains the germinal ideas which were to explode in his sombre 1977 masterpiece *Ghatashraddha*. In order to assess the peculiar originality of *Ghatashraddha*, one has to set it beside its illustrious predecessor, *Samskara* (1970), made nearly ten years earlier. Pattabhi's film, also based on an Ananthamurthy story, was more polemical in tone in its indictment of Brahminism, and through its rebel hero, Naranappa, articulated its critique of orthodoxy in somewhat simplistic, hedonistic terms. Perhaps the original Ananthamurthy novella is itself to blame here for its somewhat ill-concealed Lawrentian overtones which the film piously and all too faithfully relays. The NFDC-sponsored Hindi *Ghatashraddha* — Arun Kaul's *Diksha* — goes a whole league further, and its critique of Brahminism is fashioned on brazenly caste-based lines. In our simmering post-Mandal climate, it is somewhat opportunistically entrusted to the sole 'untouchable' character in the film who is made to 'master' Brahminism simply by overhearing Nani's ritual instructions. As if Brahminism were merely that! Kasaravalli's *Ghatashradda* approaches Brahminism more subtly, *entirely from within*, and at no point does the viewer feel any outright rejection, as was the case with the recent, almost agit-prop NFDC film.

In my own somewhat ambitious three-part critique in *Deccan Herald*

(11—13 Dec. '77), I probably went too far in suggesting that '*Ghatash-raddha* [was] a film of Brahmins, by Brahmins, for Brahmins' without quite realizing that this was precisely its strength. I now feel that it is because Kasaravalli's sensibility is so Brahminical that we feel the force of his indictment. It is, to set the record straight, a reformer's anguish rather than the iconoclast's zeal, and it was against the latter that my rather intemperate wrath was directed. Years later, in 1985, he told me in his modest Rajajinagar residence that in the original Ananthamurthy story the young Nani spits at the widow Yamunakka's tormenters, but that he himself didn't want to end his film on such a negative note. 'The present end (i.e. in the film version) expresses his [Nani's] helplessness and his willingness to understand her.' Not surprisingly, the iconoclastic NFDC film goes in for much spitting. Watching the film now, after several years and several intervening Kasaravalli masterpieces, one is struck by the boundless compassion of the closing scenes, their infinite forgiveness and, indeed, the complete absence of malice for anyone, including Yamunakka's tormenters. All the subsequent films of Kasaravalli retrace the same humble path from anger to forgiveness, from commitment to compassion.

Kasaravalli's second film, *Akramana* (1980), is only apparently con-cerned with the nature of love, but the real concern is still the same: human helplessness and the need to understand. In a moment of youth-ful, filmic self-consciousness, rare in the entire range of Kasaravalli's work, a fan approaches the hero Ravi and asks him if he is acting in a film called *Akramana*. When pressed for details of the story and what the film is about, Ravi, somewhat archly and cryptically, replies that the film is about 'seeking and understanding ... seeking people we don't know and understanding those we do know'. This dictum could well serve as the motto not only of *Akramana* but for all of Kasaravalli's films. In *Akramana*, the entire spectrum of love (in India, that is) is explored: those affairs that don't go beyond 'the chocolate and cigarette stage' (Madhu and Parvathi); those that cool after an initial ardour 'without leaving traces' (Somu and Veena); the more tragic extra-marital ones between Ravi and Laxmi, or Chamiah and his married mistress. *Akramana* is a much subdued film after the tur-bulence of *Ghatashraddha*, but it shows Kasaravalli quietly plunging into the deeper mysteries of human existence — mysteries, one might add, undreamt of by the dour, phlegmatic folk who so tormented Yamunakka. The portrait of Laxmi, in particular, is central to the film's deepest concerns. It is as if Yamunakka had been transported to the modern world and found herself, like Laxmi, not widowed but unhappily married. *Akramana* is a much better film than it looks, and the witty dialogue by Sadashiv, particularly in the early scenes, is a sheer delight. It approaches, if a little gaily, what is to be one of the central concerns of Kasaravalli's work: the plight and exploitation of women. However, the dilemma of Laxmi (played by Kasaravalli's wife, Vaishali, with her customary ease) alone is explored at any depth and at least one sequence in the film — where Laxmi recalls a childhood memory — is almost worthy of Bergman.

Oddly, *Mooru Darigalu* (1981) — according to me, Kasaravalli's best cast film — the grimmest and most pessimistic of Kasaravalli's films, is closer in tone and ambience to *Ghatashraddha* than any of the others. It catches the state of mind of a girl who comes from a north Kanara village but is rather precipitately exposed to the confusing currents of modernity in the small town where she has come to study. Nirmala (whose dour, adolescent, and annoying obstinacy is well captured in Sreeranga Krishnaswamy's playing) shows a rapidly hardening psyche attendant on too swift social change, and her horrendous suicide at the end is preceeded by an orgy of violence which she unleashes in the room where she has been virtually imprisoned by her irate and impotent father (played magnificently by C. Viswanatha Rao). None of Kasaravalli's doomed heroines, before or after, could have sought such an extreme solution to their dilemmas. The point to emphasize here is that Nirmala's suicide is deliberate in a way in which Yamunakka's attempted and aborted suicide is not. Yamunakka was helpless, whereas Nirmala is angry. Towards the end of the film, when people are being frantically blamed for Nirmala's gruesome death, Kasaravalli stages a cold sequence in the seducer Ranganath's studio. We see a couple who come to be photographed, and Ranganath is shown adjusting a lock of hair on the girl's forehead much as he had done with Nirmala. This would seem a somewhat grimly ironic comment on the nature of male seducers like Ranganath. Even Yamunakka's lover was treated with a mixture of disdain and a certain reproachful sympathy in *Ghatash-raddha*. And yet, unlike in the earlier film, Kasaravalli is not inclined to blame the man alone. Here the nature of Nirmala's own sexual vulnerability to the cunning photographer is documented in careful detail, not only in the long sequence between Tara and Nirmala, when the ill-fated rendezvous is set up, but also in that imaginatively shot beach sequence (for which the film's cameraman, S.R. Bhat, must take much of the credit) which is surely one of Kasaravalli's very best in terms of *mise-en-scene*. Nobody is really to blame then, for everyone has his reasons. This is Kasaravalli's most Renoirean film. It's a pity that seven of the film's original footage of 22 rolls got unaccountably fogged. Had everything gone well, the film might well have proved to be his masterpiece.

Tabarana Kathe (1987) came several years after the sad disaster of *Mooru Darigalu*, but the intervening years (no doubt years of frustration and bafflement) only served to deepen and mellow the cinematic art of Girish Kasaravalli. Gone is even the muted anger of the early films (particularly *Ghatashraddha*) and their dark and chilling denouements (Nirmala's suicide in *Mooru Darigalu*). There is a new compassion now, a new acceptance of life and death too (Appi's death in *Tabarana Kathe* and Sheshappa's in *Bannada Vesha* [1988] are tragic but entirely natural deaths). Religious chords are gently struck, but except in the extraordinary closing sequences of *Bannada Vesha* (of which more later), Kasaravalli remains very much an agnostic for any outright affirmation. To return to *Tabarana Kathe* which won the top national award both for its direction and its leading player Charuhasan. It is, one suddenly realizes, a less dense work than many of its predecessors, but a command performance by the lead star who lends an almost Chaplinesque dignity to the role, probably proved decisive. Its theme, too, is 'understanding' — the *Akramana* motto — but here the understanding takes on a near-religious dimension hitherto absent in Kasaravalli's films. When at the end, Tabara wipes away the tears welling in his eyes (moved by the bitter predicament of the three octogenarian pensioners patiently sitting on the bench?) there is the now familiar Kasaravalli 'reversal'. A withering indictment of society suddenly gives way to an engulfing and almost maternal compassion. That Kasaravalli decides to conceal Tabara's compassion under the cloak of madness is a measure of the constraints that a belligerently secular society imposes on all of us. We also have to remind ourselves that whereas in the Tejaswi original the Tabara character comes to us filtered through the heavy irony of the author's prose, in the film the character is elevated to heroic and saint-like proportions solely through the director's redemptive compassion. We, too, are quietly nudged into examining our own responsibility for the Tabaras of the world. Religious elevation does not negate social responsibility. On the contrary, it enjoins it.

That Kasaravalli's next film, *Bannada Vesha* (1988), takes religion less covertly as its subject-matter is eloquent testimony to the nature of the director's maturing consciousness. The film is a patient study

of a remorselessly ambitious *yakshagana* player, the Macbeth-like
Shambhu, who beginning as a bit player 'that struts and frets his hour
upon the stage/And then is heard no more', rises dizzily to the lonely
pinnacles of fame when he is identified by everyone with the god
Junjutti himself. But then he has his moment of truth in that magnificent
scene with Bhimbhatta when he learns that he is venerated not as
an actor but as Junjutti. In bottomless despair he shouts 'Who are
you?' at the awesome splendour of the rugged mountains and, like
Pilate on a famous occasion, waits in vain for an answer. This is his
night of Gethsemane. There now follows the now familiar Kasaravalli
'reversal', for henceforth he is a chastened, albeit doomed man. His
hard-won humility before the rival troupe is indicative of his newly
born self. At the end, assisted Lear-like by his young nephew, Shankara,
and hobbling about on crutches, he contemplates the insignificance
of life and vanity of all human desire. And here Kasaravalli plays his
trump card. He dramatically cuts to an overhead shot of Shambhu's
mother, in an enclosed womb-like but empty courtyard calling for
'Shankara' and 'Shambhu'. And as the camera tilts up, we glimpse
yet again the cloud-dimmed mountain that has been the monitor image
of the film. Suddenly all the submerged religious motifs of the film
— likening Shambhu simultaneously to Lord Krishna and Lord Shiva
— leap to life and explode in our minds even as we salute the serene
beauty of this cinema of transcendance.

Mane (1990) is undoubtedly Kasaravalli's *chef d'oevre* to date. Its
labyrinthine complexity may not be readily accessible even to Festival
filmgoers looking for the topical or the classical or, quite simply, for
the sensational. All this however, did not prevent Hank Heifetz of
The Village Voice from declaring in an article entitled 'Movie Madness:
1991 International Film Festival of India' that *Mane* was 'the best
and most original of the feature films' shown at the Madras Film
Festival. Mind you, that year's Indian Panorama included heavyweights
like Kumar Shahani's *Kasbah*, Mani Kaul's *Nazar*, and even the great
Satyajit Ray's *Shakha Proshakha*. So Kasaravalli's film was in very exalted
company indeed. That the film was ignored in India but invited for
the London Film Festival may be an index of the state of film culture
in India today. Indeed, the 'serious' film in the 60s or 70s sense would
seem to have gone into permanent eclipse before the combined assaults
of TV and the commercial film.

Mane is not about getting a suitable place to stay in a big city,
as in Balu Mahendra's *Veedu*, although that is its ostensible subject-

matter. It is not about noise pollution, although the film's story concerns itself with this issue as the central character Rajasekhar (played by Nasiruddin Shah with a studied wit and a, perhaps, too worldly charm) does his best for the major part of the film to get the people in the neighbouring shed evicted. It is indeed difficult to pin down the exact metaphorical implications of the title of the film. Perhaps, as the owner of the *chawl* declares in the film's very opening: 'A house is not just four walls. It is where the body grows, and the mind expands. A house is not a house. It is the path of enlightenment; it is never easy to attain. It is the stairway to heaven.' Perhaps Kasaravalli is warning us, through this most unlikely (because shady) character (played by the late B.S. Achar in what proved to be his last film), who utters several more gnomic lines shortly thereafter, not to take his title too literally. The opening scene of the film itself gives several clues, both visual and verbal, that are indispensable to any understanding of the film. The first clue promptly arrives when Rajasekhar accidentally knocks down a copper plate containing turmeric and *kumkum* powder. These two colours — turmeric yellow and vermilion red — are the master colours that internally govern the 'deep structure' (to use Chomsky's telling coinage) of the film's action. The second clue, this time verbal, comes when the owner of the *chawl*, twice in the course of the opening scene, addresses the wrong person, and this verbal *contretemps* is to be the prelude to several 'reversals' in the film. As in Antonioni's *Blow-Up* (1966), our expectations are systematically and repeatedly frustrated and, time and again in the film, even as we expect something not to happen it is precisely what occurs. Right away, in the same opening scene the owner, after categorically refusing to rent the house to Rajasekhar, is shown in the very next shot giving him the keys, accompanying his action with some philosophic profundities which have become his trademark. Likewise Geetha (faultlessly played by Deepti Naval in her most assured performance), after a little timidly refusing to lie down on what Rajasekhar has described as a 'celestial couch' (which she says may have witnessed 'many sighs and woes'), proceeds to do precisely that. And so, on countless other occasions throughout the film, except at the end when, between the intention and the ensuing action, there is no divide.

To return briefly to the action: after a swift and merry montage celebrating the couple's moving-in ceremonies, the action moves to the centre of the house which has already been described to us as 'the stairway to heaven'. Here lies Rajasekhar's 'celestial couch', which to Chikkamma on her first visit looks like a 'monster'. It is an enormous, baroque wrought-iron affair, with exquisite filigree and inlay mirror work (which only draws from Chikkamma further lascivious remarks) and bony, tubular legs that taper into the semblance of a lion's paw whose declivities Geetha languidly caresses with fingers that seem to anticipate celestial bliss. And, sure enough, the first extended conversation between the couple on the 'celestial couch' is of a dream of happiness. A small house with a garden full of flowers and a fountain, where at night in the moonlight, one can talk of one's joys and sorrows, is Geetha's little Utopia. A house with a compound to screen out disturbances is Rajasekhar's closing wish. And this is where the trouble in their particular corner of paradise begins — with that missing compound wall.

The film then proceeds to detail the gradual disintegration of Geetha's dream. The immediate cause (in the Aristotelean sense) of the disintegrative process is, of course, the noise emanating from the neighbouring shed. But there are other unknown and mysterious agencies as well, and it is here that Kasaravalli's cunningly deployed colour symbolism comes into play. The initial sundering of the auspicious vermilion and turmeric powder at the house-owner's place foreshadows the expulsion of the lovers from paradise, which is never quite regained in the film. A pale, ghostly yellow dominates all those sequences where a nameless dread pervades the atmosphere. It first appears, innocuously enough, as the colour of Rajasekhar's suitcase, faintly glimpsed outside the house as the owner talks disarmingly of the difficulty of telling 'the true from false, tinsel from rot' [*sic*]. Later, as the couple settle in, Rajasekhar half-playfully closes one of the windows with the remark that the old widow in the house opposite is actually a voyeur spying on them. When Geetha opens the window to check this, what we see is a wizened old lady staring almost sightlessly into empty space. And right beside her is a scorchingly bright, yet disquieting yellow cloth. As Geetha turns away in some alarm, a brooding flute underscores one of the *leitmotifs* of the film, which is the general unreliability of appearances. Likewise, when the people of the shed attempt to open the shed at night, an unsuspecting Rajasekhar actually goes to their help. Later, as he offers them some water to drink, a sinister gloved forearm, encased in the most sickly yellow, seems a portent of evil things to follow. And, sure enough, the people of the shed turn the couple's life into a grim nightmare. Yellow is always the fly in the ointment and all tokens of happiness for the couple turn into a mirage.

When Rajasekhar takes Geetha for a stroll in the park and sits with
her on a bench under the fragrant *champak* tree, their thoughts are
on their native village where all their favourite flowers would have
been in bloom. It is a moment of great tranquillity; the closest they
will ever come to their dreams of happiness on that 'celestial couch'.
But Evil arrives, robed in a yellow shirt, in the form of a prowler
in a car wanting to pick up Geetha. Yellow's sinisterness is most comprehensively established in the film in the sequence when Rajasekhar,
attempting futilely to call his office from a public booth, is virtually
chased down the street by a cart laden with yellow drums that are
emptied in front of his own house. The handcart has a red flag in
front and the cartmen sport dark crimson shirts. Red and yellow appear
together as the twin colours of the kites on the terrace, as Rajasekhar
seeks vainly to enlist the support of that reluctant *pahelwan* (who stomps
the ground all day and flies kites in the evening reaching for the sky).
Red appears separately as the flags of the protesting CPM marchers
in front of the sinister Corporation Office, outside whose glass-walled
corridors appear yellow sunflowers pale in their beds. But yellow does
not always hold sovereign sway. In a brief respite from his problems,
as Rajasekhar looks out of the corridor of the Corporation Office,
a gardener in the courtyard below — which even has a fountain! —
is shown watering a line of delicate red flowers. A haunting musical
theme is heard, and Rajasekhar's face is suffused with joy. And so
we come to one of the most extraordinary sequences in the film which,
for sheer thematic intensity and formal control, is surely unsurpassed
in recent cinema. The shed has finally been vacated and, after the
humanly gruesome aftermath, a disconsolate Geetha is found seated
between two empty white-painted chairs in a tight, triangular gird.
Distracted by a noise outside, she walks out into the yard below where
hang formally arranged white sheets like so many exclamation marks
against the inky black sky. She sees a little girl chasing a yellow plastic
ball picked off by diagonal red stripes. As Geetha, ball in hand against
the backdrop of a blue-white sheet, entreats the hesitant and somewhat
puzzled child, we notice a huge yellow drum looming in the background.
The yawning gulf between the two worlds — the slum child's and
Geetha's — seems wholly unbridgable. Certainly the sequence touches
on Geetha's childlessness but clearly goes well beyond it.

The film began with the metaphor of the house as 'a source of
enlightenment'. The widow's cautionary quote from the *Gita* about
human self-centredness leads eventually to Geetha's gradual and painful

realization that the people of the shed had lost more through their eviction than they, the evictors, had gained therefrom. In the film's most grimly ironic scene, Rajasekhar is shown almost missing the noise from the adjoining shed which had hitherto so bothered him. The dreadful silence that has taken over almost suffocates him. A video parlour (run by the US-returned nephew of the Police Inspector who, with his heavy moustache and ready laugh, weaves in and out of the action as the man in Chikkamma's life) takes the place of the shed and, once again, 'yellows' are much in evidence, not only in the T-shirts of the young men crowding the place but also in the stylish yellow jacket that the young nephew sports. An ambiguous gaiety pervades, and even Rajasekhar seems, momentarily, sucked into the whirlpool. It is only the realization that his wife is drifting away from him towards Chikkamma (whom he has always regarded as the personification of Evil) that awakens him. There is a tantalizingly ambiguous sequence staged inside the house before the final epiphany on the terrace that shows the extent to which Kasaravalli has subtly and inexorably drawn us into the dizzying vortex of Rajasekhar's constantly shifting moral values. Geetha has clearly returned home late — even the placement of her slippers is indicative of this — and Rajasekhar is suspiciously examining the contents of her hastily discarded bag as well as the tell-tale, still unfolded white blouse and silk saree thrown over the side of the bed. Geetha, herself, is crouched behind a pillar looking like a frightened rabbit. We have been so completely pulled inside Rajasekhar's perception of reality that we too, without realizing it, begin to suspect Geetha's conduct and actions. It is only on the terrace, ringed by those radiant white fluorescent lamps (a quiet metaphor for enlightenment?) that Geetha begins her own belated 'narrative'. As her steady indictment of Rajasekhar's lack of basic human trust begins to mount, we begin to distinguish 'the true from false' and our perceptions dramatically alter. When Rajasekhar at last confesses that he, too, has begun to feel hollow within, we recall Chikkamma's 'narrative' in the cemetery where she, too, had confessed to a similar feeling. Geetha's closing maternal tenderness as she cradles him in her arms (a shot reminiscent of the close of yet another Antonioni film, *La Notte* [1961]) need not be seen as 'regressive' in any sense of that much abused term. It points in the direction of the some healing plateau of human 'understanding' that Ravi had talked about to the bemused film fan in *Akramana* 'seeking those we do not know and understanding those we do know'. Not surprisingly, if rather belatedly,

Rajasekhar 'seeks' out the slum people (whom he hadn't till then cared to 'understand') who had earlier even promised to secure him a suitable house elsewhere. As Ravi asks a passerby (rolling a solitary yellow drum forward, which itself retreats now!) directions to an address in Sultanpura, he is directed instead to a slum which is in the process of being demolished. Rajasekhar's 'enlightenment', which had begun on the terrace, now reaches yet another plateau when he recognizes the yellow bulldozer as belonging to his own firm. The first faltering steps on that 'stairway to heaven' have been taken ...

If I began by calling *Mane* Kasaravalli's masterpiece I wasn't being, I hope, unfair to the other films. It is just that thematic concerns and formal resources were never so completely matched before. *Akramana* merely posed the problem in a spirit of youthful bravado but, except for the magnificent early failure *Mooru Darigalu*, none of the other films — neither *Ghatashraddha* nor *Tabarana Kathe* — had the necessary thematic and formal complexity. Even the 'understanding' achieved in these films was a bit too sudden to be altogether convincing.

Bannada Vesha (1988) was undoubtedly a new beginning, but its tight and exclusive focus on Shambhu made the film an account of a personal tragedy rather than the parable of an artist like Istvan Szabo's *Mephisto* (1981). In *Mane*, both the 'seeking' and 'understanding' are fought for and won at the cost of great anguish. The technical and formal complexity — the editing (M.N. Swamy), art design (John Devraj), photography (S. Ramachandra) and, to a slightly lesser extent, music (L. Vaidyanathan) — is an integral and necessary part of the film's meaning. *Mane* is undoubtedly one of the classics of modern Indian cinema.

3

Girish Kasaravalli, *Tabarana Kathe* (1987)

There is a scene towards the close of Kasaravalli's *Tabarana Kathe* where Tabara (a petty tax-collector in an outpost of one of the coffee-growing areas of Chickmagalur), his life in shambles, his wife dead of gangrene, surveys the very agencies that have brought about his ruin. He is standing outside the Tahsildar's office, the scene of many frustrating and infructuous visits to secure his provident fund, but rage gives way to a sudden and anguished pity for everyone concerned. He has just espied those hoary pensioners, patiently waiting outside, and one of them even chuckles at him. Smiling wanly in bitter acknowledgement of their common predicament, Tabara wipes away the tears welling in his eyes. It is a unique moment in the film, linked thematically to the opening shot of the film which shows Tabara atop a hill, solitary and mute in the early dawn, with the sun just cresting the horizon. He is the object of mildly derisive comment from passing hunters, as, indeed, from others in the sleepy village of Padugere who remark laconically on his 'madness'. Earegowda and Krishnappa are two such figures whose comments in a sequence before the credits prefigure the action of the film. For Earegowda, the erstwhile president of the municipality, Tabara's 'madness' is a matter of relief and, in any case, as he remarks with a lofty irony to Krishnappa — while still lathering his face — all the madmen of the village cannot be hospitalized. Krishnappa (our viewpoint character here) is rather more troubled and worries if he has, in some inscrutable way, contributed to Tabara's tragedy. The film thus quickly establishes our collective guilt for Tabara's plight and we are quietly nudged into examining our own responsibility for the Tabaras of the world.

Certainly Kasaravalli derives his inspiration for these opening sequences from Purnachandra Tejaswi's original 1973 short story masterpiece which begins with the sentence, 'The people of Padugere were talking about Tabara Shetty going mad'. But when Tejaswi goes on to liken Tabara's fate to that of other madmen in the village who didn't turn 'crazy all of a sudden ... [but] in a natural way, by gradual turns' he is careful to attribute this view to the villagers of Padugere. His own authorial judgement of Tabara's 'madness' is more political and psychological, but more of that later. Kasaravalli approaches Tabara's predicament much more equivocally, seeing it partly as social culpability and partly as in the very nature of things. The first approach leads him to bracket Tabara's 'madness' (even before the credits) and then to privilege certain scenes (by marking them off in red) and making us wonder if Tabara's fate couldn't have been otherwise. The second approach is far, far more implicit, for its focus is the presentation of Tabara himself who emerges in the film, overall, as a kind of modern saint suffering and, eventually, even taking on the mantle of madness to exonerate the guilt of his fellowmen. Which is why, iconically, his image is imbued with a faint tinge of religiosity and, as already noted, our very first glimpse of him is of a prophet in the wilderness. Lord, forgive them (he seems to be saying), for they know not what they do.

In the Tejaswi original, Tabara is less metaphysically conceived and, hence, more sharply defined. An erstwhile tax-collector under the British, showered in those blessed days 'with gifts of vegetable or fish and such by the tax-payers' and treated 'like a king', Tabara is rudely shaken from his dogmatic slumbers by the turbulence of the freedom struggle. 'Muttering imprecations at this Gandhi fellow', he gets himself transferred to a less troublesome watering hole. And, now, at the fag end of his career, Tabara finds himself once again a tax-collector but under vastly changed circumstances. The coffee-growers of Padugere refuse to cough up the tax and Tabara feels personally humiliated. It was not like this in the good old days when the British were around and 'government servants weren't harassed'. When his affairs reach a crisis — his provident fund delayed, his wife lying seriously ill — Tabara can only hark back to the days when the British would 'sanction lands in a trice ... and if something pleased them there would be rewards'. In fact, Tejaswi's Tabara is so immured in the British past that during the silver jubilee celebrations of Independence, when everyone is lavishing praises on free India, 'Tabara was said to be enlarging on the greatness of British rule'.

Now this Tabara is a very recognizable type (present-day India is full of them), and although his plight evokes pathos there is nothing essentially tragic about it. He comes to us filtered through the heavy irony of Tejaswi's prose and the author's emotional distance from him remains undiminished throughout. But Kasaravalli seeks to elevate his protagonist to heroic and saint-like proportions, and hence deliberately underplays the irony in Tejaswi's story which resulted in the creation of a Massey Sahib-like figure. A few traces of Tejaswi's Tabara linger in the opening sequence of the film between Tabara and Krishnappa, where we catch hints of Tabara's earlier corruption and braggadacio. He proudly recalls how, on one occasion, he even got non-tax paying 'Gandhicapwallahs' marching to the tune of *'Kadam kadam badaye ja'* beaten up by the colonial police. But these hints are never allowed to surface again, and Kasaravalli is careful to play down Tabara's dubious past. In an unusually explicit scene, when the coffee-grower Kalliah chides Tabara for living in the past, ('Independence for us has created too many problems for you, isn't it?'), Tabara ruefully replies, 'No. No. But still ... I feel we've lost something.' This sounds unmistakably like the director's own viewpoint, for Tabara is allowed, in the same scene, to further strengthen his case against the present order. 'Why should you rebel now?' Tabara asks Kalliah, 'Government is yours. Law, too, is yours.' Tejaswi's Tabara is treated with none of this in-dulgence. His Tabara is a man whose value-world is disrupted once and for all by the arrival of Gandhi on the political scene. He feels emotionally threatened whenever anyone raises a voice in protest (even if it is morally justified, as when Ramanna refuses to be 'taxed twice, at the depot, as well as when buying from the coffee-growers'). It is this refusal of the coffee-growers to be taxed that leads Tabara to reflect that although 'Gandhi was dead, the movement he taught seemed to be lingering on'. In Kasaravalli's film, Tabara is given the line alright, but it is more in the nature of an aside in the scene following his long set-to with Kalliah which has already been referred to. Tabara is further allowed in this scene (with wife Appi) to criticize the uselessness of revolt in present-day India because we are the rulers now. Thus by endorsing Tabara's moral uprightness, the film encourages us to treat his 'madness' at the end as the true sanity. The path is thus cleared from the very beginning for his final apotheosis.

In order, then, to achieve Tabara's innocence, Kasaravalli sets it off dialectically against the inflexibility of the system, notably the bureaucracy. But this inflexibility is nowhere portrayed as a positive evil. And, indeed, there are no irredeemably bad characters in the film, where each one seems to do good in his own way. There is the Tahsildar who, however ineptly, does expedite routine procedures and is truly responsible for Tabara getting his due — however belatedly and uselessly — at the end. You can't blame Dr Silva or Krishnappa either. The doctor treats Appi and is responsible for intervening with the Tahsildar on Tabara's behalf, while Krishnappa is clearly a source of moral support throughout. That petty shopkeeper, Nanniah, may have refused un-limited credit but against this we must set Yusuf the butcher's help in getting a loan for Tabara (from Earegowda) which enables him to take Appi to Bangalore for treatment. Which leaves us with just Bantyappa and Earegowda, the rival politicians. Can anyone honestly charge them with responsibility for Tabara's tragedy? Both of them may have had their own axes to grind, but it would be the height of unfairness — given the help they both render to Tabara at crucial junctures — to blame them for our hero's misfortunes.

No one, then, despite their guilt is really responsible for Tabara's tragedy in this extraordinary world that Kasaravalli has created for his characters. Perhaps we might seek a clue to this enigmatic world by examining the parallel tragedy of Appi, Tabara's wife. Is not her wound — that leads to gangrene and her eventual death — caused by the merest of accidents, as the new approach road is being laid? Her death is subtly linked in Tejaswi's story with the routinized delay in disposing of Tabara's pension files ('It looked as if the sore in his wife's leg was racing with the files'), but in Kasaravalli's film no such metaphorical link is established. The two misfortunes run their separate courses and merely serve to bring out the common fate that is responsible for both, as indeed for Babu's inexplicable disappearance at the end. Chance, then (or destiny, if you like), is the controlling agency in Kasaravalli's world. Human tragedy is part of the cosmic order and is, indeed, in the very nature of things.

Many of us may not share Kasaravalli's all-forgiving, almost Renoirean vision of things, but no one can deny its freshness and sheer unex-pectedness in the face of the souped-up rage and myopic vision of many of his contemporaries. This astringent, almost bracing pessimism, is ably conveyed by some exceptional performances, notably from Charuhasan, who maintains an almost Chaplinesque dignity through all the trials and vicissitudes of his life. The supporting performances are uniformly good (with the solitary exception of Nalini Murthy who is woefully inadequate as Appi); still, mention must be made of Madhav Rao who plays the head clerk in the Tahsildar's office to dew point perfection. Madhu Ambat (who photographed *Phaniyamma* [1982] and *Adi Shankaracharya* [1984] so sensitively) is always behind Kasaravalli's directorial intentions and, at least in one scene where Tabara receives the notice for misappropriation, his cinematography conveys almost mimetically the vertigo of the character. L. Vaidyanathan's music teases some useful motifs from those receding corridors and arches of the government offices. But his best moment in the film comes at the very end where the rhythm of the typewriter keys acts as the sonic fulcrum of the film's slow and elegiac finale. Kasaravalli's direction never falters, but *Tabarana Kathe* needs to be set alongside the director's neglected masterpiece, *Mooru Darigalu*, to be fully understood. *Mooru Darigalu* ends starkly and grimly on the suicide of its protagonist who was born ahead of her times, and the gloom and pessimism about the human condition seem here almost unrelieved. *Tabarana Kathe* heads off from unrelieved tragedy and its plea for universal compassion at the end sounds the note of almost redemptive optimism. Both films deal with human innocence, travestied in *Mooru Darigalu* by society and in *Tabarana Kathe* by a cosmic fate too vast for human comprehension.

4

Girish Kasaravalli, *Bannada Vesha* (1988)

Philosophy, observes the Hungarian philosopher George Lukacs, is always a symptom of the rift between the 'inside' and the 'outside', a sign of the essential difference between the self and the world. This is the agonizing conclusion that Shambhu, the tormented protagonist of Girish Kasaravalli's award-winning *Bannada Vesha* (literally 'coloured mask') arrives at towards the film's conclusion.

To begin with, he is revealed to us as a man with a grievance, and indeed his boyhood — shown to us in a series of tantalizing flashbacks — is a tale of wrongs, slights, buffeting, and unending humiliations. His earliest ambitions have clearly to do with playing the god Krishna in Yakshagana theatre and, in this make-believe world, Maabala, (his childhood playmate and now a co-artiste in the travelling troupe of players) is a willing accomplice. The initial object of Shambhu's envy and wrath is the lordly Sheshappa who has cornered all the big roles and is seen as King Partha in the film's first Yakshagana sequence; Shambhu (made up delightfully as a lion) seizes his chance to scuttle Sheshappa's performance and humiliate him. Partly through chance and partly through contrivance, he gains the role of Junjutti (one of the minor minions of Lord Shiva) in a new troupe sponsored by the Brahmin priest, Bheembhatta, to bolster the sagging fortunes of the temple.

Now Shambhu's problems begin in real earnest. Unfit to play such a major role, he resorts to stratagems and ploys to consolidate his shaky position. He uses drugs to nerve himself for the role, and when he faints from dizziness and exhaustion, he pretends to be the recipient of a visitation from the god Junjutti himself. This is the apogee of his acting career, but paradoxically, henceforth, he is a prisoner of his own success, chained remorselessly to the role of Junjutti even in 'real' life. Gradually and inexorably, the realization dawns on him that he is not venerated as an actor but as a living embodiment of the god. He confronts the priest and learns the truth in a scene of unsurpassed beauty and terror. An abyss of nothingness opens before him, and Kasaravalli's *mise-en-scene* matches the grandeur of the moment. 'Who are you?' Shambhu shouts, facing the awesome splendour of the rugged and mountainous terrain — and waits in vain for an answer. Kasaravalli cuts back to a childhood reminiscence when, coerced by his father to mend his erring ways and return to school, young Shambhu experiences mixed emotions of elevation and fear. The gulf between man and the universe seems unbridgeable. Kasaravalli's protagonist is heir here to countless heroes in film and literature down the ages confronting an alien and unfriendly universe.

Here onwards, Shambhu is a doomed man. It is this Shambhu, suspended between mutually exclusive worlds, that we see in the *dance macabre* towards the end of the film. All attempts to get out of the Junjutti stranglehold have failed and even his mother would appear to blame his impiety for Shambhu's nephew's illness. Kasaravalli meticulously annotates for us Shambhu's inner turmoil as he goes into his near-terminal dance routine. It is, additionally, a dance competition with a superior rival troupe (or so the now chastened Shambhu feels). Images of Shambhu's boyhood — and, indeed, we see several Shambhus simultaneously in one flashback — alternate with the pregnant image of the girl of Shambhu's dreams, and it is hard to tell if the two parallel images are aspects of each other or point to different levels of Shambhu's personality. Kasaravalli himself stoutly maintains that the girl (played with haunting innocence by his own niece, Smita Kasaravalli) first seen immediately after Shambhu gains the coveted Junjutti role, to the lyric strains of ' *Kamini Karedu Taray, Sri Manjunatha* ' is an aspect of his sexuality; perhaps, since she is associated repeatedly with images of playing children, she symbolizes Shambhu's immurement and permanent arrest at the stage of boyhood. This reading is reinforced by his boyish imitation of her childlike steps as she goes to fetch water the very first time we see her. However, in fairness to Kasaravalli, I must point out that when Shambhu appears on crutches after his literally 'crippling' dance, it is again to the now familiar strains of ' *Kamini Karedu Taray, Sri Manjunatha* '.

However we read these ambiguous images, what we see at the end is a much-mellowed and chastened Shambhu pondering on the insignificance and vanity of all human desires. It is a hilltop image of Shambhu, assisted by his young nephew, Shankara, and now Kasaravalli plays a trump. He dramatically cuts to an overhead shot of Shambhu's mother, in an enclosed, womb-like but empty courtyard, calling for 'Shankara' and 'Shambhu'. And, as the camera tilts up, we glimpse yet again the cloud-dimmed grey mountaintop that has been the monitor image of the film. Suddenly, all the submerged religious motifs of the film — likening Shambhu simultaneously to Lord Krishna and Lord Shiva — leap to life and explode in our minds, even as we salute the serene beauty of this cinema of transcendence.

Competent performances from a strong supporting cast (where Jayaram as Bheembhatta and Loknath as Sheshappa are outstanding) and a capital performance by the 'star' — Sridar — make *Bannada Vesha* an outstanding (and economical) production by Bangalore Doordarshan. Fluent editing (Swamy), superb camerawork (Bhasker), low-key music by the one and only B.V. Karanth, striking make-up for the Yakshagana players by Mahadeva Naika, and imaginative art direction by that Kasaravalli-faithful, young T.B. Srinivas, all fall into place to make *Bannada Vesha* an undoubtedly difficult but truly unimpeachable film.

5

Girish Karnad, B.V. Karanth, *Vamsha Vriksha* (1971)

The task of the true artist is not the solution of problems, be they ethical, social, or political but, as Chekhov once observed, 'the correct putting of questions'. The answers provided by artists are often quite unsatisfactory, but this does not vitiate the value of the artwork which has imaginatively and truthfully posed the questions.

The questions posed in *Vamsha Vriksha* are the right questions, although they are not always correctly put. One of the questions posed in the film is that of the conflict of generations, but the film attenuates the conflict through a kind of structural legerdemain, and is thus able to avoid the necessity of arriving at viable and acceptable answers. The film achieves this primarily by updating some of the characters to give itself a more contemporary appearance, but the result is not a little confusing. Historical development is muddled and several anachronisms develop, and the denouement, in particular, suffers. Part of the difficulty is the problem of rendering the novel into a film; a novel, moreover, which, though recently published (1965), is almost epic in its scope, dealing as it does with the lives of people over a period of four generations. And though the film is able to foreshorten the action and deal with the past in terms of flashbacks, the scope of the novel is so vast that some incoherence unavoidably develops. This is so particularly of the character of Srinivasa Shrouthri Sr. who is pivotally important to the development of the whole action. After being presented as the embodiment of dharma and the upholder of age-old traditions for most part of the film, he behaves strangely towards the end and, on the death of his daughter-in-law, leaves abruptly for the Himalayan retreats with what can only be described as unseemly haste. The grandson, his world crumbling around his feet, looks at the departing man with the now familiar modern bewilderment. End of film, although just the beginning of our critical perplexities. The moral of all this is that if one must have adaptations, complete disregard for the originals is perhaps the safest rule.

The principal theme of the film, as indicated in the title (literally: The Family Tree), is the perpetuation of the species: more particularly the perpetuation of the 'Shrouthriavamsha'. The desire to have children is seen primarily as the need to perpetuate the clan (as it is in Nanjunda Shrouthri Sr.), although in Katyayani, the young widow who marries again, it is a simple womanly desire to have children. It is there even in the clearly polygamous union of Ratne and Sadashiv Rao (the period of the film is presumably the 1940s) when Ratne, too, expresses a desire to have children. This desire in her is simply personal — perhaps a stay against loneliness and the interminable research of Sadashiv Rao — not clannish, and already this marks a significant change. Still, since the desire (whatever the motives) is assumed to be universal, the *modus operandi* to its fulfilment is regarded as beyond the scope of traditional morality. Thus Shrouthri's father in requesting Harikatha Shamdas to sleep with his childless wife is obeying the same fundamental laws as the sophisticated Ratne in her desire to have children. Katyayani, too, languishes when she realizes she can't have any children and her marriage with Raja Rao begins to disintegrate. Even Srinivasa Shrouthri Sr. himself is brought within the scope of this particular ambience as his wife (unable any more to have children!) arranges for her husband to sleep with the servant, Lakshmi. Although this episode is presented as an example of the 'permissiveness' of the orthodox, its true domain is elsewhere: it is part and parcel of the 'desire for progeny' theme that pervades the film like a blanketing fog. The film thus achieves a peculiar tension, as it is able to tap the very primitive instinct to have offspring to motivate both very traditional and modern people. The position has its obvious advantages, but it suffers in being unable to point out the real issues that divide the older generation from the new. Thus a biological atavism conceals cultural conflicts and relativizes moral judgements. After all, the problems of life simply cannot be reduced to the problem of having children!

Vamsha Vriksha invites comparison with *Samskara* (1970), Gold Medal winner a year earlier, but clearly survives it. Both deal with the theme of conflict between tradition and modernity, but *Samskara* rather muffled the conflict through the implausible Naranappa whose espousal of modern values was confined to playing cheap Hindi film tunes on the gramophone in front of a traditional *patasala* where teaching was in progress. Otherwise he remained a remote and shadowy non-person, at best the stock figure of melodrama — the familiar dipsomaniac with mistress in tow — with few positives and his chief 'disciple', Sripathi, a sexual degenerate with homosexual leanings and a definite proclivity to rape. *Vamsha Vriksha* fills in the blanks on the positive side of modernity, and both Raja Rao and Karunaratne are very sympathetically drawn although the ultra-sophisticated and anglicized Visalam who, playing Karunaratne, manages to alienate our sympathies with her la-di-da accent and her stiff British diction. Tradition is equally well drawn through the figure of Srinivasa Shrouthri Sr., perhaps rather too well drawn. Shrouthri is given a personality so compounded of the classic old-world virtues and a sympathetic heart that we are made to wonder how on earth we could have come away from all that. He is 'complex' in a way no Brahmin of his generation could have been. For instance, he is 'liberal' in allowing his widowed daughter-in-law to continue her studies, but the orthodox manner in which he brings up his grandson seems, as a friend suggested, an unconscious retreat and reaction to his own 'liberalism'. His need to seek forgiveness from his daughter-in-law at the end is again somewhat improbable, as is the swift attrition of his character which follows the discovery of il-legitimacy. His generation (he is about 75 in the film) lived the old Brahminical life without overt conflict, and if they sent their sons to school or college in the mid 30s and early 40s it was the only adjustment they could make to the changing world. The Nanjunda Shrouthris no doubt went to college with their tufts and their caste-marks on their foreheads with an unselfconsciousness impossible for the next generation. The too modern Raja Rao, in spite of his English trip, seems an unlikely contemporary of such a person, although, in the novel, he is more realistically portrayed as a man who would 'act out' Shakespeare in class. Staging Shakespeare, too, was the done thing then and the Raja Raos of that era literally acted their hearts out. It is this middle Nanjunda Shrouthri generation, now in its late forties or early fifties, that experienced all the conflicts between the pull of the past and the demands of the present. By transferring some of his conflicts to his son and some to his father, the film falsifies historical development and blurs the process of social change. Similarly, Prithvi and Srinivasa Shrouthri Jr., too, seem unlikely contemporaries, and if someone argues that these discrepancies simply measure the social

distance between urban Mysore and rural Nanjangud, I can only say
that the distance is exaggerated.

The film would have had a truer and surer focus (as *Samskara* did
by centring the conflict in Pranesachar) had it concentrated on the
conflict in Raja Rao and Katyayani. But, as already pointed out, Raja
Rao is too ostentatiously modern and agnostic in the film: he repeatedly
criticizes the concept of sin and takes his sister-in-law to task for writing
umpteen Sreeramajayams. The novel is more realistic in showing the
'modern' Raja Rao as absolutely contrite at the end when he falls
at Shrouthri's feet and asks for his forgiveness. So Katyayani alone
is made to carry the burden of the real conflict. As she grows older
and finds she cannot have children she caves in psychologically, unsure
if her second marriage was morally right, and can only long and pine
for her absent son. But instead of allowing Katyayani to carry the
burden of her conflict right up to the bitter end, the film shifts the
key to Shrouthri's 'conflict' as he discovers his illegitimacy. By updating
Shrouthri and adding 'conflict' to his character, the film assumes a
double focus that suggests that both the older and the younger generations have their own conflicts, which is beside the point. It thus manages
to run with the hare and hunt with the hounds. Byrappa's novel is
more truthful. It does not modernize Shrouthri's character. It is true
that he breaks down during his father's *shraddha*, but the breakdown
is only temporary (the film treats the whole episode melodramatically),
leaving the essential character of the man intact. And even his purpose
in visiting Katyayani at the end is because he hasn't seen her for nearly
14 years and Mysore is on the way to Haridwar or Rishikesh where
he intends to go. The film makes it appear that he has expressly come
for forgiveness — which he doesn't get — and since Katyayani too dies
before she can gulp the sacred Ganges water (in the novel she swallows
the water before dying) there is a distinct impression created that both
the older and the younger generations have to suffer in their own
ways for their past mistakes. By thus isolating the two conflicts, the
real conflict between the generations (which just surfaces twice in the
film; once, seriously, in the heated exchanges between Katyayani, on
the one hand, and her lawyer father and Bhagirathamma, on the other,
and the other time, less seriously, in the differences in outlook between
Raja Rao and his orthodox sister-in-law) is obscured and tricked away,
and the film becomes strangely evasive. Thus the climactic scene of
the film becomes wholly incredible. After Katyayani's death, Srinivasa
Shrouthri Sr. walks away abruptly after mumbling that he had come

to ask for forgiveness — thus wiping out in one stroke our whole conception of his character. In the novel he leaves only after advising his grandson not to sit in judgement over what his elders have done and asking him to perform his mother's *shraddha*. The novel is thus unashamedly on the side of tradition, but the film equivocates, intent no doubt on holding the scales evenly between tradition and modernity. It thus leaves the problems it raises not just unanswered but unanswerable. Here we have the classic dilemma of the modern Indian liberal who retreats into his shell of scepticism by criticizing both positions: tradition and modernity. The old liberal of the nineteenth century used to see truth on both sides; the modern liberal, taking a step further, sees it on neither side!

Difficulties in delineation

The film's difficulties are not confined to the main plot. *Vamsha Vriksha* attempts to unify and generalize its principal theme through a subordinate plot which, although played down in the film, still demands to be taken seriously. This is the Karunaratne—Sadashiv Rao affair which is the structural analogue to the Katyayani—Raja Rao relationship. We are meant to see the two relationships in terms of each other and, indeed, at various points they are juxtaposed. Thus Katyayani's conflict before she marries Raja Rao is counterpointed with Sadashiv Rao's conflict before Karunaratne returns to Mysore. Again towards the end, Karunaratne briefly returns to Mysore after the death of the hapless Sadashiv Rao, and her final departure from India is a prelude both to Katayayani's death and Shrouthri's final pilgrimage. She, too, is briefly 'reconciled' with Prithvi — Sadashiv Rao's son through his first marriage — and this prepares us for the thematically significant reconciliation of Srinivasa Shrouthri Jr. with his mother, Katyayani, just before her death. But neat as all this sounds theoretically, it doesn't work too well in the film. The truth is the basic implausibility of the Karunaratne — Sadashiv Rao relationship. Here is an extramarital affair between an over-forty college professor and a youngish Sri Lankan research student that rings false right through. Her la-di-da is matched by his 'awl-rite' (for 'all right'), and he invariably replies in Kannada to her clipped and unrelenting English. To make matters worse, it looks like a case of platonic adultery because they never give the impression of having gone to bed together, and his evasions to her desire to have children and his subsequent illness and death are all too tell-tale and over-explicit. The whole affair is pitched in the wrong key (the tip-off is the modern pop song used as the background score after the intermission, as they trudge up to their lodgings), and Karanth's interpretation of Professor Sadashiv Rao is downright comic. We get a clown instead of an infatuated academic, and their conversations (with parallel Kannada text when Karunaratne is speaking) are incredible. One feels that she simply wouldn't have fallen for a creep like him. The debonair and rather dashing Raja Rao seems more her type, and even their few exchanges in the film are suggestive. The result is that the sub-plot, so important to the principal theme, jars the rhythms of the main plot, and when, towards the end, we cut from the *shraddha*, where Srinivasa Shrouthri Sr. collapses, to Karunaratne in a traveller's bungalow leaning on a table (in a most studied pose to the background score of a violin concerto) we recoil in sheer horror. Are we watching the same film? — is our first thought. Our second thoughts depend; I myself am tempted to rephrase Eliot's famous lines in *The Waste Land*:

When Sri Lankan woman stoops to folly
And learns too late that professors are lousy
She sums up her life with automatic phrases
And listens to a record on the wireless.

Yet, with all these qualifications, it must, however, be said that *Vamsha Vriksha* is one of the great films of modern India. It does culture history on a scale not attempted before and does it on a scale that challenges us to re-examine our immediate past. How many problems get focused here if only marginally! I can remember no other film that did this before, and *Vamsha Vriksha* achieves all this by not sentimentalizing the past or unduly falsifying the present. Those two episodes that deal with how the older generation managed their sexual problems, with sheer brutal realism, rip off the lid of hypocrisy that has hitherto veiled accounts of the recent past. The episode of Srinivasa Shrouthri, in particular, being asked by his wife to sleep with the servant Lakshmi is beautifully paced, edited, and photographed, with the least suggestion of vulgarity. Yet the sequence eerily evokes the erotic mood, and one magnificent zoom-out punctuates the episode with metronomic precision.

Technical triumph

The film is also a technical triumph in many ways. Its generous use of South Indian musical instruments in the background score — with the *thambur,* the violin, the *veena*, the flute, the *kanjira*, and several varieties of percussion instruments with the *mridangam* prominent — is just right, and as the film got away with some brisk cutting to melodious 'Hamsadhwani', I knew it could not go wrong. 'Hamsadhwani' was followed by 'Charukesi' (as Katyayani goes to college in Mysore for the first time by train), and thereafter 'Charukesi' in its many keys and tempos — plaintive and time-inudated on the flute, regal and euphoric on the *veena* — almost caresses the delectable heroine till melody and maiden become one. Outside this, just one song is verbalized (if we except Bhagirathamma's casual off-key humming just after the credits), a haunting lyric (by Chandrasekhara Kambar, the poet) sung at several of the film's key moments, notably the scene just before intermission when Shrouthri comes upstairs to find to his immense relief, Katyayani gone, leaving her son behind. The lyric 'overflows' (in the Shelleyan phrase) into intermission time: the words of the song being truly the perfect correlative for Katyayani's personal dilemma which is here objectified. If only the talented Bhasker Chandavarkar had left out that wretched violin concerto and had not overloaded his soundtrack with all that 'atmospheric' Harikatha!

Sheriff, the cameraman from the Film and Television Institute of India also had obviously to contend with a defective camera and consequently some of the frames are wobbly. But after the intermission, the lighting is toned down (except for one bad miss in the attic scene), and the film achieves an almost three-dimensional solidity with great depth of field — notably in the scene when Katyayani collapses near the sofa, where the effect is one of a luminous transparency. The long takes after intermission, the thick, succulent shadows, the brilliant chiaroscuro suggest and reinforce the dramatic nature of the second half, while the first half bristled with special effects — the freezes in opening credits, the fluent and telling images, the flash forward of the narrative aided and abetted by the rapid cutting. One is almost tempted to attribute the first half to Girish Karnad and the second half to Karanth who is primarily a theatre man. Perhaps this unevenness in camera and film style is a symptom of the continuing pressure of the commercial cinema with its emphasis on narrative and emotional conflict in the second half (*Vamsha Vriksha* is an incredible 17 reels!).

First-class editing

The editing by Aruna Vikas (another Film Institute product) is first-class (there is a solitary lapse in the Shrouthri—Lakshmi encounter) with absolutely dizzying bits of cutting in Katyayani's nightmare where music and image coalesce, achieving an almost synaesthetic unity, that is otherwise so rare and fortuitous. The idea of the sequence (the protagonist dreaming of herself as dead) could have been inspired by the Bergman of *Wild Strawberries* (1957), but the rhythms and the shaping are simply inspired. The central charge for the sequence derives from the fact that Katyayani had, earlier in the film, seen a smouldering corpse and this menacing image ominously surfaces during the nightmare. And whereas in the earlier episode she had all too rhythmically climbed the stairs to the temple on the summit, in the nightmare she gropes her way up along untrodden paths. The contrast is complete.

Needless to say that Sharada (a newcomer to films) is memorable as Katyayani. She has very Mysorean Brahmin good looks, with just that touch of sophistication that gives her movements and gestures a deliquescene and an almost languid fluency. Hers is a very difficult role, and Sharada walks the tightrope of interpretative playing with such lambent ease that we marvel at the sheer delicacy of the performance. We see her in the classroom 'falling' ever so delicately in love (a fleeting blush caught, almost magically, by the camera) and her embarrassment and confusion on the lawn, as Raja Rao proposes, vitally connect our memories of famous love scenes in literature with our own youthful loves. She is equally marvellous in her scenes with Shrouthri — with whom she has a mysterious rapport — although the chemistry of motherly love is strangely absent in her scenes with her son. Ill and dying, she is not given much to do and recedes, a forlorn and dilapidated figure, into the background. This was a mistake, prompted no doubt by the need to foreground and highlight Shrouthri's 'conflicts'. Still, Sharada's Katyayani is a masterpiece: it will (to quote Shelley again!) 'vibrate in the memory'.

Absolute tonal control

Talageri Venkatrao — in private life a retired Railway official — is equally splendid as Shrouthri. An entire bygone era of pious orthodoxy is at once evoked in his beautifully underplayed performance, and his tonal control, in particular, is absolute. Here is a true Shrouthri come to life! The role is the aesthetic fulcrum of the film, its veritable centre of gravity and, such is Talageri's triumph, that the actor disappears into the role. He is absolutely at ease in all his scenes (except when he is senselessly called upon to be contrite at the end) and his great scene of temptation and self-conquest, prefaced and rounded off by a lone kanjira, is firmly anchored in the deepest reaches of true Brahminical dharma. Girish Karnad, after his undoubted triumph in *Samskara* is disappointing as Raja Rao. He is probably still suffering from 'limelight burns'! He pales besides the lovely Sharada and his scenes with her are rather wooden and tame. But teaching *Coriolanus* or *Twelfth Night*, or reciting bits of the ghost scene from *Hamlet* or ragging Karunaratne, we see glimpses of a different and more assured man. Visalam as Karunaratne doesn't really belong in *Vamsha Vriksha*. Hopelessly miscast as she is, she is evidently no mean actress herself. Somebody ought to introduce her to the Ivory—Merchant team: they should surely be able to use her talents in their films. The other subordinate players — Bhagirathama (Shanta), Nagalakshmi (Goda Ramakumar) — are very well cast, all playing well within their roles except Lakshmi (Uma Shivakumar) who is unaccountably made a *sumangali* in the film although in the novel she is a widow. Was it to pep things up a bit and add some spice to Shrouthri's programmed adultery? Karanth as Sadashiv Rao is best forgotten and simply remembered as the co-director of the film. His direction and Karnad's (whatever their respective contributions) must be reckoned among the great strengths of the film. Seldom has such undoubted finesse been witnessed, especially in south Indian cinema. And, finally, something had to be bad in such a good film and that is the sound recording. What a pity!

Vamsha Vriksha surely establishes Karnataka as a new centre for art films, an honour that has hitherto been enjoyed exclusively by Bengal. The film owes a great deal to Ray, whose shadow is everywhere, and indeed the film would have been impossible without his pioneering work. Still, *Vamsha Vriksha* is a landmark, a milestone in the slow march of Indian cinema to artistic maturity. It is certainly the cinema of tomorrow.[*]

---

[*] After this essay was written Karnad and Karanth received the Award for 'Best Direction' for their work in *Vamsha Vriksha* at the Nineteenth Annual National Awards in 1972 and the film was also declared the 'Best Kannada film' of the year.

6

B.V. Karanth, *Chomana Dudi* (1975)

People should desist from making films based on 'literary masterpieces'. Especially is this the case in Karnataka where literature enjoys a high reputation and writers metamorphose into film directors overnight without necessarily shedding their literary prejudices. *Samskara* (based on U.R. Ananthamurthy's novel) teemed with symbols whose sources lay chiefly in Europe, and in 1973 Girish Karnad came up with the abominable *Kaadu* (novel again!) which was a veritable treasure trove of 'symbols' and 'meanings'. And now comes *Chomana Dudi* (based on a 1930s 'masterpiece' by that doyen of Kannada novelists, Dr Shivarama Karanth) so chock-full of 'significance' and 'symbolism' that one does not know where to look.

The trouble with *Chomana Dudi* is not Choma (admirably played by Vasudev Rao with a lean, wiry gauntness) but with his *dudi* (drum) which gets in the way so often that Choma himself looks like a useless and redundant appendage. I am reliably informed that the dudi is so important in Dr Karanth's novel that it makes its appearance at the very start of the book. Its sound fills the darkness, we are told. At one moment the sounds fill the air, at another they slow down. Very good. There seems to be a living power behind it. And so on. Excellent. But when the cinematic transfer is sought to be made, the results are none too happy. After the quiet fluency of the opening frames where we see villagers walking towards us with flaming torches, there is a bit of a let-down when we come to Choma himself and his drumming. It doesn't seem much — just routine family entertainment.

But in the novel we are told that Choma returned early from the fair, that there was no food, that he thrashed the complaining children and turned to his dudi, that Belli who was singing fell asleep but Choma continued to play. In the film we learn nothing about why Choma even plays the dudi till much later. The excellently produced handout informs us that it is 'to express his happiness, sorrow, and other emotions', and this is as may be. But drumming in itself isn't visually exciting, and it doesn't help matters to get Choma to prance on his feet like a restive horse while doing so. Only once in the whole film is his drumming eerie and effective. This is when Belli, Choma's daughter, has been raped by Mingela, the estate owner. This sequence, sensibly underplayed, is immediately followed by a mid-shot of the lone Choma drumming. The remorselessly tracking camera adds to the sense of a bleak and awesome desolation.

Erotic interest

Getting away from Choma's dudi and settling on the more human aspects of the story, we have Choma and his family of five children (four sons and a daughter). Of these, two sons (Chania and Neela) are lost through death , one through marriage to the 'hateful' Christians, and the daughter, the adored Belli, deserts the good cause by making love to Manvela, the estate writer, in her own house. You see, the *Nirmalayam* touch! But whereas the sexual capitulation of the Velichapad's wife was tragic but internally necessary, given the grinding poverty, here, in *Chomana Dudi*, it is merely gratuitous. Nothing in Belli's character (nor in Choma's situation) prepares us for it. She is presented throughout as the apple of her father's eye, the central pillar of the family and, indeed, as the cement holding the whole structure together. And, certainly, in none of the four separate visits that Manvela makes to her house, prior to her departure to the estate, is there the faintest hint of attraction on Belli's part.

It is true she smiles faintly at him during the bus ride to the estate, but that is more in a socially ritualistic way than anything else. Not even when Manvela brings medicine and generally ministers to her ailing brother, Neela, in the estate, is there any hint of weakening on Belli's part. It is only when we come to the actual seduction scene that she suddenly exhibits signs of erotic interest. But even here it is only his present of a sari to her (which he avers he got for her specially from Chikmagalur — well, what about the blouse?) that evokes a shy response. One could explain her surrender here (a bit practised, what!) as being triggered by Manvela's declaration, at a crucial point in the proceedings, that now her father's debts are paid up. That Manvela takes her to Mingela (that very night? certainly the unbroken soundtrack suggests no time lapse) should, if anything, have angered her against her paramour. And, certainly, she leaves the estate that same night in a huff (in the novel Manvela not only unsuccessfully pleads with her but gives her money as well — all of which makes him an altogether different character from the cardboard villain of the film).

Under these circumstances it is hard to see just what caused her to yield to Manvela once again (before doing so she even rests her head momentarily on her father's dudi with a blissful lack of guilt) back home. In the novel, Belli is no paragon of virtue, and her surrender, if not exactly convincing, does not pose any serious problem. But here, in the film, where she is shown as the moral fulcrum of the family, her fall is plainly incredible. This scene, then, is stuck in the film as a catalyst for the denouement, *Nirmalyam* style. But it is wholly unconvincing. This, in turn, makes Choma's suicide pathetic instead of tragic. The film thus depicts the plight of one man, not that of oppressed mankind. And this, in spite of the psuedo-universalization sought by dowering Choma with a drum. Choma never becomes his drum, he remains apart from it. And it is the drum, destitute of all human substance that we are left with at the end of the film.

Crucial failure

Apart from the failure of the central character, there is a more crucial and larger failure. Although the film arouses New Left expectations with its land-for-the-tiller theme, it fails to live up to them. This is chiefly because of its obsession with religion. The novel itself does not pay undue importance to religion, and the only place that it comes under sharp fire is in the scene of Neela's drowning. Brahmins stand watching as Neela drowns, and one of them plunges in only after Choma shouts, and returns rather crestfallen with Neela's corpse. In the film even this is softened and we are left with the feeling that Neela drowns in spite of the Brahmin's efforts. Since some Brahmins on the bank do try to prevent the rescue, Brahminism, with its pollution taboos, does come in for some mild reproach. But the real evil — Brahmin landlordism — goes scot-free.

Sankappaiah, for instance, is portrayed most sympathetically, as is his wife, and one is left with the impression that he doesn't give land to Choma only in deference to his mother (and since there is an actual scene in the film in which he refers the matter to her in Choma's hearing, it is difficult to treat Sankappaiah's plea as simply a ruse).

Choma is all too Brahminical himself, as witness the purificatory dip that he takes in the stream after the visit to the padre. Both Choma and his director are too concerned about Hinduism to bother about a piece of land for the former. Both the editing of the film as well as the screenplay make this clear. Religion is in the foreground in the film's major transitions. For instance, the scene where Guruva listens amorously to Mary's song next door is immediately followed by a shot of Choma and the Christian convert, Jardu, who begins to ply him with drink. Again the scene of Choma's visit to the padre is followed by a shot of Guruva being ministered to by Mary, not without ulterior designs.

Further, at the level of the screenplay (which is by the novelist himself), the whole development of the Guruva—Mary relationship is viewed through Chania's eyes, Chania who has the same hostile attitude to Christianity as his father. All these nuances are absent in the novel where the Guruva—Mary episode is treated so casually that Guruva is not even properly aware that Mary is a Christian. And, finally, when Guruva and Mary are shown as being visited by the priest (an odd sequence this, which seems to have been specially created for Choma's discomfiture), Choma curses every Christian in sight while reserving his special venom for Mary. Even at the end, after Neela's death, when capitulation to Christianity seems inevitable (both Belli and Choma feel so) and Choma is on his way to Kakkada, he has a sudden change of heart. Trembling and penitent before his tribal God he vows not to leave the ancestral faith (a scene taken straight from the novel). It is on his return that he finds Belli and Manvela (another Christian, if you please!) in *flagrante delicto.*

Thus the ruin of Choma's family — first Guruva's defection (followed immediately by Chania's moral collapse, his illness and death) and then that of the adored Belli — is directly traced to Christianity and not as being due to the rapacity of landlords, both Christian and Hindu. Choma's tribalism is held under the same Hindu umbrella that holds Sankappaiah's Brahminism and only the odium of untouchability in the Hindu caste structure is attacked. This should please BJP sympathizers in the audience, but what does this have to do with class oppression? Neither Mingela, the blond estate owner, nor Sankappaiah, the Brahmin landlord, are looked at from a class perspective. Manvela becomes the scapegoat for Mingela's sexual and economic exploitativeness, and Sankappaiah's ageing mother is used as a cover-up for Sankappaiah. But neither is judged for what he stands for. Christianity, generally, is the whipping boy for Choma's misfortunes, and he dies a martyr not of the politically oppressed Harijan class but of sacred Hinduism. Better a dead landless Hindu than a live landowning Christian seems to be the message.

Uneven casting

The casting of the film is uneven. Padma Kumta who plays Belli is hopelessly middle-class and Brahminical in her accent and gestures to be a convincing Harijan. Yet her 'speechless' scenes with Manvela are restrained and good. The sons of Choma are uniformly terrible except for Jeyarajan who plays Chania. His illness and death are among the two most moving things in the film (the other is the scene where Choma collapses in the field after almost insanely driving his bullocks well into the dusk; and as he lies forlornly, in long shot we get a terrifying picture of a man caught and mangled by poverty and circumstance).

In spite of certain limitations in the original conception of the character, I can't help liking Honnaiah's Manvela: a certain leery, brittle, yet all too human venery comes through. But the prize error in casting and costuming (Nagabharana, please note!) is Leena Goveas as Mary. Pantied and braed suitably, if not for the actual occasion, Leena—Mary has a fashion model walk that ruins that extraordinarily rich, throaty, hill-drenched folk song that fills the air like some invisible native aroma as the coolies wind their way to the estate. She is a disaster in the film. And Mary, mind you, is not the only girl in the film to wear panties ... Our directors should depict not only the surfaces of life realistically but also the hidden depths!

Still, in spite of many, many failings, the patent sincerity of its direction and a certain choking pathos in the playing of Choma shine through. B.V. Karanth will surely make more and better films.

7

Pattabhi Rama Reddy,
Chanda Marutha (1977)

In Godard's *Wind From the East* (1969), there is a sequence where the Brazilian film-maker Glauber Rocha is asked by a young woman with a movie-camera: 'Excuse me for interrupting your class struggle, but could you please tell me the way towards political cinema?'

If she asked that question to any Indian film-maker she would get very confusing answers. It is true that Ray's *Pratidwandi* (1970) and Mrinal Sen's *Interview* (1970) showed the way, but Ray muffled the radical thrust of his film by deducing the Naxalite's motivation from a childhood predilection for killing chickens and Sen screened off his protagonist's rebellion through a framing device. Since then, other attempts have been made but all have been forced to compromise with the prevailing ideology, either through a lingering aestheticism and/or through a meek acceptance of the narrative tradition of 'realist' cinema, while being belligerently anti-establishment in content.

Chanda Marutha (literally 'Wild Wind') was made just before the declaration of Emergency but languished in the cans in the duration. And, just before its scheduled release, all hell broke loose once more as the censors at Madras and Bombay successively refused the film a certificate.

Reddy's appeal went up to Delhi where L.K. Advani's advisory panel finally cleared the film. And, then, in Bangalore, in the august (and appropriate) presence of George Fernandes, the film at last saw the light of day. Appropriate because George Fernandes has long been a friend of the Pattabhis and, quite possibly, was given asylum by them during the early days of the Emergency. Such, then, are the blinding ironies brought about by the whirligigs of time!

The film begins with a hunger-strike, Gandhian-style; the period is April 1975; the strikers, students of a college; and their slogans are mostly about unemployment. A student, Haridas, dies in the process but the fire-eating professor, Bhagwan (played with aplomb and a passing ease by the President of the Film Federation of India, Bhaktavatsala) sees nothing but futility in this. He urges his student Dinakar (Ashok Mandanna) to action, pressing upon him a paperback on guerilla warfare.

Dinakar, in his faded denims, is initially one of the idle rich (his uncle is a revenue minister and his father has made his pile through permits and licences) with the usual upper-class guilt towards the doers, in this instance, the strikers. His classmate and friend Vilasini (Nandana, the late Snehalata Reddy's daughter) is a devotee of Shiva, the destroyer, and also an instrument in Dinakar's political education. First she asks him to cover a students' demonstration (we are into the Emergency by now) which he does innocently from the wings. This results only in his Minolta being nabbed, he himself being clapped in jail and just as summarily released. A waiting Mercedes outside underlines his affluence and his company with it and, true to class, he is expected to go abroad for 'further studies'. This, Dinakar, freshly reinforced by Ho Chi Minh's *Prison Diary* which Vilasini has given him, turns down in a dramatic gesture by tearing his air ticket. He is now properly inducted into an underground terrorist group and quickly foozles his first assignment — he can't hurl a hand grenade at a chosen victim's car because there are children inside. He acts more single-mindedly in his next assignment, a do-or-die attempt on a black marketeer's life. In the process, he kills a police sub-inspector and, from then on, is on the run.

Professor Bhagwan gives him shelter despite protests from his wife Sudha (played in her farewell role by the late Snehalata Reddy), and it is from this point onwards that the film is set on its remorseless course that ends in the death of both the professor and his pupil. The professor is presented to us through the refracting lens of his crumbling marriage, but otherwise politics for him is an ego trip — merely an occasion for public performances. A natty dresser, pipe always in hand, he has one of those roomy post-war Dodges and is always in a hurry. His wife is a born clubber, one of those vaguely humanitarian social do-gooders and, clearly, their marriage has gone stale (they have no children). A party they attend, one of those cocktail affairs with a lot of informal dancing, defines their lifestyle.

A horrifying sequence of the police torture of Vilasini who, too, has been arrested, is intercut with this heartless upper-class vacuity and the comment leaps at us out of its celluloid reality overwhelmingly and inescapably. This is the visual and sonic fulcrum of the film, particularly as the girl's torture is plainly and directly shot.

For once, historical fact and cinematic fiction collide and coalesce in a memorable image of desolating reality. Meanwhile, Dinakar bides his time in the professor's house, locked in his room (to appease Sudha's fears about harbouring a killer), reminiscing about his childhood, spent in idyllic parks with pets, now all lost forever. Eden is behind for sure, but is Utopia definitely ahead?

But before he can glimpse the Promised Land, he has his moment of truth in that long encounter with the thief who has been weaving in and out of the film as a leitmotif. Presumably this was the thematic fulcrum of the Lankesh play, 'Here comes the Revolution', and certainly our young terrorist gets his come-uppance here. Worse: his bourgeois instincts are aroused by the spectacle of the thief trying to make off with the valuables in the house, and quoting Proudhon ('All property is theft') in the bargain! In the ensuing scuffle he is accidentally shot and, as the professor returns from a Hindi film, Dinakar shoots his mentor whom he has come to see as the real enemy. The holocaust is complete.

The political meaning of the film is very ambiguous. Like an ellipse it has two foci: one is that encounter between Dinakar and the thief just alluded to and Dinakar's rout here, taken together with the professor's rather mysterious change of heart at the end, point towards the internal collapse of the philosophy of violence. The other is that tantalizing encounter between Sudha and Dinakar in the kitchen where, despite her initial resistance, the woman is obviously drawn to the man and, by implication, to his way of life. The following scene, where they embrace violently, has several pointers in it that hint at a transformed Sudha. But the implications of this 'political embrace' are not worked out in the film.

Censorship problems have obviously forced Pattabhi to play things down, with the result that we get a film coming apart at the seams. But then this splitting, through the tension generated by the contending and rival philosophies in the film, while causing artistic incoherence, is really a mark of the film's integrity.

The film closes with a blow-up of the late Snehalata Reddy, and as the commentary takes up the politics of the Emergency, one leaves the theatre with a sense of having been close to history, to real events, instead of the usual let-down even after seeing the best of films. The shortcomings of the film are completely swallowed up, for those who knew Sneha, in the implacable reality of her harsh and terrible death.

8

Prema Karanth, *Phaniyamma* (1982)

Prema Karanth's *Phaniyamma* has been widely received as striking yet another blow at the decaying corpse of tradition. And, indeed, there is plenty in the film (particularly in the Dakshayini episode towards the end) that lends plausibility to this view. More, the M.K. Indira novella itself bristles with iconoclastic dicta directed at the shackles of tradition — some put in the mouth of its eponymous heroine and some issuing from the author herself. Iconoclasm has so often been the stock-in-trade of the socially marginalized classes (and of late, it seems, also of the upwardly mobile classes!) that it has ceased to have any shock value whatsoever. Masti's Sheshamma and Shivaram Karanth's Mookajji (both widowed, like Phaniyamma, before their prime) come at once to mind. The latter, in particular, with her dubious archaeology and mystical visions is presented as a repository of wisdom 'unfettered by traditional values'. And thus does Karanth succeed in turning the grim tragedy of a woman literally beaten into submission into a transcendental triumph of Indian womanhood. In *Phaniyamma*, too, an identical process of idealization is at work, leading inexorably to the apotheosis of the heroine. But *Phaniyamma*, even more than *Mookajji Kanasugalu*, reveals the other, darker side of the picture: the human cost that has to be paid for the usual triumph and shabby martyrdom. The film, in particular, lays bare the psycho-sexual roots of Phaniyamma's scorn of tradition by locating its origins in a disgust with the very mechanisms (menstruation, copulation, marriage, childbirth, etc.) that sustain and nurture life.

The film opens with the groans of a woman in labour (the pains, we are informed, have been going on for four days), and it is left to Phaniyamma of the 'healing touch' to work the miracle. Her skills,

hitherto, have been post-parturitive — not those of midwifery — but
she goes through the necessary motions, oiled hands and all, with
that dour, unsmiling idealism that is to remain her permanent trademark.
An ever so slight revulsion does snake its way to the surface, but one
could put it down to her inexperience and so wholly justified under
the circumstances. It is only in the scene that follows that we get
a different picture altogether. After ritually cleansing herself in a 'holy
river', Phaniyamma reflects inwardly on the nature of women who
persist in 'going' to men even after such travail as we have just witnessed.
The entire episode is found in the novella (Chapter XI, p. 69 *passim*)
and since Indira's treatment of it is rather more explicit, I take the
liberty of quoting the relevant passages (the translation is by M.U.
Jayadeva):

Once when [Phaniyamma] was staying with relatives at Konandur, she came
to know of an untouchable girl having trouble with the delivery of her child
with no midwives to help. Her help was sought as she had very small hands.
   Overriding the objections of the people in the family, she went there. As
directed by others, she was able to extricate the baby. Blood flowed in profusion.
A shock ran through Phaniyamma's body. She thought, 'God, how dirty is
your creation. You saved me from this ugliness. No matter if it made me
a widow'. She remembered Subbi and Puttajois. 'Why this human life? God,
if I am to have another life, make me a flowering tree. I have not sinned
in this life. I don't want any more lives.' After exhorting them not to tell
anyone that she had delivered the baby she went back. She was fed up seeing
the rumpus made by that mass of blood-and-flesh. 'God, what is this *maya*
of yours? This suffering, this ugliness, and still women forget them and go
near men. What strange forgetfulness? And still they breed ten—fifteen children.
I don't want any more human life. And certainly not the life of a female.'

   This passage occurs more than midway through the novella but
the film plants the episode at the very head and front of the narrative.
It establishes at least four major themes that will recur in different
keys through the whole body of the film.
   They are: (a) the revolting process of childbirth; (b) the shamelessness
of women who persist in their folly by breeding prolifically ; (c) disgust
with the entire human condition; and (d) the misfortune of being
born female. Reinforcing this misanthropy concerning childbirth, indeed
following it, is the spectacle of the Brahmin changing his sacred thread
(the Indira novella, by the way, does not link the two episodes in
any way). Initially Phaniyamma can make nothing of what she sees,
but on being enlightened by that worthy's wife, she is led to reflect

on the inequality of the sexes and on the irrationality of traditions. Both the opening episodes of the film then — the pains of childbirth and the Brahmin's sexual peccadilloes — trigger off the same scorn of tradition in Phaniyamma. A wholesale rejection of sex results — both inside and outside marriage — with its necessary corollary of a rejection also of tradition. Not surprisingly, the Indira novella ends on a note of unqualified triumph for the Phaniyamma *Weltanschauung*. Going to deliver yet another child — and given her disgust at such things, such an act of seeming benevolence can only feed her tireless and gargantuan masochism — Phaniyamma is accompanied by Premabai — a Christian — who is apparently so dazzled by our charismatic heroine that soon she not only gives up eating meat but holy matrimony as well! Total sexual abstinence then — the oldest inhabitant in the musty cupboard of Indian culture — is surely the ideal preached not only in the book but in the film as well.

We read the film wrongly by paying overzealous attention to the Subbi—Dakshayini episodes without realizing that they are fundamentally refracted to us through the commanding and enclosing framework of Phaniyamma's consciousness — the Subbi episode wholly so and the Dakshayini story perhaps only partially. But their fundamental meanings, given the bracketing, cannot be autonomous but only derivative and parasitic on the Phaniyamma value—world. Let us take a closer look at the Subbi—Puttajois episode because we will discover how it is organically linked in Phaniyamma's mind with the horror not only of sex but also of childbirth. This discovery is essential if we are not to persist in the delusion that Phaniyamma's broadsides against tradition are the result of some quiet, rational enquiry into their foundations. Her rejection of tradition, on the contrary, is wholly irrational (and given her illiteracy, this is inevitable) and has its origins in a psycho-sexual neurosis that is precipitated when she witnesses what, following Freud, we will describe as the Primal Scene. (Of course, it would have been clinically far more accurate to have a teenaged Phani witnessing this than a woman so much more advanced in years. In the novel she is a ripe forty — a terrible mistake, I think — but in the film she is — given that expert transition at the well — at least meant to be much younger.)

Let us reconstruct the episode. After the return of a weeping and barren Subbi — her husband having spurned her — things start to hot up with the arrival of the irrepressible Puttajois. A series of beautifully executed scenes (and none more so than the taut and witty 'grinder sequence') — Prema's favourite and mine as well — with its teasing riddles and phallic symbolism) leads inexorably to the midnight rendezvous of the lovers. Soon their nocturnal revels bring Phaniyamma to the window, and she watches transfixed (the novel adds to the gore by disclosing that Phaniyamma was menstruating during this scene). Her reactions are finely calibrated and L.M. Sharada misses none of the nuances of this difficult scene whose importance was brought home to me by none other than Adrienne Mancea of the Museum of Modern Art: a naïve if mounting curiosity (as Puttajois entreats his mistress) travels rapidly to a steady plateau of wide-eyed bewilderment (the lovers now begin to embrace) before abruptly rising to the crescendo of an overwhelming disgust (as the bedding begins). Unable to look any longer, Phaniyamma plops down and buries her head between her knees. The glass of water she resorts to now is — as my wife has suggested — not symptomatic of any incipient sexual desire but of an over-mastering unpleasantness that she has to literally gulp down. The morning after reveals the true scale of the trauma. Drawing water from the well, Phaniyamma looks rather querulously at Subbi (Sharada is quite simply marvellous here) who is busy recollecting her midnight rapture in tranquillity. Phaniyamma's mental reactions, as given in the film, are: 'This is the story of Subbi who grew up before me. I never had a man in my life and I have to sit before a man (now). It is more vulgar than the Puttajois—Subbi affair'. (In the Indira novella Phaniyamma's physical revulsion from the act of sex is even stronger after witnessing the Subbi—Puttajois coupling, but it is in no way linked with her decision not to sit in front of a barber). But let us make no mistake: Phaniyamma's refusal of the ministrations of the barber is not to be construed as her first act of rebellion — as Adrienne Mancea, with her typical Western notions of subjugated Indian womanhood, told me — but springs essentially from her newly-developed physical revulsion from men. It is more a rejection of sexuality and men (with its necessary corollaries of 'marriage, initiation, pregnancy, childbirth, worship, purity' — the words are from the Indira novella) rather than of tradition.

The Dakshayini episode, too, as treated in the film, only reinforces this reading. True, almost the first thing that Phaniyamma does after the newly-widowed Dakshayini falls weeping into her arms is to repeatedly caress her hair. But surely it is not its impending loss that can be worrying her! After all she herself sat through her own ordeal stoically — leaving it to the barber to shed a few tears. What worried Phaniyamma is, 'Why should a grown-up woman sit in front of a barber *scantily clad* '?' (emphasis mine). In the Indira novella, clearly Dakshayini is not the formidable stalwart, the awesome Kali-like figure, that she is in the film and hence Phaniyamma's plea that she should be allowed 'to eat and play as she wants' makes better sense there than in the film where it sounds downright ridiculous. Revulsion from physical proximity to man is Phaniyamma's ruling passion in life, and it is this that acts as a solvent of those traditional ties that bind men and women together. Otherwise her outlook remains quite traditional, and she approves of Dakshayini's remarriage (to her brother-in-law) chiefly on the grounds that the property will remain within the family. Significantly, Dakshayini's morning sickness is staged after Phaniyamma has left the house. We can be sure that had Phaniyamma witnessed this it would have provoked the now familiar nausea in her just as much as the earlier spectacles of childbirth and copulation. In this respect, at any rate, Phaniyamma's sexual education in the film is somewhat incomplete!

Unfortunately Prema Karanth seems insufficiently aware of the conflicting fields of force of her three principal women, and so plays them all up simultaneously. Thus we have a kind of Laurentian paean to sex in the Subbi—Dakshayini episodes, and at the same time Phaniyamma's near-ascetic revulsion seems to merit authorial sanction. There should have been conflict but this is the cinema of idealism and Phaniyamma's is the overarching and commanding consciousness, indeed, the synthesis reconciling no doubt, in its own fashion, the warring claims of the barren Subbi, on the one hand, and the all too fertile Dakshayini, on the other!

And it is her shining example that the film celebrates both at the beginning (when she is likened by Sinki's husband to a '*rishi*') and at the end in that dazzling Kambar lyric. This haunting song (in marked contrast to the Bendre epigraph of the Indira novella that talks of the tragedy of 'a naïve artless maiden' who languished 'suppressed and smothered') is not only celebratory but also an act of anguished affirmation of Phaniyamma and her entire way of life; this is true especially of its closing lines ('Let there be a thousand thorns but let there bloom one flower, O God, among them'). In other words, all hardships borne by Phaniyamma (as a result of the rigours of orthodoxy, what else?) are to be written off if such a flower-like human being like her can emerge from them. When I asked the author of the song, Chandrasekhar Kambar, about this he smiled and said, 'The song is probably sung

by a man (unlike the earlier 'Runner' song) because this brings out
the latent sympathy of the oppressor for the oppressed!' It also expresses
the 'secret admiration for Phaniyamma by the male-dominated society
of her times'. Agreed. Only if we grant this secret admiration, will
it make nonsense of the brave, instinctive defiance of tradition by
both Subbi and Dakshayini — particularly the latter. Will such women
never merit celebratory lyrics? But our viewpoint character in the film
is Phaniyamma (it is her story, remember?), and it is her values that
are eventually endorsed. Prema Karanth herself told *The City Tab* :
'Every woman should be like Phaniyamma'.' Not like Subbi or Dakshayini, mind you, but alas, like Phaniyamma! And so a lordly and
withering contempt for tradition results and, of course, this readily
fits in with the positivistic temper of our times where the reigning
orthodoxy is defined by 'A Statement on Scientific Temper'. But all
social traditions are not necessarily crippling, and some may even turn
out to be guardian angels of the instinctive life. There is, indeed, a
belated recognition of this truth in the film (and this surely is a measure
of its strength and its undoubted claims to greatness) in the spectacle
of a now happily married Dakshayini (with *kumkum, mangalsutra,*
bangles, et al.), and her husband participating not only in domestic
chores but also in a religio-social festival of lights which clearly involves
the entire village community. (It is another measure of Dakshayini's
relative freedom from the Phaniyamma value—world; Dakshayini who
had openly proclaimed her right, 'to give water to an untouchable'.
For Dakshayini — like her mythological counterpart — has both a
destructive and a benign nurturing side.) But this precious insight is
soon forgotten and buried ten fathoms deep in the film's terminal
question to the audience: 'Nature may do wrong sometimes, but this
tradition...?' And so we return to a wholesale slaughter of traditions
rather than a measured critique of them. What I have been struggling
to establish in this essay is, I hope, by now clear. A critique of social
traditions has to start from the instinctive side of life if it is not to
end in the Phaniyamma kind of sterility and sexual asceticism. In scything
our remorseless and 'rational' way through the thicket of native traditions,
we may unwittingly inflict untold damage on the very springs of life.
It is well to remind ourselves occasionally of Santayana's dictum that
reason may be the differentia of the human condition but never its
essence or basis.

9

Baragur Ramachandrappa, *Koté* (1989)

Koté (The Fortress) is the story of Putti, a newly married Harijan girl, who comes with her husband Rama to start life in an unnamed village of Karnataka. Right at the beginning, her husband tells her the folk-tale about the Seethamma Kola in the village. According to the myth, the *kola* (pond) was created by Sri Rama for his wife, Seethadevi, during their *vanavas*. But social convention forbids the use of Seethamma Kola by the untouchables of the village. Putti is troubled by this convention which claims that the polluter will die if he touches the waters.

One day she sees a piece of silk on top of a hill and, Seetha-like, demands it. In attempting to climb the hill, her husband injures himself, and is unable to continue his profession as a cobbler.

Two upper-caste men of the village (a *sahukar* and a Brahmin, a priest) try to take advantage of Putti's helplessness. The Brahmin attempts to lure her into his net with a silk blouse (not unlike the one Putti desired in the first place) but she is unyielding. Later, driven by hunger and desperation, Putti turns to the sahukar, but this leads only to unmitigated disaster. Putti is raped and her agonized husband dies, after a bout of non-stop drinking.

Roused to consciousness and anger at the indignity of her situation, Putti decides to act. Breaking the age-old caste barrier surrounding the Seethamma Kola, she 'defiles' the water and even drinks from it. The upper-caste members now unite and decide to punish Putti. She is asked to walk across fire to prove her innocence. But, at the last moment, she takes evasive action. The final sequence of the film shows Putti — now united with the other villagers — trying to bring down the *vadha-stambha* (the pole of authority) at the head of the fire-pit. The film freezes on the image of the half-bent stambha.

Koté is Baragur Ramachandrappa's fourth film and, like his previous film, *Surya* (1987) (which featured Rohini Hattangadi), this, too, focuses on the subjection and plight of rural women. But the emphasis here is not on sexual subjection but on bare, physical survival. The story is narrated against the mythic backdrop of the *Ramayana* story, and in Brechtian fashion attempts to work against the myth. As in Brecht, there are songs — here the ballad form, the *kathanagesthe* is used. The attempt is always to weaken the hold of the myth on people's minds. For instance, the song that accompanies Putti's final act of rebellion is as follows:

'There Mother Earth came to rescue Seethadevi/But no one around us to help or tell of our pain/...We ourselves are the way, we have to lead on to the light of salvation.'
Chorus: 'We ourselves are the way to the light of salvation/We ourselves are the way to the light of freedom.'

Directorially too, Baragur attempts to break the myth through sound and visual devices. As Rama is shown climbing the hill to fetch the silk cloth fluttering at the top, the Rama of the *Ramayana* is shown aiming his arrow at the climbing man. This is probably the film's best edited and directed sequence (not to mention the brilliant photography and the stunning music accompanying it), and it makes its point tellingly and economically. But the same, alas, cannot be said for the sequences likening the rape of Putti by the sahukar to the abduction of Seetha by Ravana. For one thing, the accompanying song is too eulogistic in its characterization of Ravana to carry conviction. On the whole, the parallels with the *Ramayana* are probably overworked, with the result that the understanding of the film relies far too heavily on a one-to-one comparison with the epic . Paradoxically, the film leans far too stubbornly (rather like a tired heavyweight boxer!) on the very object (i.e. the *Ramayana*, which it seeks to discredit). This is perhaps a true measure of both the film's strength and weakness.

Tara, in the pivotal role of Putti, doesn't put a foot wrong and her performance is outstanding. But Sundar Raj seems far too obese to play the impoverished Rama — as Sunder Raj himself confessed to me with disarming candour! Guruprasad is so perfect as Sri Rama that admirers of Arun Govil are bound to do a double take. Sadly, Prameela Joshai is miscast as Seetha: far too sluttish in her movements, compounded with a roving eye! Chandrashekhara Kambar's music is appropriate throughout, and bears its heavy burden in this 'silent' film very adequately. Baragur Ramachandrappa should be commended for his courage in making such an 'uncommercial' film.

10

Adoor Gopalakrishnan, *Swayamvaram* (1972)

Swayamvaram has two separate beginnings. The first, which lasts about three and a half minutes, shows the eloping lovers, Viswam and Sita, arriving at dusk in Trivandrum by a *mofussil* bus. The camera is inside the bus all the time and there is no back projection of the usual tell-tale variety to suggest the passing scene. The soundtrack with a solitary interruption, is monotonous but almost deliberately so, it seems. There is, significantly, no background music, just the sound of the bus moving at an unvarying speed. Neo-realistic, cinema *à la mode* — I almost said *à la Pratidwandi* (1970), with whose opening *Swayamvaram*, at this point, boldly invites comparison. With the next group of sequences (the couple are by now installed in a hotel room), Gopalakrishnan seems to make yet another kind of beginning diametrically opposed to the first, both in style and temper. In an insert which the director claims is 'neither a dream nor a flashback', we are treated to various possible developments of the plot of the film we are about to witness. In one sequence there is clearly a reference to *Chemmeen* (1964), with the lovers (Viswam and Sita) lying side by side in an affectionate parody of the famous last scene of the Kariat film. This is followed, immediately, by the lovers walking together down the beach, arm linked in arm — garland and all — with all the syrupy romanticism of a toothpaste commerical. This is evidently yet another story-line development that Gopalakrishnan rejects. There are other developments, stated a shade too conceptually, too abstractly, with perhaps too private a symbolism. Who indeed would have guessed that the *bhajan* music which is heard a little before the whole sequence starts, and which extends into the insert some 20 or 30 seconds, was an attempt to divinize the lovers and assimilate their love-making to the *mithuna* concept? Such is the director's avowed and formal intention, but it is an intention, which remains largely unrealized in the arcane symbolism of the film's second opening.

Luckily, perhaps *Swayamvaram*, which won plaudits from British critics in *The Times* and *The Guardian* at the London Film Festival reverts soon afterwards to the style of the first opening. Gopalakrishnan has mastered the lessons of neo-realism, and the film has passages of great beauty and delicate, unobtrusive social comment. Madhu as Viswam sheds some of his customary screen glamour and Sharada — at any rate here, has little of it to need shedding — make as good a team as we can hope for these days. The minutiae of their suddenly impoverished lives is documented meticulously through Ravi Varma's always sober camera. The domestic scenes are intimate and underplayed, and when Sita sends a neighbourhood boy out on an errand or soaps her arm to remove a tight-fitting bangle to procure a *thali*, everything sounds right, just right and, generally, Gopalakrishnan's grip on the *mise en scene* never falters. Likewise, the scenes outside the house are economical and precise. The atmosphere of the Tutorial College where Viswam teaches Zoology (predictably his lecture on the splitting of the amoeba is succeeded by the announcement that Sita is *enceinte* !) is evoked by a few telling strokes. The sawmill where Viswam works later comes off less well but, early on, the sleazy two-bit hotel where the couple briefly stay is etched with a cruel accuracy: the dirty sheets and the empty liquor bottles grimly foreshadowing the late night imbroglio and the faintly sinister lechery.

Occasionally it would appear that the film could take some compression, especially in the sequence that commences with Sita giving Viswam a list of provisions to be procured forthwith. Certainly Gopalakrishnan's long *detour* here — although it is a critical situation in the plot — would appear somehow justified. The scene in the bar itself — to which the Principal of the Tutorial College takes Viswam for a drink — if visually rather cluttered, is a little gem of telling characterization. But when Viswam returns home, rather the worse for liquor minus the provisions, there is some melodramatic dropping of empty vessels into other empty vessels to underline the obvious. A more effective way here would have been to cut directly to the shopping list still in Viswam's pocket the following morning. This particular scene is there all right in the film but its impact is greatly reduced by the earlier hurly-burly. Then, too, Gopalakrishnan labours the odd social comment, as in the lingering shot of the overloaded handcart struggling up a steep lane after making way for a taxi. But, generally, the editing is brisk: a brief shot of strikers taking out a procession is intercut with a poor man at a municipal water tap who stares uncomprehendingly at the hero. The spectre of unemployment — a major *leitmotif* of the film — is there in the faintly sinister figure of the displaced worker in the sawmill (whom Viswam replaces) weaving in and out of the narrative, creating a sense of menace, of obscure evil, which falls like a dark shadow across the latter half of the film.

The film is rich, too, in the detailing of social character types — perhaps this is the real strength of the regional cinema. The prostitute, Kalyani, who lives directly across where Viswam and Sita live, is not as sentimentalized as she might have been: her place in the rigid caste hierarchy is brought out in her relationship with Janaki Amma, the impecunious widow, whose heart of gold is, under the circumstances, perhaps both an economic and structural necessity. The smuggler Vasu has a couple of good scenes to himself (his last one, late in the plot, is a trifle puzzling though, probably, deliberately dysfunctional), but the Principal of the Tutorial College with his old Hillman, his feckless love of films and good times is straight out of life. The line-up of famous writers in the editorial office — in a spirit of 'Let Us Now Praise Famous Men' — does not come off too well, which only goes to show that writers do not make good actors!

A great first film then — it took 22 shooting days and 3 months to edit and cost 2.5 lakh of rupees — which would have been much, much better without the redundant ambiguities of the end. If the film had two beginnings, it has likewise two endings. The first one (and, in my view, the better one) shows the widowed Sita gamely turning down both Kanakkapillai's offer of help and Janaki Amma's suggestion that she should return home with the child. The last scene shows her determinedly boiling milk for her infant daughter (her face is in grim shadow through all this particular sequence), and then feeding the child. Gopalakrishnan could well have ended his film here. But the man who revealed self-consciousness of an unusual kind in the abstract insert that followed the dry, empirical opening, reverted to that mood in the final freeze frames and the repeated shots of the bolted door that bring the film to its enigmatic close. Reason: to insinuate alternative endings in the same way that the second opening had insinuated alternative developments of the plot line. The freeze itself is so extraordinarily achieved — a slow progressive high-key freeze after the multiple fade-ins and fade-outs cleverly employed after Viswam's death to achieve an emotional diminuendo — that one hates to cavil. Still I am unable to fathom the thematic purpose served by the freeze. One thinks of the end of Truffaut's *The Four Hundred Blows* (1959), Polanski's *Knife in the Water* (1962), Ray's *Charulata* (1964) or even Mrinal Sen's *Bhuvan Shome* (1969) and wonders what on earth Adoor accomplished by this unexpected and bewildering freeze. Not surely any controlled ambiguity — and even that would have been a poor substitute for the first straight-forward ending.

Instead the freeze merely annoys with its technical dexterity but thematic incoherence. For what do we really learn of Sita's past during the course of the film that can help us to get behind her glassy stare at the end? Next to nothing, really, beyond the fact that she has a father who mysteriously surfaces during her nightmare. How, then, can we be legitimately asked to speculate about her future? But such is the confusion unwittingly generated by the freeze that one reviewer (*Link*, 17 Dec. '72) has even surmized that Sita has, at the end, made a 'difficult decision to sell her flesh'! Of course nothing could be more absurd in this picture of suffering, brave endurance, and sad, melancholic dignity that the Sita character projects so unremittingly in the film through the subdued pathos of Sharada's finely shaded portrayal. This Sita of *Swayamvaram* is a distant, if unmistakable, cousin of her namesake in the *Ramayana* who, too, chose her spouse in a *swayamvaram* and who, too, endured countless indignities and tribulations. Let us make no mistake about that. In this sense, *Swayamvaram* is truly mythic in its range of almost subliminal suggestion. Evidently this dimension is not so easily accessible to those British critics who praise it for its sombre modernity. In this vein Verina Glaessner writing in *Time Out* (19 Jan. '73) observes that 'the most important thing about *Swayamvaram* may be that it poses new questions'. Even if this is so, the question posed to the audience at the end of the film through Gopalakrishnan's freeze is certainly not one of them. That the preference questions over answers is one of the bugbears of modernity and is in danger of canonization in the arts is the great cliché of our time. It is rather a pity that Gopalakrishnan decided to end his film on an interrogative note. Yet, despite this, *Swayamvaram* is a major achievement.

M. T. Vasudevan Nair,
Nirmalayam (1973)

It is indeed an indisputable fact of our recent cultural history that the conflict between tradition and modernity (despite strenuous denials by neo-apologists of the caste system like Rajni Kothari and the Rudolphs in *The Modernity of Tradition*) provides the chief subject-matter of most of our so-called 'art' films. More specifically, while tradition is centred around religion and its various allotropes, modernity is invariably symbolized by sexuality in its disruptive and less sanctioned forms. Especially is this the case with some of the recent triumphs of neo-realism in the cinema. I am thinking of *Samskara* (1970) where the high priest of orthodoxy, Pranesachar, succumbs to the charms of the untouchable, Chandri, precisely at the moment when he is seeking Divine guidance from the God Maruthi. Similarly, in *Vamsha Vriksha* (1971), the venerable Srinivasa Shrouthri discovers his illegitimacy, ironically, on the eve of his father's *shraddha*. And in *Maya Darpan* (1972) (although this is not made in the neo-realistic modes), the girl attains her freedom from the shackles of a crumbling tradition — embodied in the person of her father, the aging Dewan — by giving herself to the young engineer who represents in her mind the forces of progress. And now in M.T. Vasudevan Nair's *Nirmalayam* the breakdown of the ethos of the Velichapadu is signalled by the sexual unchastity of his wife Kalyani. The scene of the revelation (*anagnarosis* in the Aristotelian sense) has been carefully prepared for. The Muslim shopkeeper, Moimunni, haunts the Velichapadu *ménage*, and one early scene, in particular, is noteworthy. The Velichapadu is not at home and yet Moimunni sits down on the steps in full view of the Velichapadu's only son, the perennially unemployed Appu. As the Velichapadu's wife appears in the doorway

it is clear from her unease that there is something brewing between
the woman and the man. Moimunni even cryptically reminds her not
to forget 'their business'. After he leaves, the son upbraids his mother
for not clearing the shopkeeper's debts but the woman wryly remarks
that there is nothing at home to sell to raise money. A later scene
shows Moimunni at the gate of the Velichapadu's house asking a bemused
Appu why he is standing there doing nothing. The petulance in Appu's
reply not only recalls his earlier terseness with his mother but also
acts as a bridge sequence and subtly paves the way for the 'obligatory'
scene of the film: Kalyani's fall. So when the blow comes it has all
the credibility of a probable impossibility which, to quote Aristotle
again, is to be preferred to a possible improbability. True, the Velichapadu is spared the spectacle of witnessing a *flagrante delicto*, but what
he actually sees is enough to make his world totter. Let us return
to the scene. It is the eve of the *kurudi* and the Velichapadu, now
at the very nadir of his fortunes but nevertheless making a brave attempt
to regain his erstwhile glory, is home preparing for the big event.
He speaks to his old and dying father of the grand preparations for
the festival and, stepping inside, asks his wife for a glass of water.
Consternation seizes him as Moimunni emerges from an adjoining
room, shoving money into his purse and the Velichapadu's wife herself
follows. In the ensuing scene she is harshly unrepentant: 'When your
children were starving it was not your Bhagavathi who brought them
rice,' she says, and the implications are all too clear. She has been
unchaste for quite some time, an unwilling hostage to brute necessity.
The whole axis of the Velichapadu's life snaps with this shocking disclosure and henceforth he is a broken man. With just the kurudi to
go, the drama now has all the lineaments of classical Sophoclean tragedy.
The converging lines of action from now on are remorseless in their
logic. The Velichapadu goes to his doom, a heroic suicide if you like,
slain by his own hand, his empire of faith in ruins and his life itself
a mockery and a vast uselessness. It only remains for his lifelong friend
and well-wisher, the pious Wariar, to voice the elgaic epitaph: 'Oh
Devi! May the bleeding stop.' But as the blood trickles away from
the bleeding forehead and collects in vast and dismal pools beside
the dead Velichapadu and the soundtrack suddenly picks up the ghostly
jingle of the Velichapadu's ritual vestments, we know better. For what
is bleeding to death is a whole way of life, of which the Velichapadu
is only the most eloquent symbol. Not even the copybook romanticism
of the closing shot of the faded flowers (and hence the film's title)

can quite take away the violent and shuddering impact of the iconoclastic
end.

The integrity of a film can invariably be gauged by the integrity
of the denouement. John Howard Lawson is surely right in holding:
'The climax concludes *what* happened in a particular system of events;
it is also a judgment on *why* it happens, *what* it means and *how* it
affects our lives and conduct. The *why, what*, and *how* are embodied
in every part of the story; the end refers back to every part and summarizes
the total result. Since the climax is the key to the story, it reveals
the creator's purpose — or his confusion or lack of purpose — in the
sharpest form.' Here the limitations of the modern film are most evident.
On this criterion it can be seen how the closing scenes of *Nirmalayam*
are the most eloquent commentary on the problems posed at the very
start of the film. However we read the implications of the Velichapadu's
extraordinary closing mime (and of this more later), the end remains
faithful to the premises of the film. We have only to compare *Nirmalayam*
to the overrated *Garam Hava* (1973) where, after wandering discon-
solately for a large part of its Eastman-coloured footage among the
melancholy mausoleums of the Mughal Empire (pitifully yielding now
to the blandishments of the marbled Taj and now to the fabled Sikri),
the film does a predictable cop-out at the end when that arch bourgeois,
the God-fearing Salim Mirza, suddenly and inexplicably turns radical
and joins the student demonstrators instead of catching the train to
Pakistan. The journey from the hard Right to the soft Left may altogether
be more admirable than the journey from India to Pakistan, Third
Class, but surely it is not a journey undertaken by Salim Mirza but
by his spiritual overlord, the puppet master M.S. Sathyu. M.T.
Vasudevan Nair, with greater integrity, has refrained from modish and
trendy panaceas and the false comfort of easy solutions. His film, on
the contrary, is open-ended, inviting the question, but sphinx-like refusing the answer. Does this make M.T. an 'uncommitted' film-maker?
So much the worse then for commitment!

Nirmalayam has epic scope. Even the principal theme, of the decline
of religious faith, is articulated in several keys carefully modulated to
bring out the poignancy of the Velichapadu's fate. The film indeed
starts on this note with the resignation of the *shantikaran* who abandons
priesthood for business (he starts a tea-shop off the highway). He complains that there is no *neivedyam* in the temple, no *payasam*, and
not even betel leaves necessary for worship. Later in the film, this
same ex-priest shows scant respect for tradition when he is willing

to part with only eight annas as donation for the kurudi. His place as temple priest is taken by the hero who, somewhat ironically, is in the process of preparing himself for the UPSC examinations. But probably more to the point is the fact that he hasn't in the past observed any of the proprieties traditionally associated with the vocation of priesthood. He confesses at one point to having taken tea in a *Moplah* shop when still a student. He even lets Ammini prepare tea for him and is rather surprised when she respectfully addresses him as *adiyan*. He doesn't even stay for the big festival at the end although the Velichapadu earnestly entreats him to do so. Although he has his reasons for going (his marriage has been fixed by his father to raise money for his sister's dowry), one does get the feeling that his faith is rather tenuous. (And as played by the ever so good-looking Ravi Menon, the young Namboodri lacks all plausibility as a priest, and even that solitary scene showing him performing *pooja* in the Melakkav is most unconvincing.) In a wholly different key is the sceptical religiosity of the woman who brings her whimpering child to be ministered to by the Velichapadu. She leaves without paying, although she says she will later. This scene is more symptomatic of the decline of faith than, for instance, the rather more blatant atheism of Appu, the Velichapadu's son, who says at one point that he too sees God but 'in a *beedi*, a *chaya*, or a meal provided by a friend'.

Parallel to the decline of faith in religion is the decline of traditional mores. For instance, when the Velichapadu takes to begging he is not treated in all houses with the customary respect due to him, although the outbreak of the epidemic restores him, quickly enough, to his wonted place in the village hierarchy; reminding us of Valery's maxim that superstition has deeper roots than religion. Later, when the Velichapadu goes round on his mission of collecting funds for the kurudi, the rich Brahmin shows scant respect and makes the Velichapadu wait an unconscionably long time even as the American tourists are treated to an exclusive Mohiniattam performance. (Incidentally, one may add, that this particular scene has its *longeurs* and could have done with a bit more attention from editor Ravi.) Two lone instances are poignant reminders of the older hospitality. The first is the way the elderly Brahmin woman shows respect to the Velichapadu in the process of giving him alms. To begin with, she brings him a fistful of rice, but discovering it is the Velichapadu she goes through the ceremonial ritual, brass candelabra and all, and, in doing so, memorably evokes the traditional ethos that is far from being extinct, at least in some of our obscure southern villages. The second instance is when Ammini, in spite of her own starving sisters, hands over the leftover rice that the young priest gives her to the 'madcap' Gopal who looks at her imploringly. That this is dharma in the true sense of the term, a dharma that exists outside the pale of economic considerations, is beautifully brought out in that little vignette with the street-hawker. The latter refuses to buy from Appu the Velichapadu's sword and other ritual paraphernalia (the *chelambu* and *aramani*) because, he says, 'they belong to Devi'. The remarkable thing about all these instances is that they in no way reflect the personal virtue of the individuals concerned. These scenes are in the nature of epiphanies revealing the *whatness* (in the Thomist sense) of the culture even as they serve as memorials for a vanishing past.

Perhaps saddest of all declines is the decline of the arts. In one of those artless little scenes in the film, a scene between the Velichapadu and the Brahmin's *karyasthan*, the Velichapadu recalls the forgotten glories of the past: Ramunny Nair's Bheeman, Nami Nair's Thadi, Poduval's drum, and Nambeesan's songs. But where, oh where, he might cry with the poet, are the snows of yesteryear? Ramunny Nair himself (played symbolically with a limp by Sankaradi) cannot even raise money to keep the Kathakali costumes in good repair, and his solitary scene with the rich Brahmin is symptomatic of the whole state of affairs. The Brahmin makes it clear that Kathakali is only for tourist consumption but is otherwise not worth its keep. During this harangue the humiliated Ramunny has a vivid — indeed, an almost angry — remembrance of happier days (the brief Kathakali insert of the killing of Dushyasana featuring Ramunny himself is perhaps the most telling of the film's many flashbacks) but the writing is on the wall. Ramunny is summarily dismissed from service and as he takes leave of the karyasthan, who sheds a silent tear for him, we sense the end of an epoch. Ramunni has been there in the village, boy and man, for nearly forty years and has literally nowhere to go. The karyasthan's voice quails in regret and helplessness (and M.B. Sreenivasan's austere musical score hereabouts, is almost ascetic in its self-effacement). A lump rises to our throats as Ramunny limps away, a pathetic and forlorn figure, mercilessly ground under the juggernaut of the Brahmin's chilling indifference.

In the presence of such august themes, it is indeed a pity that M.T. has made concessions to the box-office by introducing a romantic by-plot involving the young Namboodri priest and Ammini, the

Velichapadu's daughter. The romance sets up a discord beside the overarching theme of the decay of tradition. The discord is patent in the soundtrack where M.B. Sreenivasan's otherwise sensitive score is forced to accommodate, and indeed orchestrate, the gambols of the lovers under varying climatic conditions. The plaintive violin theme of the Velichapadu (taken from the beautiful composition in *arabi* of the Pullavan's song which we hear during the film's most poignant and moving flashback) gives way, in the scenes delineating the various stages of the heroine's erotic pilgrimage, to a strange medley of sounds. This apart, the values governing the growth and development of the love story are not, and indeed, cannot be, wholly the values of romantic love in the strictly modern sense. True romantic values govern its development up to the moment of Ammini's sexual surrender, but thereafter we are asked to accept the inevitability of the lovers' separation. Twisted and claustrophobic branches of a knot of trees form the depressing visuals as the hero confesses his plight and his decision to leave the village, and Ammini's fatalism at this point has the effect of almost making a martyr of the hero! (And, certainly, his own grim fantasy of his impending wedding serves to reinforce this impression.) And such is the lyric charm of the parting scene on the banks of the Bharatapuzha, so mellifluous the sonic backdrop of the euphoric wedding song as the hero takes his leave of the girl that we, too, accept the situation 'philosophically'. Indeed, we are so hypnotized by the visual symmetry (the hero returns by the same route along which we first saw him enter the story) that we masochistically decline to judge his actions by any of our customary moral standards. The fact that *Nirmalayam* completely reverses the order of the commercial film where such a character would have been judged a 'villain' shows not emancipation from conventional moral standards but only their total suspension. It is another of those unholy triumphs of 'aestheticism'.

Fortunately, however, at least in the early scenes when the Namboodri arrives to take his place as the temple priest, both Ravi Menon and Sumitra show remarkable restraint and a surprisingly unforced naturalness and spontaneity. But, alas, the deterioration starts even with their second meeting pitched in the wrong key when Ammini shows an alarming familiarity in her witticisms and runs playfully in a manner that is as familiar as it is *filmi* (she repeats this 'run' later in the film, underlining the basic conventionality of the film's love scenes). The now obligatory *Aradhana* drenching in the rain is too remorselessly followed by the first fumbling embraces to compel anything but sexual titillation and anticipation in the audience. True, this particular scene is handled with somewhat unusual restraint, but M.T. throws all caution to the winds in the ensuing scene depicting the heroine's sexual fantasies. Her palpitations are annotated laboriously with the touristy skills of Khajuraho and a general quivering and rustling of leaves whose symbolism is more remote from common understanding. The culminating scene of her sexual surrender (signalled by guttering wicks nearby) is in rather dubious taste, set as it is inside the temple precincts, and the hero himself, after the initial moves, is so completely absent from the proceedings that one gets the feeling that either the heroine is masturbating or the audience is making love to her. Even technically the scene is so over-lighted (almost suggesting 'fantasy' again, so reminiscent is it texturally of them) and so unimaginatively photographed by Ramachandra Babu whose work in the film as a whole shows little evidence of Film Institute discipline. (Just look at that post office scene!) The editing just about saves the scene from outright disaster with a quick cut of a still glowing Ammini now back in her house followed by a mid-shot of her bemusedly watching water spilling over a vessel in which rice is boiling. The cut would have been *witty* had we gone straight to the brimming vessel from the doings in the temple. But then between the temple and the vessel lies the long shadow of Khosla!

Thematically, then, the love story has little significance. Had it been muted to a minor key sans all the carnal writhing in the vertical and the horizontal, it might have attained the status of a minor melody in the grand concerto of the Velichapadu's fate. As it stands, it is merely cloying, an irrelevant parenthesis, wholly external to the sublime and heart-rending pathos of the Velichapadu's decline and serves little or no purpose in the architecture of the film.

But otherwise the film is rich in moments of detailed observation unobtrusively tucked away in the magic weave of the narrative. For instance, when the young priest has just arrived in the sleepy village, 'half as old as time', the ever courteous Wariar offers him sleeping accommodation at his own house (there is even a faint suggestion that the young, handsome Namboodri reminds him of his own son who has committed suicide). The next scene, at night, shows him installed in a room in Wariar's house reading a *General Knowledge Refresher* for his UPSC exams (appropriately a later scene shows him getting stuck on Rio de Janeiro when memorizing the capitals of the world). Wariar comes in to make routine enquiries, to be followed, a few moments later, by his wife, Lakshmi Kutty, who brings water and some milk. It is clear she is faintly attracted by the young priest, and as she leans over to put the vessels on the window sill she almost brushes him. The Namboodri draws back and stammers his answers to her somewhat contrived efforts at a conversation. The little scene is left tantalizingly incomplete. From his next scene with Wariar we know that the young Namboodri has gone back to sleep in the temple premises under the pretext that he needs to read all night. And since his sleeping alone in the temple is made the subject of teasing innuendoes by Ammini, the earlier scene with Wariar's wife is thrown into subtle, shaded relief.

M.T.'s social comment, too, is telling even when brief. For instance, in noting the distinctions of caste he is acute even as he remains a neutral, non-partisan observer. The caste proprieties between the Namboodri and Ammini are all quietly noted in the first stage of their relationship. In the 'cooking' scene, for instance, she merely blows the fire while the rice is being cleaned by him, but she doesn't touch the vessel when it is brought. She addresses him after the first worship as adiyan, much to his embarrassment, and it is only after promises that he won't tell anyone that she prepares tea for him. Even here she drinks her tea from his unwashed cup although he asks her to clean it — surely a wishful gesture on her part but also one that underlines her caste subjection. In a like vein, in the scene in the tea-shop, the ex-priest who runs the shop won't even touch the non-caste Hindu's hands in serving him (he discreetly places the plate on the bench), but is willing to treat the Velichapadu on terms of social equality, albeit the Velichapadu's missing son, Appu, comes in for some witheringly condescending remarks.

Only once does M.T. really overplay his hand. This is the scene when the 'madcap' Gopal (clearly an echo of Velayudha of M.T.'s earlier script, 'Iruttinde Atmavu') after unsuccessfully appealing to the Velichapadu for a *beedi* scorns the *beedi* thrown to him by Moimunni, the Muslim shopkeeper, with the remark that the action has 'polluted the place'. He braces himself up for the remark and clearly M.T. is suggesting here that human dignity comes before everything else. But this is a luxury that, nowadays, only madmen such as Gopal can afford. Brecht wrote, 'Food first, morals later,' and M.T.'s reversal of the Brechtian dictum here is rather too idealistic and reactionary. This reading is confirmed later when the same Gopal chases Ammini and the audience, to a man, thinks 'rape'. But on catching up with the fleeing girl, Gopal merely comes up with, 'Are you hurt?' before asking her for an anna (incidentally the use of the now defunct system of coinage makes the period of the film hard to place, but then the cars and the tourists and especially the Ranji Trophy cricket commentary make it definitely a sixties film). These are the vestiges of a decadent bourgeois humanism in a film otherwise free of ideological sentimentality. In fairness, perhaps, I should add that Kalyani's capitulation to Moimunni for the sake of food is treated by M.T. with the least trace of sentimentality. Had the Velichapadu shown moral indignation here (as Gopal had earlier with Moimunni) he would surely have lost the sympathy of the audience which rests hereabouts — and such is the mood of bitterness of the times in which we live — squarely with the 'fallen' Kalyani. Instead the Velichapadu merely hangs his head down in hopelessness, thereby ensuring for himself a certain measure of tragic dignity.

But these shortcomings do not really mar or in anyway diminish the overall splendour of the film. *Nirmalayam* has the sweep and majesty of a major symphonic movement. The first preludial movement culminates in the first flashback when the Velichapadu has just returned home at night after a rather thankless day (the priest in the Melakkav has resigned and the pipers are testy over the payment). In a mood of sheer despondency he harks back, in fond memory, to a remembrance of happier days when religious festivals were momentous occasions marked by music and merriment and hectic fireworks. The whole flashback sequence is punctuated at either end by the melancholy croaking of frogs. The second movement starts with the morning when the Velichapadu's children are shown doing their lessons and terminates with the departure of Appu, the Velichapadu's eldest son, from home. The violin theme (or should one call it 'the Velichapadu theme'?) is heard throughout this sequence and, indeed, is heard even during the earliest exchange in the film between the Velichapadu and his son who wants some money to go to Trichur to look for a job. In thus stressing the importance of the father—son relationship the violin theme becomes the *leitmotif* of the film; significantly it is heard for the last time towards the end of the film as the Velichapadu has his ritual bath before the start of the kurudi. The third movement, the shortest and the most euphoric, shows a brief respite in the Velichapadu's fortunes (M.T. uses a most telling symbol to convey this: Ammini helps a struggling beetle drowning in an oil lamp in a night scene of characteristic brevity). The movement (whose start is signalled, ironically, by the breakout of smallpox in the village) shows a return of the Velichapadu to his most imperious manner. As he supervises the arrangements for the forthcoming festival, the Velichapadu recovers his *élan* and his voice takes on a sumptuousness and pride as he negotiates the vexing business of the pipers. That old stage hand, P.J. Anthony, is indeed learned in all the devices of voice and attack. His regal disdain in dealing with the alleged recalcitrancy of Achuta Marar is matched by the authority with which he requisitions the services of Kunhikrishnan. The whole passage is marked by an urgency hitherto lacking in the Velichapadu's actions. The same controlled emotion, without the rhetoric of the 'actor's business' is evident in the earlier scene at home when he asks his wife for the wherewithal for the kurudi. When it is revealed that she has spent the last quarter of an anna on domestic necessities the Velichapadu's anger flashes forth with the fluency of one who is accustomed to being obeyed. Perhaps P.J.'s finest moment in the film comes in that unforgettable scene, already referred to, when the Velichapadu stands before his wife, a shamefaced cuckold, shaken and overwhelmed by the revelation of her unchastity. It is a sombre scene, and P.J. plays it with a surefooted and unimpeachable dignity. An unforgettable and monumental creation, P.J.'s Velichapadu is a tiny miracle of sustained power and imperishable glory.

The final movement, which commences with the Velichapadu's 'moment of truth' sweeps the film irresistibly to its tragic denouement. As the Velichapadu greets people going to the festival, his face (already fallen to one side) wears a wan and dejected smile. As he bathes in the river and is greeted by his lone friend and well-wisher, the loyal Wariar, his face momentarily lights up in that now familiar smile. The final *dance macabre* soon begins. These scenes are paced and played to an absolute perfection. As the Velichapadu's frenzy mounts, in an unforgettable and breathtaking moment, alone and before the Goddess Bhagavathi, whose worship and service have sustained him all his life, he *spits* in her face the blood that is her offering and breaks his ritual sword. It is an act compounded of belligerence and defiance, bitterness and despair, but, in all, wholly irrevocable. The Velichapadu has indeed crossed the Rubicon of the spiritual life. It is an act, too, that in its seeming refusal of transcendence and scorn of the gods, recalls the withering, terrible and, yes, lofty atheism of the Camus of *The Myth of Sisyphus*. Still, the final significance and meaning of these extraordinary closing scenes of *Nirmalayam* must remain a matter of controversy and debate. M.T. himself (in a letter to me) has said that 'an archetypal character like the Velichapadu cannot lose complete faith ... He is in a dilemma at the end ... Yes, an angry offering it is.' But, much as I respect the intentions of the maker of *Nirmalayam*, I remain unconvinced by this line of argument. The Velichapadu has, for me, at this point, crossed the line into despair and hence into the twilight zone where such belief as still survives is too vexed by unbelief to be really distinguished from it. Perhaps the closet drama of the Velichapadu's 'crisis of faith' has too 'private' a setting for the outcome to really matter. After all, it is only we in the darkness of the auditorium who are privy to his possible 'loss of faith' but not the multitudinous villagers assembled outside the Melakkev. But the crucial question here, in terms of the film's initial premises, is simply: Has the Velichapadu, too, lost his faith or merely his life? For me, at any rate, the total impression created by the symbolism of the discarded sword, the faded flowers, and the bleeding forehead is one of a finally sundered belief.

Still, however elusive (not ambiguous) the import of the terminal images, *Nirmalayam*'s boldness and departure from social placebos make it — in the annals of Indian cinema — something of a unique phenomenon, the most authentic product of what I will call 'the secular imagination'.

P. Madhavan: Mythological Syndrome in Tamil Cinema

With the outstanding success of both *Vietnam Veedu* (1970) and *Nilave Nee Sakshi* (1970) at the annual State Awards in Tamil Nadu, director Madhavan must be said to have definitely arrived. *Nilave Nee Sakshi* is as unlike *Vietnam Veedu* as it is possible to be and does not bear even a 'family resemblance' (in the Wittgensteinian sense of the term) to the latter. Since I hold no brief for the auteur theory of the Cahierists, Continental or American, this does not cause me any embarrassment beyond the critical inconvenience of being unable to talk about them together as illustrative of some directorial obsession.

Still, *Nilave Nee Sakshi* has some important structural features which I would like to single out since the same features reappear in Madhavan's subsequent films, *Sabadam* (1971) and *Thenum Palum* (1971). For want of a better name, I will call this the 'mythological syndrome', taking the liberty of borrowing the latter term from medical science. Briefly, the 'mythological syndrome' is the use of the mythological past (the *Puranas* and the great epics) in popular films to identify and ratify the present. What this really amounts to saying is that while in the 20s and 30s we were making only mythologicals, now we are supposed to be making socials, only they are mythologicals in disguise. My present thesis is that the recent work of Madhavan represents a new complication of this strategy which possibly portends a new trend.

Interesting twists

To begin with *Nilave Nee Sakshi*. For a good two-thirds of its length, the film ambles along, accoutered with all the paraphernalia of 'contemporary' films: campus love, domestic bitching, the old classmates lore, psychistric jazz and a 'hot' scene in a jammed elevator, straight from *Sweet Charity,* between Jai Shanker and K.R. Vijaya to get the younger crowd in. Where *Nilave Nee Sakshi* gets interesting is towards the end where hero Jai Shanker has lost his memory (due to disappointed love, of course!) and psychologist Muthuraman is put on the job. After doing his best in the clinic, Muthuraman takes his patient home for a change and then for a long ride to all possible old haunts in the hope, perhaps, that Mother Nature will do the trick. A sundered branch of a tree almost seems to do it, the name of the street where his sweetheart once lived inches the memory further up, and finally the song (sung by the old darling, of course) which sealed the 'true love' in the first place — the song from which incidentally the film takes its title (literally, 'Moon Be My Witness') — brings the hero whistling back to life. Trouble is the old sweetheart is the doctor's wife, and although the doctor himself takes it in his professional stride, his mother and brother take a different view of it.

And here is where the film turns towards the *Ramayana* for salvation. The *Ramayana* has been mysteriously present all through the film through deliberate misquotation and jumbling of episodes by Muthuraman's mother who, in good company with that old wizard, Thangavelu, takes care of the lighter side of the film. Suddenly even the playful parody of the *Ramayana* abruptly stops as the plot takes a more serious turn and the presence of a possible unchaste woman on the premises (namely, the heroine) enables the script-writer and the director to tap directly on these episodes in the national epic when Sita returns from Lanka and has to go through the *agni pariksha*.

A modern film

But *Nilave Nee Sakshi* is a modern film: you have to find equivalents of the agni pariksha and our modern film-makers come up with psychiatry. If Muthuraman can cure Jai Shanker and restore his memory, then his (Muthuraman's) wife is sexually pure! It is an odd inference indeed and one which would have puzzled both Aristotle and Nagarjuna, but this is film logic and the hero's memory is restored so that the heroine's domestic life may remain unimperilled. The film is interesting because it invokes the epic situation only to show the inadequacy of an older reaction. It is a mild plea for tolerance of pre-marital affairs, but manages at the same time to keep its respect for the strict monogamic ideals of the great epic. The last scene in the film is highly symbolical: it shows Thangavelu's wife quoting correctly from the *Ramayana* for the first time, and in this oblique way, perhaps, the *Ramayana* may be said to have the last word.

Sabadam again shows Madhavan's exploitation of the 'mythological syndrome'. This time it is the *Mahabharata*; that notorious episode — the disrobing of Draupadi — is on call and her vow to avenge the dishonour is what gives the film its title. Indeed, the use of the epic episode is so blatant that it is employed as a pre-credits metaphor to cue us to the meaning of what is to follow. The whole episode is enacted at a furious pace in a dance—drama (featuring L. Vijayalakshmi, star of yesteryear) to quickly set the stage for the drama of deceit and lechery to follow. The epic story culminating in that epic battle undergoes what can only be described as 'topological' displacement; nevertheless it is there for those who care to look at the repeated shots of a dice game and in the story of the evil Dorasingham (a Duryodhana figure) wrongfully dispossessing his elder brother, the virtuous Selvanayagam (a clear echo of Dharmaraja, the eldest of the Pandavas), of his property. The wronged 'Pandavas' suffer in silent exile before returning for the final showdown which is staged with such a revolting admixture of righteous indignation and glee that an unconscious sympathy for the cornered 'Duryodhana' develops.

Mechanical and schematic

The film is altogether too mechanical and schematic, and seems the product of a fevered and melodramatic imagination. The dialogue, for instance, is rampant with crude animal imagery and a key song towards the end is punctuated visually with shots of a dummy tiger and two stuffed goats with the intellectual subtlety of kindergarten. Only that veteran stage actor T.K. Bhagavathi and the generously proportioned K.R. Vijaya do something to mitigate the elephantine heaviness of the plot, but then the impossible Ravichandran is on hand undoing, with smart-alecy smirks and pseudo-heroic posturing (derived from the local school of Bond, of which he himself is the undisputed headmaster), all the good work of the rest. His two fight scenes in the film — nightmares of limb-twisting — are aching dissonances in the ruthless chiaroscuro of the film. Still, *Sabadam* is interesting because it invokes the epic parallel in a story more concerned with the class war between the rich (Dorasingham) and the poor (Ravichandran and Co.) than with personal morality. Here, a watered-down Marxism is grafted on to the *Mahabharata* structure to yield the kind of ethic that could loosely be called egalitarian were it not for the overall crudeness. It is to be hoped that Madhavan will not be tempted to repeat its methods in the future.

Mythological syndrome

With *Thenum Palum* we find we run head on into the 'mythological syndrome'. Since Madhavan himself is responsible for the screenplay and direction, it would be relevant to examine it in some detail here to gain a clue to the ascendancy of this unusual phenomenon in the work of this man. The film is basically the story of a married man (Ramu—Sivaji Ganesan) who gets involved with a rather flighty girl (Thangam—Saroja Devi). During a business visit to her father's house in Ramnad, he seduces her, ostensibly under the influence of a spot of gin (which fools really nobody!) The seduction scene (cunningly prepared for from the start of the film) is staged with the customary overdrafts from Mother Nature. While a storm rages outside, the lovers are transfixed, with the aid of some rapid cutting, a few yards apart in the privacy of her bedroom while tumultuous background music is poured on relentlessly, as if pleading with the pair for some quick action.

Forced, after the storm — inner and outer — has subsided, by the girl's mother to make the best of a bad job, the contrite hero sets up the girl in a separate establishment near his own home town, Madurai. His wife (Janaki—Padmini) is a chaste, devoted woman, much given to singing the praises of Lord Rama when not engaged in plying her husband with sweetmeats. There are indeed faint hints of a sexual malaise about the marriage, possibly aggravated by her unyielding religiosity and frigidity. As the plot develops, the underlying mythological parallels are fully exploited; while Padmini harps on Lord Rama's monumental monogamy, Sivaji plays up Lord Muruga's more elastic domestic life, featuring Valli and Devayani. The sexual ping-pong between man and wife is thrown into hectic relief in the sub-plot where Nagesh and Sacchu lower the mythic temperature by parodying the tensions of the main plot.

Here we have a fun-loving, frivolous, but clearly frigid wife (in the second scene between them at night she expressly refuses him her sexual favours) who is slowly brought around through a false double of her husband (the beard-sporting, dashing, debonair Duplex) and a false mistress (the all too plausible Rosie). Even this spider-thin plot is beefed up with loaded and pointed references to the great Sangam classic, *Silappadikaram*, where Kovalan has a merry time with mistress Madhavi while wife Kannagi keeps the home fires burning. *Silappadikaram* itself is roundly parodied in the sub-plot where the wife's interest in dance (she even has a tutor) is our surest clue to the tie-in with the Tamil classic where Madhavi is an accomplished dancer and courtesan.

Eternal triangle

The eternal triangle situation of *Silappadikaram* is, indeed, more appropriate to the main plot where a married man has both an adorable wife and an adorable mistress. The parallel is in fact kept down — in deference no doubt to the middle-class obsession with pre-marital chastity — but, just once, almost miraculously, it surfaces even in the main plot in a song sung by Janaki during the beautiful Adi-Perukku festival, only to be explicitly denied there. She thanks her stars that unlike Kannagi in *Silappadikaram*, there is no Madhavi to foul up her own life ('Oh Tamil which sings the praises of both Kannagi and Madhavi/There is no Madhavi in my husband's life, Oh Tamil!'). It is doubly ironic because, at this very moment, a formidable Madhavi-figure (Thangam) is around also to participate in the festival and, in true Tamil-film style, she turns out to be a bosom pal of the heroine! The plot gets a much-needed push with the advancing pregnancy of the Madhavi-figure, and the whole thing winds up on the precipitous brink of tragedy: a seriously injured Ramu marries the young mother, Thangam, in the presence of her parents with Janaki herself doing the honours — and providing the *thali* herself (Lord Muruga and his two wives)! But the monogamic ideal of the *Ramayana* is asserted by both women, and the now-wedded Thangam leaves with infant in tow, leaving Janaki to the joys of undisturbed matrimony.

Limitations

To sum up: Madhavan's recent work is controlled by mythological and literary references which somewhat limit the social meaning of his plots because of the concomitant reduction of the present to the terms of the past. His earlier films, *Raman Ethanai Ramanadi* (1970) and the sophisticated *Vietnam Veedu* do not move on mythological levers but were nevertheless more successful on all counts, particularly the latter. The technical fineness, the expert cutting, and the low-keyed compositions of *Thenum Palum* (aided by some splendid camerawork by Sundaram) are continually undercut by the banal Rama—Sita story that we have heard so often before. One can only regret that such a fine talent is pressed into the service of such basically unserviceable beliefs — and unserviceable, I mean, in the context of complex modern living — and a retrograde *Weltanschauung*. One hopes that Madhavan will soon revert to his *Vietnam Veedu* manner and give us similar, carefully observed portraits of the boredom and the horror and the glory of living in the world of today.

13

K. Balachander, *Arangetram* (1973)

Balachander's *Arangetram* marks a new beginning, a fresh approach, and is a veritable oasis in the dreary desert wastes of Tamil cinema. I had criticized his *Nootrukku Nooru* (1971) for a certain want of originality (the film being rather implausibly based on the French film *Professional Hazards*). I missed his next film *Punnagai* (1971) — which Balachander has admitted to being his personal favourite — and then comes *Arangetram* which has taken Madras virtually by storm. It has achieved by now something of a *success d'estime* but, ironically, for what seem to me to be the wrong reasons! The theme of the film is by no means novel in the Balachander canon. Indeed, sexual impropriety of one form or another is one of the recurring themes in Balachander's films. No — the film succeeds for other and altogether more praiseworthy reasons. It is the tightly woven and superb screenplay by Balachander himself (which deserves to be published separately in its own right), the remarkably imaginative editing by Kittu which establishes a coherent visual syntax for the film, and the magnificent low-key photography by Lokanath that chiefly contribute to the film's signal triumph.

Arangetram has a subdued, austere opening. An establishing pre-dawn shot places us squarely in the sleepy little village of Puliyampatti. The life of the village is deftly evoked through brief but telling touches: a deserted street at night with a lone beggar's voice asking for food, the faintly sinister *kudukudupandi* doing his rounds in the early hours, a bhajan *ghoshti*, with cymbals clashing to the strains of 'Hare Rama Hare Krishna' walking down the village street at break of day while adolescent Brahmin girls are shown decorating the front of the house with *kolam* ; these and countless other 'atmospheric' details bring the slumbering village achingly to life. This superb opening sets the key for the film's real beginning: a developing crisis in the life of Rama Sastry (played by Subbiah, especially early on, with a certain abrasiveness and rancour). But the crisis itself — the slow erosion of faith in ancestral ways in the lives of Brahmins which directly threatens Rama Sastry's very means of livelihood — is allowed to develop not through melodramatic situations as is customary but in strict accordance with the ground rules of cinema.

Subtly woven mosaic

Scenes are visually linked, sometimes verbally linked, and through this subtly woven mosaic of interweaving details — all evocative of the south Indian Brahmin ethos — we are brought to an understanding of the grinding poverty of Rama Sastry and his family of ten children. When into this situation comes Janaki (played with superb nonchalance by that old Gemini hand, Sundari Bai) and her half-wit daughter, the scene is set for the unfolding of the iron laws of economic necessity that drive the eldest daughter (played with insouciant charm by newcomer Pramila) first into a neighbourhood job and later — in far-away Hyderabad — to prostitution. The film is thus concerned with the colossal price that a lower middle-class Brahmin family pays for wanting to keep up with the Joneses of the aspiring middle class: the eldest boy, Thyagu, wants to be a doctor while the second eldest girl, Devi, wants to marry a man with 100 acres! The latter half of the film is thus inevitably melodramatic, but this is the price that art has to pay to the box-office to stay alive. Yet, the first hour and a half of the film are pure magic.

Extraordinarily competent is the screenplay which, by being broken up into shot scenes, is precise and without verbosity. Instances abound, and I will choose just one to illustrate the point. When Lalitha comes to the bold decision to go to work, she is shown requesting Natesa Odayar (a family well-wisher and President of the local Panchayat Board) to get her a job. The shot opens with Odayar weaving a thatch, and he continues to do so during the ensuing exchanges between them. At the end of the sequence we close to a shot of his hands still weaving — suggestive of his whole character and temperament. Lalitha is shown next, preparing to go to work (she has finally landed a job) and the scene — which opens with a shot of her sister Mangalam playing the harmonium — shows Lalitha asking her father's blessings. The *varnam* which Mangalam is playing serves, with clever interruptions, to cue the scene and serve as background score and the next shot shows Lalitha walking jauntily down the street — handbag in one hand and tiffin box in the other — to the derisive remarks of old diehard Brahmin types rapping away in front of a house.

The next shot shows Janaki asking her brother, Rama Sastry, for a loan of two rupees and, even as he tells her to ask in the right quarters, Lalitha returns home with her first month's pay packet. Then follows a shot of Lalitha playing dice with Natesa Odayar — apparently on a holiday — when a telegram arrives with the news that Natesa Odayar's son is dead. (This scene has, in addition, some very good lines.) We cut from the grieving father to a shot of Lalitha in office. The tear in her blouse invites the attention of the leering males in the office and a colleague offers to buy her a saree. In the next scene, to music, rather reminiscent of Michel Legrand's score in *Summer of '42* (1971), Lalitha is shown preparing to wear her new saree. Simultaneously we hear the voices of her younger sister Girija and her mother engaged in argument. Girija, who was earlier shown as coming of age (a rarity in Indian films; indeed menstruation is referred to obliquely thrice in the film) will not go to school without a half-saree. So, for a second time in the film, Lalitha is unlucky with sarees!

The next shot shows Thyagu reading for his PUC exams late at night — it is 2 a.m. — but through two lap dissolves (showing Lalitha engaged in domestic chores) we are taken to the point where Thyagu has passed his examinations. There is next a shot of Mangalam — who is evidently having her periods as she is lying apart from the rest — asking her sister to arrange for her music lessons. The next shot shows Girija taking leave of her mother before going to office. The camera angle is high, enabling the pan further upwards to show the *dharbai* and *samith* — indispensables for a Rama Sastry's *purohit* calling — lying unused in a dusty corner full of cobwebs. Thus does Balachander keep us aware of Rama Sastry's earlier decision to leave his ancestral profession, a dramatic decision that has been transformed now due to the magic of art to the purely graphic. And so on, each shot preparing the ground for the next.

Masterly transitions

Transitions and connections are masterly in the first half of *Arangetram.* When Lalitha requests her Hyderabad boss for a loan of Rs 300 and she is asked to come home the next day which happens to be a Sunday (we remember her father asking her to leave Puliyampatti on Thursday which would have enabled Lalitha to reach Hyderabad via Madras on Saturday), the scene does not terminate here as would normally happen. The camera pans to a flower vase in the corner of the room and there is a cut to flowers in a vase in the house of the Managing Director, and Lalitha herself emerges from behind it. Likewise, early on, the three faithless Brahmins performing *Amavasai Tharpanam* (when Rama Sastry leaves in a huff) empty their tumblers into the pond. There is a cut from this directly to Visalam (M.N. Rajam in a brave and well-deserved comeback is very good in this role) emptying grain from the depleted granary in an exact visual parallel of the earlier shot. The verbal continuities and felicities are too numerous to be cited here, but all of them add up to some of the best cinema the Tamil screen has witnessed in a long, long while — perhaps since Jayakantan's *Unnaipol Oruvan* (1965).

Wages of prostitution

Alas! all good things come to an end. In *Arangetram* the intermission is the true end of the film with the mad Thangam drumming away on her empty Dalda tin in the hope of seeing her lover return from faraway Singapore. Lalitha's future is mirrored in this demented girl on the seashore; she, too, will one day meet a like fate. Her *arangetram* in Madras — a gruesome rape which is intercut *Samskara*-fashion with Mala's Bharatanatyam debut six times — is really the beginning of the end. But the box-office is a bloodthirsty monster that must be appeased and Balachander proceeds to do so in the second half of the film. I won't carp here except to make a brief point. The moral degradation of Lalitha — which is shown in a beautifully executed montage — is treated, somewhat inexplicably, purely externally. I say this on the evidence of the Dorian Gray-like portrait of her in her Hyderabad house which undergoes a progressive decline as she plunges headlong into the abysses of her profession.

But the wages of prostitution — no matter how nobly motivated and especially if undertaken, as Lalitha is shown to, in a spirit of unguarded bravado — have always to be paid for heavily: both in terms of the flesh and the spirit. But the spirit — or the soul — of Lalitha is shown as inviolate till the very end. The internal rotting, consequent on a flouting of moral values, is inevitable, but of this there is — unlike as in the Wilde masterpiece — no evidence. The punishments accorded to her for her life of ignominy are all external: excommunication from the family and, eventually, madness. Thus is Lalitha morally exonerated by her creator for her life of scarlet sin. As to the price paid by the body: real thematic boldness here would have shown her at the end a victim of disease. Madness, pure and simple, would seem to be too facile and faulty a diagnosis! Still I won't press the point. There is enough as it is in *Arangetram* to enthuse over. It is an achievement of a very high order; an achievement besides which the cinemascopic nightmare of *Raja Raja Chozhan* (1973) and the mindless opulence of *Ulagam Sudurum Valiban* (1973) pale into ghostly insignificance. Truly, Balachander's *Arangetram* ushers in a new age of the Tamil cinema.

14

J. Mahendran, *Udhiri Pookal* (1979)

'Some men are born great, some achieve greatness, and some have greatness thrust upon them,' muses Malvolio while pacing Olivia's garden in Shakespeare's *Twelfth Night*. But, equally, one might argue, 'Some men are born evil, some achieve evil, and some have evil thrust upon them.'

Certainly in the case of Sundaravadivelu in Mahendran's *Udhiri Pookal* it is a case of evil being thrust upon him. For not only is he held morally responsible for his wife's unhappiness and eventual death, but right from the start of the film the people around him spare no epithet to malign him in our eyes. The 'hero' schoolteacher, Prakash, who has just arrived at Palayampatti glibly joins the chorus of the other two masters just because he has been told to turn up in school in the regulation white *jhubba* rather than in coloured shirts of his own choosing. When this prize idiot turns up in a pair of trousers and a plain white banian the next day and has again to be ticked off, we are supposed to take this as one more instance of Sundaravadivelu's infamy.

Still, the incorrigible Prakash continues to go his own wilful way for he is soon seen sitting in a wayside *mandap* instructing Sundaravadivelu's children in some inconsequential game with a stone. Once again Sundaravadivelu's displeasure at this delinquency (it is all during school hours, mind you!) is chalked up against him. On his very first appearance in the film, Sundaravadivelu's brother (an assistant in the local health centre) villifies his brother in no uncertain terms. Why, even his gentlemanly father-in-law, Thambuswamy, reacts with almost obscene outrage ('I am a father, not a broker', etc.) to Sundaravadivelu's fairly innocuous proposal of marriage to his sister-in-law. But surely this must be considered pretty routine behaviour (when you take into account Lakshmi's poor health) in villages in the not too distant past.

Later, when he convenes a *panchayat* to secure a legitimate separation from his wife whose fidelity he suspects (which is a whole lot more than what that paragon of Hindu virtue, Lord Rama in the *Ramayana,* did under similar circumstances), he is fairly shouted down and a howling mob soon takes the law into its own hands. And yet he has pretty strong grounds for suspecting his wife (consider, from his point of view, first, the gifts for the children and, later, the unsecured loan from the handsome doctor!). And then, when he arrives with his newly married wife, he is greeted derisively in the song, 'Kalyanam Paru Appavoda Kalyanam Paru', by a mocking Senbagam fairly armed with her sister's children. And yet what is so morally obnoxious about it? Later, when his sensuous young wife (played by the delectable Charulata) neglects to feed his two young children, the same Senbagam turns up and asks him to drop them into a well instead of starving them to death. She even threatens to burn his house down if it happens again! Indeed, he is provoked continuously and unremittingly throughout the film.

A couple of days before his own marriage, Prakash shows up at Sundaravadivelu's place not to invite him for the function, mind you — although he brandishes an invitation at his former boss's face — but to taunt him into leaving town, *before the marriage,* because his school was likely to be soon wound up. Senbagam soon follows suit. She repeats her fiance's palaver and demands custody of the children in the teeth of Sundaravadivelu's own claims to their legal custodianship. Now can you blame this man for retaliating? True, by humiliating Senbagam, Duryodhana-style, he does incur a great deal of moral odium. But, then, the punishment meted out to him — death by drowning — is not only hideous but out of all proportion to the nature of the offence. Certainly, on balance, this man appears far, far more sinned against than sinning!

Certainly, viewed impartially, Sundaravadivelu (excellently played by Vijayan) seems, at worst, like Malvalio, 'sick of self-love', but he is surely not without redeeming qualities. He has a certain natural dignity — what Bertrand Russell has called 'proper pride' — which blazes in contrast to the cringing self-effacement of the others. He has courage, both physical (witness his taking on the doctor against all odds) as well as moral — both essential ingredients of the textbook hero. These qualities don't desert him even in his final hour of ignominy and defeat where they shine in all their glory. Further, he is no ordinary debauchee (unlike the stock villain of Tamil films) but lawfully seeks to marry Senbagam with the consent of his wife and father-in-law (he even suggests that they all live under the same roof). He is, of course, a strict disciplinarian, a believer in order, and this results (as it so often does in life) in the complete absence of a sense of humour. No, he is not exactly likeable. Further, he is vulnerable to suggestions from that toadying parasite of a music teacher who is, arguably, the one really bad character in the film if you except Sundaravadivelu's ghoulish mother. But all these are minor human failings to which all flesh is heir and cannot, by any stretch of imagination, be identified with the principle of Evil. He is repeatedly referred to as 'beast', but his own heartbreaking plea that he be allowed 'to live like a man' (by being allowed to separate from a sick wife and marry again) is rudely ignored. And except for the solitary instance where he slaps her, he is not shown as particularly unkind to her (his criticism of her cooking, early on, surely is trivial) although we are continually told that he is an ogre.

Even his behaviour throughout to his children is unexceptional (his one *seeming* callousness when Bhavani is ill is redeemed when it turns out that Lakshmi's fears that it is smallpox are groundless), and his final parting from them is strangely moving but thoroughly unsentimental. And so he remains a renegade to the bitter end. Remember it is not he but his tormenters and principal accusers who break down and weep at the end! Truly, his fall is that of a towering titan, and not untouched by a certain tragic dignity. Why then, does the film unremittingly slander and morally crucify him?

A structural clue is provided by the recurring image of that demented character who is constantly threatening to chop off his absent wife's head while, at the same time, is clearly solicitous for her return. Now there is a wholly gratuitous hint at the very beginning of the film that Sundaravadivelu was responsible for driving this girl out of the village because he was envious of the man for having such a beautiful wife. But this is clearly malicious since the 'chopper' himself doesn't show the least resentment towards Sundaravadivelu. On the contrary, he plays *tavil* during Sundaravadivelu's second marriage for which he is roundly abused by the barber. There is, indeed, a clear hint at the end that it was the 'chopper's' cruelty rather than Sundaravadivelu's machinations that drove her out.

In stark contrast to this blighted marriage is set the one shining example of blissful matrimony in the village: that of the ageing widow who sings that unabashed eulogy to her husband's sexual prowess. They had nine children, yodels this model matriarch, and her husband died yearning (they had never been separated, you see) when she was away having her tenth. If he was alive, the concluding lines of her song proclaim, they would have populated the entire village. Further, the first line of the same song ('Poda Poda Pokkay') openly mocks Sundaravadivelu as he walks away from the wedding preparations. For, you see, he doesn't belong — to that Club Elect of Matrimonial Bores!

Children and motherhood (the opening and closing images of the film centre on them) are the very fulcrum of the film whose very title refers to children as 'scattered flowers'. If the widow's song celebrated the earthy joys of having numerous children, the song Lakshmi sings (Lakshmi, by the way, is marvellously, if a trifle too Brahminically, played by the Kannada actress Ashwini), 'Azhakiya Kannay', is concerned, more ideologically, with the very meaning of children who are here declared to be the very *raison d'être* of womanhood. But all these resounding hosannas to the wedded state should not blind us to the cruelties it inflicts on the losers.

What if your wife dies (as in the case of Thambuswamy), or falls sick (as in the case of Sundaravadivelu), or just leaves you (as in the case of the 'chopper' or Sundaravadivelu again)? Or what if you have no children (as in the case of the doctor and his barren wife)? And, in any case, in these days of planned families, nobody is going to have nine children, going on ten! This is arrant nonsense. In any case Sundaravadivelu, married off at the ridiculous age of sixteen, simply didn't get that second chance (his sexually provocative but cold second wife eventually leaves him after being, initially, brainwashed by the villagers). But the film has no compassion for losers and loners but only for winners and belongers.

Instead of compassion, the film offers the atavistic satisfaction of a swift and terrible justice, Khomeini-style. In a ghastly reprise of the panchayat scenes, an unprincipled and vicious mob of villagers (led significantly by a *pahalwan*) gather at Sundaravadivelu's house, force him out, and march him belligerently to the river. Their purpose is clear for the film has already established that he can't swim. The final scenes are truly macabre in their unmitigated but complacent sadism but nevertheless serve, however unwittingly, to bring out the truth in Sundaravadivelu's parting shot to his butchers: 'You were all good people. My only mistake was to have made you all like me.'

Films, these days, faithfully reflect (so much for people who think that our films are 'unrealistic') what, in fact, is daily happening around us; public redress of wrongs in blatant disregard of the law. (Consider for a moment what happened a few days ago to the alleged child-lifters in Dharmapuri who were burnt to death with the aid of public subscription for the kerosene.) The Law makes a token appearance in *Udhiri Pookal* after the panchayat riots where it is effectively silenced. What we are witnessing these days (on and off the screen) is a steady erosion of true democratic norms and a slow and gradual eclipse of the rule of law.

Conversations

1

Alea and the Cuban Revolution

Tomas Gutierrez Alea is not young. His high-domed forehead speaks of a speculative cast of mind while the humorous lines around his mouth point to an appreciation of the good things of life. He is, in fact, a Marxist by conviction (he spoke, more than once, of 'the determination in the last instance') and a religious man by temperament (he listens to Bach every day). Almost the first thing he asked us was about the 'strange' Buddhist chant at the end of Sukhdev's documentary, *An Indian Day*. He had hopefully accepted a tape of vedic chants, the experience of listening to which he described as 'hallucinatory', something 'that transported you to another dimension.' But he added, somewhat later in the day, that the moment of revolution, too, was religious. 'The fault lay in 'absolutizing' that moment. Then 'Revolution becomes an empty word, a myth'.

We had now reached the Blue Fox, a Bangalore nightclub, and were ensconced in the doleful comfort of its Saturday afternoon doldrums. A few young bucks and their girls were gyrating to the strains of 'Billy Joel' which Alea informed us was very popular in Cuba. We ordered three bottles of Kingfisher while I stayed, safely put, on the salty tang of a Limca.

Alea had been very religious till the age of 15 and in those days he actually thought that 'Religion could bring about regeneration'. Then came Marxism and the Revolution in Cuba. 'When you live in the middle of a revolution you realize that the revolutionaries also have a religious attitude.' Marxists tend to overrate the 'will', but you have to count on feelings, passions. People will continue to be ambitious, selfish. As for himself, he said that while he wanted to be scientific, he did not want 'to close the door'. Shades of Pascal's diatribe against

Descartes! As I have said, Alea is very Catholic, very religious by temperament and attitude.

But he is also a votary of Beauty — especially in women. He was now admiring a particularly attractive girl on the floor. I regretfully pointed out that in India sexual attitudes were very rigid. This led to a discussion of Cuban sexual mores and particularly to the attitudes to homosexuality there. I told him I had read some very negative reports. He agreed on that but said that things were fast changing. A book by a German sociologist on homosexuality recently translated, was widely read. In fact, Cuban newspapers carried a column on sex every day. But in Muslim countries things were quite terrible. He was in South Yemen four years ago. All windows were closed there albeit etched with delicate arabesques. The sexual repression was grotesque. 'Men disguised themselves as women in order to fool husbands,' he observed wryly. They had enacted a new law to stop the selling of women at high prices. There was, as a result, a 'fixed price ceiling'. 'This,' said Alea with a mixture of passion and indignation, 'was the most revolutionary law at that time!'

We talked of his film *The Survivors*. He confessed to being in Bunuel's debt, particularly the Bunuel of *The Exterminating Angel*. The point was to trap the bourgeois in a situation from which they cannot get out, where their customary 'masks' fall off. 'In comedy you can push things far but because of the realistic base there is no metaphysics.' During a revolution — and *The Survivors* is set during the Cuban Revolution — older 'forms of life survive but lose their former significance'. That is why the bourgeosie in *The Survivors* are so ceremonious even in their 'cannibalism'. Surely decadence can go no further.

We talked of film-makers. He didn't like Godard except his *Vivre sa Vie*. 'Still I like the way he destroyed bourgeois cinema,' he added by way of qualification. 'But his cinema is not popular.' Bergman he liked for his 'intense metaphysical perception'. Whereas Fellini was 'artificial' and he only liked *La Strada* . Otherwise he was 'so spectacular, so ambitious'. He liked Ray's *Pather Panchali* and Dos Santos's *Barren Lives* (it struck me that they were very similar but approached with different sensibilities). Mrinal Sen, he knew and obviously liked (Alea was there at Alankar to see *Ekdin Pratidin*). I asked him about the political cinema of Latin America. What about Solanes's *Hour of the Furnaces*? 'Oh, he worked with publicity,' Alea replied brusquely.

The lunch finished, two more bottles of beer were ordered and, of course, another Limca. Indian women were beautiful, our guest observed. He drew his wallet and showed us a photograph of his family. His wife was beautiful, with the Latin allure of Maria Montez. She was 18 years his junior and had starred in his *The Last Supper*. He wanted to take a saree for his wife (cotton, not silk, he corrected me) and presents for his children but the Cuban government had allowed him only 100 dollars. He consequently felt insecure outside Cuba because of money (but 'secure inside Cuba', he added quickly). 'They don't understand you have to take presents home,' he said simply, uncomplainingly. But last year he had enjoyed himself hugely in New York with the 2000-dollar prize money for his film, *Memories of Under-Development.*

Driving back he asked us about M.V. Krishnaswamy with whom he had studied in Italy way back in the fifties. Could he meet him? But, of course! After leaving him at the hotel we found ourselves troubled at that 100-dollar budget of Alea's. Some brisk discussion was followed by an even brisker drive to 'Handloom House' and soon a flaming red saree (cotton, of course!) set off by an ochre yellow border was acquired. We were soon back at the Ashoka. But who should we meet at the lobby but M.V.K. himself looking as immaculately fresh as ever, and all set to show his documentary on Tirupati to some friends. We virtually kidnapped him to Alea's room and soon we witnessed the embarrassed reunion of old friends.

We then hesitantly offered Alea our little brown parcel. Without the least self-consciousness he unfurled the garment in one sweeping movement on the sprawling bed with the grace of a matador passing a bull with a swirl of his cape. And now, in its new setting, the saree looked exotic, almost Spanish you might say, beside him and would no doubt look positively Castillian on his gorgeous young wife. And, all the while, Time stood politely still.

It was left to another film-maker, M.V.K., to break the spell by inviting us all to his film which was due to start in the next few minutes. And so we adjourned to a little room where Alea was traditionally welcomed with *kumkum*. The film was in progress for by one of those mysterious paradoxes of Fate we seemed destined to 'visit' Tirupati after all on that eventful day. And soon the rhythmic notes of the Vedic hymns that Alea had so innocently — but oh, so prophetically! — captured on tape began their swelling diapason inside the darkened auditorium. Unbelievable! But fact — even documentary fact — is stranger than fiction, Lumiere more fantastic than Melies.

And so it was on that near miraculous day as more than one wheel came full circle that it struck me, then: that Alea could listen to his Vedic tape every day back in Cuba along with the obligatory Bach without feeling unduly 'strange', 'hallucinated' or 'transported to another dimension'. For would he not be safely, securely, astride the magic carpet of the Cuban Revolution?

2

A Portrait of Polanski

An ill-wisher once described Roman Polanski as 'the original five-foot Pole you wouldn't touch anyone with'. And certainly 'nobody is harder to faze', as even his friend Kenneth Tynan has written of him, 'than this cocksure Polish gnome'. He is certainly a hard man to please. Interviewing him turned out to be like trying to fly a kite during a storm.

We talked of his early childhood. His father had worked in the Mauthaussen quarries in Austria and his mother had died in the concentration camp at Auschwitz. Perhaps his life had been marked by his experience in a ghetto in occupied Poland? Not a bit of it! He didn't believe that suffering produced great art. 'It is a very Jesuit way of expressing it — suffering as an inspiration for the artist. I would not like to live like Van Gogh,' Polanski observed grimly. It was living under Stanilism that was the decisive influence. Art, during the Stalinist period, was suffocated; 'Even Impressionist painters were not allowed. The reason why most Polish films were about war was due to lack of freedom. The Government would not let you film the contemporary scene with integrity.'

Still the art and later the film schools at Lodz were a great experience. 'I had never known that such things existed. And I was certainly influenced by teachers who could not hide their love of painting just because of the official Party.' Gombrowicz and Schultz were the earlier writers he had read. Kafka came much later. *Waiting for Godot* was staged in Warsaw in 1956. But his interest in absurdist philosophy had waned as the world itself had become more and more absurd. *Tess*, for him represented a return to basic human sentiments. Yes, he had lost faith in political nostrums, in political films. Look at Ireland where society had really degenerated. Look at Cubans in Africa. Look at Vietnam now. It struck me that Polanski was probably turning religious. He was certainly wearing on his wrist a talismanic thread which a Buddhist monk had given him in Thailand 'for good luck'.

His literary heroes were Tolstoy (*War and Peace*, not *Anna Karenina* he said), Dostoevsky, Balzac, Dickens and Stendhal. Freud he didn't like at all. He kept referring to him as 'that bearded gentleman'. Kenneth Tynan, his buddy, was great. What was his philosophy? 'Not to have any principles at all but to listen to my instincts, to my feelings.' He spoke briefly of Sharon Tate. 'She completely changed my life. It was the beginning of a new thing and it didn't last long.'

Who were his favourite film-makers? Wrong. It should be: What were his favourite films? Right. Welles. No, not *Citizen Kane* but *Touch of Evil*. Felini's *8 1/2* and *La Dolce Vita* but not *I Vitelloni* which was sensational. Kurosawa's *Seven Samurai* and Carol Reed's *Odd Man Out* which was — and here Polanski groped for the *mot juste* — 'insolite', strange, bizarre, not ordinary. And Chaplin, of course. *City Lights, Modern Times* and *Gold Rush*. He had seen *City Lights* in Bangkok in a huge theatre holding some 3000 people. But the film, with its universality, spoke to these people from a different race, speaking a different language. Olivier's *Hamlet* he had seen some thirty times. 'Everything I have done has some connection with *Hamlet*,' he said cryptically.

I sought valiantly to renew myself in the healing waters of the Polanski masterpieces. *Repulsion* was indeed a great experience. This was the day before I saw Polanski. After seeing him, however, I, too, must have changed, for the magic had strangely fled (*Tess* excepted of course, but is *Tess* authentic Polanski?). It was *Cul-de-Sac* I went to see for Polanski himself had called it the most 'cinematic' of his films. The theatre was bursting to capacity but I didn't give up. Flaunting my delegate's badge I pleaded with the Manager. Alright, I could sit anywhere.

Anywhere turned out to be the floor to the left of the screen, with my back to the wall, both literally and figuratively. As Polanski's nightmarish story unwound on the screen, I felt something eerie was happening to me as well. I felt something sticky in the spotless mosaic of Abhinay theatre but managed to dismiss it from my thoughts. After the intermission, things got worse both on and off the screen. A little child, feeding bottle in hand, kept charging up and down the aisle. For variety, rolled the bottle, which was full of milk. No wonder I had found the going sticky! After a while, the child started hurling the bottle in my direction, squirting milk all over, and gleefully running forward to retrieve it.

Much later, musing about Polanski, it struck me that he himself was like that child: wilful, spoilt and almost totally without interest in anybody but himself. The world was his oyster to do with as he pleased. He certainly made films with the facility of that child with the bottle. It was for other people to understand him, love him, nurture him, and clean up the mess he often made in their lives.

Youssef Chahine, 'Lilli Marlene' and the El Alamein Battle

Underneath the lantern
By the barrack gate
Darling I remember
The way you used to wait:
'Twas there you whispered tenderly.
That you loved me,
You'd always be
My Lilli of the lamplight
My own Lilli Marlene.

The Desert War was fought out by the Allied and the Axis powers between 1940 and 1943 in Egypt and Libya. It had its own rugged flavour ('This land was made for War,' wrote one of the Desert poets) as the God of War favoured now one side, now the other, in what historians have laconically dubbed 'The Benghazi Handicap'.

Some reputations were enhanced and Rommel, in particular, gained the sobriquet of the 'desert fox' but many British generals (Wavell, Auchinleck, Ritchie) fell by the wayside and bit the dust. Of course there was Montgomery, victor of Alamein, but his victory constitutes more a victory of British arms than of British strategy as Correlli Barnett has pointed out in his *The Desert Generals*.

The historic battle of El Alamein was not a battle of manoeuvre like Marne or Bulge but a battle of sheer attrition with victory going to the stronger but not necessarily more skilful foe. 1942 represents, in many ways, a watershed: it was the hinge on which the wheel of fortune eventually turned. In Stalingrad, Paulus' Sixth Army perished to flatter a whim of Hitler and at El Alamein, Rommel's famed Afrika Korps were halted only 60 miles from Alexandria ('Alexandria! You are mine,' thundered Hitler).

The rainbow of victory had once again eluded Rommel and on 24 October, Monty began his counter-offensive which was to drive the Axis powers finally out of Africa. Youssef Chahine's remarkable film *Alexandria — Why?*' is set against the background of those turbulent African years when the tide turned from certain defeat to glorious victory.

I had looked forward to *Alexandria — Why?* for several reasons. And when I did get to see the film I was late by several minutes, delayed at a nearby hotel due to a friend's most inopportune appetite. It was quite a while before I properly 'connected' with the film but much was clearly lost. I left the theatre with a sense of gnawing incompleteness. Luckily, as it turned out, I was introduced to Chahine the next day and there ensued the most bewitching half-hour for me during the entire Festival.

Chahine had just given a most explosive press conference and some of that fire was still with him. We soon got round to talking about *Alexandria — Why?*

I remarked that the best thing in the film was the homosexual relationship between the aristocratic Adel Bey and the young British soldier, Oswald, who dies at El Alamein. Chahine looked agreeably surprised and added that some critics had asked him whether the friends had slept together during the night the soldier spends in the Egyptian's room: 'May be they did. How should I know? It isn't important.'

I said I didn't like the 'Hollywood' ending of the film on Yehia's triumph, especially since the rest of the film had so many complex strands of narrative. Chahine looked annoyed. For him, that was the whole point of the film, what the film was leading up to — Yehia's faith in himself, in his talent. When I looked a bit puzzled, he added with ill-concealed savagery that this theme 'occurred about 500 times in the movie'.

'Don't you remember the scene when that lady tells the hero not ever to betray his talent?' he asked, visibly annoyed with me. And when I said I didn't, he burst out: 'You must consult a psychiatrist at once.' Since there was no psychiatrist around, we talked of other things.

Deciding to get my own back, as it were, I attempted to impale the Egyptian visitor on the numerous *Hamlet* quotations that fairly litter his film. But of course *Hamlet* was his favourite play. He had seen the John Gielgud production. 'But I loathe Olivier's film,' he said with unexpected heat.

I asked him about the location shots at the El Alamein cemetery where Adel Bey mourns his dead friend and told him I found the sequences very moving. He said that he had acquired the battle footage from the Imperial War Museum at enormous expense. I now asked him about the Hollywood film clips and he laughed and said that the use of the 'bathing beauty' sequence in the opening of the film (there is a brief shot of Esther Williams swimming) was anachronistic since the film itself was made much later! In fact, both the hero and the hero's father are incorrigible movie buffs and the film is replete with references to Hollywood. The hero goes to see *Ziegfeld Follies* at the beginning of the film and somebody or other is 'lovelier than Hedy Lamaar'. As Yehia and Mohsen go picnicking we hear the jazzy strains of 'Lady Be Good'. Glenn Miller, Ella Fitzgerald and the liquid notes of Harry James's trumpet, one and all, drench the soundtrack. Yehia's English teacher (an American) talks about doing a new version of Spencer Tracy's *Boom Town* and Yehia goes to drama school at Pasadena (where Chahine himself studied). I may add, parenthetically, that none of our own film-makers makes even a passing reference to Hollywood although, for most of us, that is where it all began.

And then I asked him about 'Lilli Marlene', the artless little song which beyond the insanity of war appealed to the heart of every soldier. It is originally in German (written by a German soldier Hans Liep in 1917 and set to music twenty years later by Norbert Schultze) but achieved such popularity that more than a quarter of a century later, in 1967, it was still being played all over the world. It was the Eighth Army's most alluring conquest from the Germans and it certainly kept the Army going all the way back to Tunisia in pursuit of Rommel. For sheer popularity, it probably has the measure of 'Tipperary' and 'Pack up Your Troubles' of World War I and apparently there is even a Lili Marleen Club in Glasgow. Many women have sung the song, the first being Gale Anderson and the most famous being Marlene Dietrich.

Ironically, the sense of the song demands that it be sung by a man and it is true that even Bing Crosby has recorded it but nobody associates it with him. Different countries have their own version, expressive, no doubt, of national character. In the German version it goes ('In front of the barracks, before the heavy gate, there stood a lamp-post and it still stands there. Let's hope we meet again there and stand, beneath the lamp as we used to, Lili Marleen'); in the Italian, there is a verse (not in the original), 'Give me a rose, and press it to my heart'; in the French version, characteristically, there is a little attempt at erotic disguise, '*Et dans la nuit sombre Nos corps enlaces*'. The English version, predictably, goes squarely down the middle and it is the one that adorns the head of this essay.

It has always intrigued me, this sad song of love in 'battles long ago'. I asked Chahine why he had left it out in his film. 'No,' he cried out. 'It is there at the beginning, heard faintly behind the titles.' And then he hummed it artlessly, in a voice all his own and, on request, sang it too, in a rough, masculine tenor. As the melancholy strains of 'Lilli Marlene' floated around the table, time rolled back and the guns of Alamein boomed softly once more. The next night I went to see *Alexandria — Why?* again at Abhinay just to hear 'Lilli Marleen'. I was not very late this time — I made sure of that. But, unaccountably, once again I missed 'Lilli Marleen'. Heard melodies are sweet but those unheard are — we have it on the highest authority — sweeter. Perhaps.

Marianne Ahrne and the Invandrare

'*The Swedes...call them* invandrare, *which means simply 'immigrants' and is used in a welcoming way for everyone who comes to settle in the country. They pay their foreign workers handsomely, house them comfortably, encourage them to bring their families, educate their children, study them with the earnest curiosity of anthropologists, chart their happiness with psychiatric concern, fight for their rights, and write endlessly about their problems...(But) the* invandrare *in Sweden soon discover that they are isolated — and they sense that, somehow, their isolation goes deeper than the volatile, defensive separateness of foreign workers in, say, France and Germany. If those workers are 'the niggers of Europe', which is how they have described themselves lately, then the Swedish* invandrare *are a little bit like the sad, nervous boys in a Strindberg book — well fed, well groomed, well cared for, but unacknowledged as fellow human beings...The confusion the* invandrare *feel is deep and bitter because they have so few practical complaints to corroborate their eerie sense of being in terrible error by being themselves.*'
Jane Kramer, *Unsettling Europe* (1980)

Marianne Ahrne is a fortyish, auburn-haired film-maker from Sweden. Lean and stringy, she is not an easy person to draw out.

To begin with, she seemed quite sceptical of Indian journalists and hence about my own ability to write objectively and accurately about her. Hadn't that man from *The Hindustan Times* messed it up pretty thoroughly? I did my best to dispel her fears. And, then, when we got on to the subject of her own film, *Roots of Grief,* things started sliding from bad to worse. Had I noticed that the projection at the Plaza was poor? When I looked a bit uncertain (it turned out that she was merely referring to the brief interruption of the screening during the restaurant scene) she sternly reminded me that the film had been screened only three days back. At 8-30 p.m., too, I might remember. I had hardly regained my composure when misfortune struck again.

My recall of certain scenes of her films didn't match hers, one to one, and this annoyed her no end. She just flung her arms about her in despair and asked me quietly just how I was going to write about her film. I assured her that *that* was not my intention; I was merely going to write about meeting her. And here we left the subject of *Roots of Grief* (which is about the situation of an Argentinian immigrant, Sergio, in Sweden) much to my — and, no doubt, hers as well — relief.

Born in Lund in 1939 to a Czech father and a Swedish mother, she didn't set eyes on Czechoslovakia till she was 25. She studied French and American literature at Milwaukee before returning to study in Lund. Camus was an early enthusiasm and she had read all his novels in her 20s. I told her that I, too, had done the same and, secretly hoping to get even on the subject of my feeble memory, I started talking of Clamence's guilt in *La Chute* (we had just been discussing Sergio's guilt in her own film). Luckily for me it was Marianne's turn to scratch her auburn head in vain. She turned with some relief to the subject of another French writer: Simone de Beauvoir. She had collaborated with Simone ('an honest intellectual' Marianne called her) on the making of a film on old age, *A Walk in the Land of Old Age* and planned to make a feature film based on the same author's *She Came to Stay*. A writer, too, like her incomparable model, Marianne regards herself as a very solitary person. Still there were differences between writing and film-making: 'When I'm writing, nothing is lacking in the world but when I'm making a film everything is lacking' (I am still trying to figure out the difference between those two 'lacks'). Marianne has also recently published an autobiographical novel, *Apple Blossom and Ruins* (1980), based on her own experiences with a schizophrenic (who is called Rune in the novel) over a period of seven or eight years. She had taken a flat in a suburb and had seen him twice a week. She had even travelled to Denmark and Finland with him on holidays. It had been 'a very deep experience' for her in which she had 'matured'. He had been well for two years since then and in the last four and a half years had been back in hospital only for short spells. Wasn't the experience of being with a schizophrenic so long a bit unnerving, I asked her. She was 'stable', she said simply.

Confident at last of having got on to the same wavelength, I asked her about the anti-psychiatric movement of R.D. Laing in which I myself was deeply interested. Did she find his work, for example, in *Sanity, Madness and the Family* useful? 'Yes and no,' she said and added, 'But it's more complicated.' And, then, emboldened, I asked her about the original of Rune in her novel. This proved to be the moment of truth. Marianne looked as if I had dropped a bomb. Clearly I had violated some personal code, trespassed unwittingly into forbidden territory. She drew herself up and reminded me coldly that we were merely discussing the Rune of the novel; she didn't feel obliged to reveal anything about the 'real' Rune. And that, simply, was that. Our interview was over.

As Marianne walked away without so much as the slightest gesture of leave-taking or farewell, I had a sudden sense of what I can only describe as Scandinavian chill. I, too, was like Rune to be filed away in the freezing cabinets of her polar mind. Sweden had no problems, she had told us cheerfully in her press conference, and now I could see why. Because the real problems had been shifted on to the thousands of *invandrare* (400,000 to be precise in a population of 8 million) who had flocked to this northern El Dorado of welfare-State capitalism. 'The Swedes treat foreignness as some sort of congenital indiscretion,' observes Jane Kramer in the same book, and this accounts for their 'calmer, quieter disapproval of anything foreign'. Ironically enough, at the very start of our interview, I had asked Marianne about the Swedish word for 'immigrant' while attempting to place Sergio's plight in her own film. She had great trouble in getting the word and now I can see why. The focus in her film is not on the plight of the immigrant, Sergio, but on the dreams and sufferings of the two women (Anita and Karin) with whom he gets involved. Karin, in particular, looks clearly like an author surrogate (the screenplay is also by Marianne Ahrne): she is a translator by profession and has dreams of writing a book. It is she who has that extraordinarily recurrent dream about a house with many rooms of which only one is furnished. She walks and walks through the empty rooms and finally screams in terror. If that room with the furniture (amidst all those empty rooms) is a microcosm of Sweden today, then Karin's restless pacing like a ghost culminating in that shriek of terror could well signify the protest of humanity against dehumanizing conditions. A different kind of spectre — different from the one Marx espied — is haunting Europe today (particularly northern Europe), threatening to unsettle it anew.

Annotated Bibliography

This bibliography refers to most of the materials referred to in the text as well as further references by no means confined to the cinema and is certainly not meant to be comprehensive. The references listed below are strictly personal.

HISTORY, THEORY AND AESTHETICS OF FILM

Barthes, Roland. *Mythologies*, Jonathan Cape, 1972.
  Left-of-centre, readable. The piece on Garbo is exquisite.
Bazin, Andre. *What is Cinema?* vols. I, II, tr. Hugh Gray, University of California Press, 1967 and 1971.
———. *Jean Renoir*, tr. W.W. Hasley II and William H. Simon, ed. Francois Truffaut with an introduction by him and a short preface 'Andre Bazin's Little Beret' by Renoir himself, W.H. Allen, 1974.
———. *Orson Welles: A Critical View*, tr. Jonathan Rosenbaum, with a foreword by Francois Truffaut and a profile of Orson Welles by Jean Cocteau, Harper and Row, 1978.
  Inspirer of the French New Wave, patron saint of neo-realistic cinema, Bazin has been described by Renoir as 'the incarnation of one the saints of the Cathedral of Chartres'. Argued all his life against 'montage'.
Bluestone, George. *Novels into Film*, University of California Press, 1973.
  Discusses filmic adaptations of *The Informer, Wuthering Heights, Pride and Prejudice, The Grapes of Wrath, The Ox-Bow Incident* and *Madame Bovary*. Seminal study; theoretical.

Bresson, Robert. *Notes on the Cinematographer*, tr. Jonathan Griffin, with an introduction by J.M.G. Le Cleazio, Quartet Encounters, 1986.

'[Bresson] is the French cinema, as Dostoyevsky is the Russian novel and Mozart is German music' (Jean-Luc Godard in *Cahiers Du Cinema*). Aphorisms on cinema, reflecting a lifetime's toil. A current cult book.

Eisenstein, Sergei. *Film Form, Film Sense*, Meridien Books, 1957.

———. *Notes of a Film Director*, Dover, 1970.

Both highly theoretical and path-breaking works. The former introduces the concept of 'montage'; also includes his well-known essay, 'Dickens, Griffith and the Film Today'.

Kracauer, Siegfried. *From Caligari to Hitler: A Psychological History of the German Film*, Princeton University Press, 1947.

———. *Theory of Film: The Redemption of Physical Reality*, Oxford University Press, 1965.

———. *Caligari* is a must for all serious students of cinema. A model of research, it has 16 pages of stills from early German cinema. Indispensable for a study of the growth of fascism and the rise of Hitler.

Theory is a rigorous exposition of the principles of 'realist' cinema, minus the metaphysics of Bazin. Carries a discussion on Renoir's filmic adaptation of *Madame Bovary*, which is found wanting.

Both works, particularly *Theory*, carry substantial bibliographies.

Lawson, John Howard. *The Creative Process: The Search for an Audio-visual Language and Structure*, Hill and Wang, 1964.

A vastly underrated book that is seldom listed in bibliographies. Lawson wrote several successful screenplays (including *Sahara* , *Algiers* and *Action in the North Atlantic*) but as founder of Screen Writers Guild and ideological guru of the Hollywood branch of the Communist Party, USA, he fell foul of the House Un-American Activities Committee and, after serving a year in jail, never worked in Hollywood again. He died in 1977 at the age of 82. Magnificently written, without the least trace of jargon.

MacCabe, Colin. *Theoretical Essays: Film, Linguistics, Literature*, Manchester University Press, 1985.

———. *High Theory/Low Culture: Analysing Popular Television and Film*, Manchester University Press, 1986.

The witty cartoon illustrations on the covers of both books say it all!

Metz, Christian. *A Semiotics of the Cinema: Film Language*, Oxford University Press, 1974.

———. *Language and Cinema*, Mouton, 1974.

———. *Psychoanalysis and Cinema: The Imaginary Signifier*, tr. Celia Britton, Annwyl Williams, Ben Brewster and Alfred Guzzetti, Macmillan, 1982.

The most important post-war theorist of cinema since Eisenstein, Metz destroyed the very possibility of a 'grammar of cinema' by showing that cinema has no dictionary of common denotations like *Webster's*. In his later essays, he examines, with the aid of psychoanalysis, the implications of the analogy between film and theory, which has given a boost to feminist film criticism.

Rhode, Eric. *A History of the Cinema From the Origins to 1970*, Allen Lane, 1976.

Beautifully produced, a mine of readable information with over – believe it or not – 300 illustrations! Handy reference book.

Tarkovsky, Andrey. *Sculpting in Time: Reflextions on the Cinema*, Bodley Head, 1986.

The most original theorist of the cinema since Eisenstein. Beautiful stills; elegantly produced. Very, very influential, particularly in India.

Wright, Basil. *The Long View*, Paladin, 1976.

Massive (752 pages), useful, readable; very good on Satyajit Ray to whom he devotes several pages.

Wollen, Peter. *Signs and Meaning in the Cinema*, Secker and Warburg, 1969.

———. *Readings and Writings: Semiotic Counter Strategies*, Verso, 1982.

Wide-ranging, Wollen is the first British theorist of distinction, a true votary of the 'auteur' theory. His later *Readings and Writings* combines insights from Marxism, semiotics and the history of art as well as psychoanalysis.

PRACTITIONERS

Agee, James. *Agee on Film: Reviews and Comments*, Beacon Press, 1964.

All that he wrote between 1941 and 1948. Includes his famous *Life* essay, 'Comedy's Greatest Era'.

Boyum, Jay Gould. *Double Exposure: Fiction into Film*, Mentor, 1985.

Indispensable for the teacher of film. Discusses sixteen adaptations from literature, including *The Great Gatsby, Apocalypse Now, Women in Love, A Clockwork Orange, Death in Venice, Slaughter-house Five* and *Swann in Love*. Excellent bibliography.

Crist, Judith. *The Private Eye, The Cowboy and the Very Naked Girl*, Paperback Library, 1970.

'You'll find no theories about theories of film criticism here' Mrs Crist warns the reader in her introduction. What we do find is exhilarating stuff, including her prize-winning negative reviews of *Cleopatra*, *The Sandpiper* and *Hurry Sundown*. Mrs Crist was President of the Columbia Graduate School of Journalism and Vice-President of the New York Newspaper Women's Club.

Farber, Manny. *Negative Space*, Studio Vista, 1971.

There has been no one quite like Manny Farber, individualist and stylist *par excellence*. The opening essay on the 'Underground Film' (the American ganster movie) is already a classic. His 'White Elephant Art vs Termite Art' deserves to be yet another, with its brilliant put-down of the European avant-garde. An art critic as well, Farber brings to film insights from painting.

Kael, Pauline. *I Lost it at the Movies*, Jonathan Cape, 1966.

——. *Kiss Kiss Bang Bang*, Calder and Boyar, 1970.

——. *Going Steady*, Temple Smith, 1970.

——. *Deeper into Movies*, Little, Brown, 1973.

——. *Reeling*, Warner Books, 1975.

——. *When the Lights Go Down*, Holt, Rinehart and Winston, 1980.

——. *Taking it all in*: *Film Writings 1980–1983*, Arena, 1987.

——. *State of the Art*: *Film Writings 1983–1985*, Arena, 1987.

——. *Hooked*, E.P. Dutton, 1989.

——. *Movie Love* : *Complete Reviews 1988–1991*, Plume, 1991.

Pauline Kael is the High Priestess of film criticism, undoubtedly the most prolific in living memory. Not intellectual at all, but has savvy, nerve and gut-level enthusiasm. Champion of the popular film, her enthusiasm for Ray notwithstanding. [For a generally sympathetic estimate see *Nine American Critics* by Edward Murray, Frederick Ungar Publishing Co., 1975, pp. 110–140. For a reverse view see Sarris's 'The Auteur Theory and the Perils of Pauline', *Film Quarterly* (Summer 1963) and Renata Adler's 'The Sad Tale of Pauline Kael', NYR (14 April, 1980)].

Kauffmann, Stanley. *A World on Film*, Delta Books, 1964.

——. *Field of View*, Paj Publication, 1986.

Macdonald, Dwight. *On Movies*, Berkeley Medallion, 1969.

> My earliest guru, immensely readable. Read his famous list of 'Marked Men' (bad directors).

Pechter, William. *Twenty-Four Times a Second: Films and Film-makers*, Harper and Row, 1971.

> The title derives from a line in Godard's *Le Petit Soldat*. Pechter is described in the jacket as 'educated at New York's High School of Music and Art, the liberal arts college of Columbia University, the film auditorium of the Museum of Modern Art, and along Broadway and 42nd Street'. His criticism certainly bears the marks of this varied education! Read his essays on Ford and Eisenstein.

Sarris, Andrew. *Interviews with Film Directors*, Discuss Books, 1969.

——. *Confessions of a Cultist: On the Cinema, 1955/1969*, Simon and Schuster, 1970.

——. *The Primal Screen*, Simon and Schuster, 1973.

——. *The John Ford Mystery*, Secker and Warburg 1976.

——. *Politics and Cinema*, Columbia University Press, 1980.

> Urbane, witty, polemical and a tremendous stylist, tending to epigrammatic formulations. Great champion of American auteurism.

Simon, John. *Private Screenings*, Berkeley Medallion, 1967.

——. *Movies into Film*, Delta Books, 1971.

——. *Reverse Angle*, Clarkson N. Potter, 1982

> My present idol. Immensely erudite (has a Ph.D. from Harvard, where he taught) and an expert at demolition. His 'Godard and Godardians' (running into some 26 pages!) in *Private Screenings* is the *locus classicus*. Certainly the critic you love to hate!

Tyler, Stephen. *The Hollywood Hallucination*, Simon and Schuster, 1940.

——. *Magic and Myth in the Movies*, Horizon, 1947.

——. *Sex, Psyche, Etcetera in the Film*, Horizon, 1969.

> The most prolific writer on film with some 26 titles, of which I have listed only three. Psychoanalytically-oriented, Tyler is often dense. Gets a chapter all to himself in Gore Vidal's best-selling novel, *Myra Breckenridge*.

Warshaw, Robert. *The Immediate Experience*, Doubleday, 1962.

> A cult book, but deservedly admired for its two notable essays, 'The Gangster as Tragic Hero' and 'Movie Chronicle: the Westerner'. Warshaw is much admired by fellow film critics for his sanity, as

witness his remark: 'A man watches a movie and the critic must acknowledge he is that man.'

Young, Vernon. *Unpopular Essays on a Popular Art* , Quadrangle/The New York Times Book Co., 1972.

Brilliant stuff. He writes in his Preface: 'the film ... is in nothing more wonderful than this: it brings us not simply a world we never made but worlds we could not otherwise glimpse. It compensates us for all those lovely dawns we slept away, the sycamore trees under which we never awakened, the rivers we never crossed, the fugitive friendships that never ripened, the south-west canyons or Bavarian churches we never reached'. Read the penultimate essay 'A Sad Tale's Best for Winter' to see film criticism approach the condition of literature.

INDIAN FILMS

Satyajit Ray

Das Gupta, Chidananda. *Talking of Films*, Orient Longman, 1981, pp. 55–75.

——. *The Cinema of Satyajit Ray*, Vikas, 1980.

——. *Film India: Satyajit Ray*, Directorate of Film Festivals, 1981.
Pioneer among Indian film critics. Wide ranging, very readable, Seminal on Ray.

Gilliat, Penelope. *Three-Quarter Face*, Secker and Warburg, 1980, pp. 61–9.
Sensitive appraisals of *Charulata, Nayak* and *The Chess Players* ; Gilliat describes Ray as 'really a novelist working on film'.

Kael, Pauline. *I Lost it at the Movies*, Jonathan Cape, 1966, pp. 245–55.
First serious estimate of Ray by a Western critic.

Kauffmann, Stanley. *A World on Film*, Harper and Row, pp. 367–74.
Discusses the Apu trilogy, *Three Daughters* and *The Music Room*.

Pechter, William. *Twenty-Four Times a Second* , Harper and Row, 1971, pp. 254–8.

Ray, Satyajit. *Our Films, Their Films*, Longman, 1976.

——. The Apu Trilogy, tr. Shampa Mukherjee, Seagull, 1985.
The first is delightful, if somewhat blind on Hitchcock and Antonioni. The second has 24 pages of sketches by Ray.

Robinson, Andrew. *Satyajit Ray: The Inner Eye*, Andre Deutsch, 1989.
Beautifully produced, authoritative, with nearly 150 stills.

Excellent up-to-date bibliography. Still, stays away from evaluative judgement.

Seton, Marie. *Portrait of a Director: Satyajit Ray*, Dennis Dobson, 1971.
Informal, relaxed inside view by someone who knew Ray well. Glorious photographs, running into several pages.

Sharar, Abdul Halim. *Lucknow: The Last Phase of Oriental Culture*, trs. E.S. Harcourt and Fakhir Hussain, Paul Elek, 1975.
Indispensable guide to an understanding of 'The Chess Players'.

Tyler, Parker. *Classics of the Foreign Film*, Spring Books, 1996, pp. 201–11.
Discusses the trilogy.

Wood, Robin. *The Apu Trilogy*, Praeger, 1971.
Very analytical but achieves at best an external understanding. Nevertheless, the first serious study by a major critic.

Wright, Basil. *The Long View*, Paladin, 1976, pp. 459–70.
Extended and extremely sympathetic treatment of Ray.

Periodicals

Dev, Ajoy and Nandan Mitra eds. Special Ray Number Itson, August 1992.
Uncollected film criticism of Ray. Extremely valuable.

Dey, Ajoy and Nandan Mitra eds. Montage special issue on Ray by Anandam Film Society, Bombay, July 1966.
Indispensable for the student of Ray. Collector's item

Krupanidhi, Uma ed. Montage Special issue on Ray by Anandan Film Society, Bombay, July 1966.

——. *Special Ray number*, Ifson, August 1992.
Uncollected film criticism of Ray. Extremely valuable.

Attenborough's Gandhi

Abraham, Abu. '*Gandhi* : A moving film with serious setbacks', *The Sunday Observer*, December 1982.

Attenborough, Richard. *In Search of Gandhi* , B.I. Publications in association with Bodley Head, 1983.

Bachchan, Amitabh. 'On *Gandhi*', *The Week*, vol. 1, No. 6.

Draper, Alfred. *Amritsar: The Massacre that Ended the Raj*, Macmillan, 1981.

Grenier, Richard. 'The Gandhi Nobody Knows', *Commentary*, March 1983.

Hertzberg, Hendrick. 'True Gandhi', *The New Republic*, 25 April 1983.

Kael, Pauline. 'Gandhi' in *Taking it all in*, Arena, 1987.

Kauffmann, Stanley. 'The Man Who Could Not Lose', *The New Republic*, 13 December 1982.

Kedourie, Elie. 'False Gandhi', *The New Republic*, 21 March 1983.

Malik, Amita. 'The Book of the Film', *The Sunday Observer*, January 1983.

Mehta, Anita. 'Gandhi and Colonialism', *Encounter*, June 1983.

Nanda, B.K. 'The Gandhi Film' in *Gandhi and His Critics*, Oxford University Press, 1985, pp. 1–3.

Patwardhan, Anand. 'Gandhi: Film As Theology,' *Economic And Political Weekly*, vol. XVIII, Nos. 16–17, 16–23, April 1983.

Rudolphe, Lyold C. and Susanne Hoover Rudolph. 'Gandhi Critic's Article Distorts History', *Indian and Foreign Review*, vol. 20, No. 13, 15–20, April 1983.

Rumbold, Sir Algernon. 'Film, Facts, History', *Encounter*, March 1983.

Rushdie, Salman. 'Attenborough's *Gandhi*' in *Imaginary Homelands*, Granta, 1991.

Sarin, Ritu. 'Reincarnation of the Little Man', *Delhi Reporter*, vol IV, No. 4 May 1983.

Singh, Bikram. 'A Mahatma For the Masses', *The Sunday Observer*, January 1983.

Watson, Francis. 'Getting Gandhi Straight', *Encounter*, August 1983.
    Discusses all the views of the *Encounter* correspondents; also Grenier and Rushdie. Knew Gandhi personally. Liaised with military intelligence during the Second World War.

Additionally, two supplements by *The Hindu*, Madras ('In Search of Gandhi', 27 February 1983) and *The Sunday Observer* ('Gandhi For Everyone', 12 December 1982) are very useful. The latter carries impressions from 9 well-known Indians and 6 foreign critics.

SCREENPLAYS

Antonioni, Michelangelo. *Screenplays of Michelangelo Antonioni*, Orion, 1963.
    Contains narrative–dramatic versions of *II Grido*, *L'Avventura*, *La Notte* and *L'eclisse*.

Bergman, Ingmar. *Four Screenplays of Ingmar Bergman*, Simon and Schuster, 1960.

Contains narrative–dramatic versions of *Smiles of a Summer Night, The Seventh Seal, Wild Strawberries* and *The Magician.*

——. *The Marriage Scenarios* , tr. Alan Blair, Pantheon, 1978.

Contains *Scenes From a Marriage, Face to Face* and *Autumn Sonata.*

——. *Fanny and Alexander*, tr. Alan Blair, Pantheon, 1982.

Briley, John. *Gandhi: The Screenplay*, Grove Press, 1982.

For a criticism of the factual errors in the script, see 'There are nearly 100 errors in *Gandhi* ', Sunday, 19 April 1981.

Fassbinder, Rainer Werner. *Querelle: The Film Book*, Grove Press, 1982.

Contains commemorative tributes from Vincent Canby, Derek Malcolm, Andrew Sarris and Douglas Sirk. Also has 118 massive colour stills from the film.

Fellini, Federico. *La Dolce Vita* , Ballantine, 1961.

——. *Federico Fellini's Juliet of the Spirits*, ed. Tullio Kezich, tr. Howard Greenfield, Ballantine, 1965.

Contains lengthy interviews with Fellini. Especially noteworthy for offering two versions of the screenplay – the final script, then transcription and translation of finished film to script form.

Ray, Satyajit. *The Apu Trilogy*, Seagull, 1985.

Robbe-Grillet, Alain. *Last Year at Marienbad* , Grove Press, 1962.

SUGGESTED READING FOR INDIAN FILMS

Banerji, Bibhutibhushan. *Pather Panchali* (Song of the Road), tr. T.W. Clark and Tarapada Mukherji, Unwin Hyman, 1968.

Barnouw, Eric and S. Krishnaswamy. *Indian Film*, Columbia University Press, 1963.

Still the most reliable guide to Indian cinema. Regrettably not updated.

Baskaran, S. Theodore. *The Message Bearers*, Cre-A, 1981.

Excellent on early Tamil cinema.

Das Gupta, Chidananda. *Talking of Films*, Orient Longman, 1981.

——. *The Painter's Eye*, Roli Books, 1991.

——. ed. *Satyajit Ray: An Anthology of Statements on Ray and by Ray*, Directorate of Film Festivals, 1981.

The first book has nine essays on Indian cinema, the second is the first serious study by an Indian of India's popular cinema and the third is an excellent collection, straight from the horse's mouth as it were.

Ghosh, Sital Chandra, and Arun Kumar Roy. *Twelve Indian Directors*, People's Book Publishing, 1981.

Useful book with 20 stills and a filmography.

Indira, M.K. *Phaniyamma*, tr. Tejswini Niranjana, Kali for Women, 1989.

Krishen, Pradip ed. *Indian Popular Cinema* vol. 8, No. 1, March 1980. Special issue of *India International Centre Quarterly*.

Seven essays, three interviews and an overlong, erratic bibliography.

Kumar, P. Shiv and T. Vinda ed. *Double Vision: Literature and Films*, Nachson Books, 1994.

Proceeding of the 'International Seminar on Indian Languages and Film'. September 24–6, 1992, Kakatiya University, Warangal, Andhra Pradesh. Discussion and essays on *Bharat Ek Khoj, Mathilukal, Samskara* and *Kanyasulkam.*

Mahmeed, Hameduddin. *The Kaleidoscope of Indian Cinema*, Affiliated East-West Press Ltd., 1974.

Introduction by Khushwant Singh who begins by saying 'I know very little about the [sic] Indian films', the book has nonetheless some interesting snippets about Indian film personalities. An interesting read.

Malik, Amita. *Brief Encounters*, Polytechnic Press, 1982.

Interviews with leading American, British, European and Indian film personalities. Informal and entertaining.

Menon, T.K.N. ed. *Indian Cinema* 1978, Kerala State Film Festival Committee, Cochin.

Contains Ray's views on script writing (as told to Gaston Roberge) and 15 other entries by leading film personalities. A most interesting essay by G.S. Panicker on Godard's critique of Z, *Battle of Algiers* and *Zabriskie Point.*

Padgaonkar, Dileep. 'Satyajit Ray' in *Focus on Directors, Cinema in India*, NFDC, 1994.

Roberge, Gaston. *Another Cinema For Another Society*, Seagull Books, 1985.

Except for a five-page discussion of Utpalendu Chakraborty's award-winning *Chokh*, Fr. Roberge's book has little to say on Indian cinema.

Sarkar, Kobita. *Indian Cinema Today: An Analysis*, Sterling, 1975.

Diffuse, lacks focus.

Sen, Mrinal. *Views On Cinema*, Ishan, 1977.

Personal, stimulating, readable, Contains controversy with Ray over *Akash Kusum*.

Symposium on Cinema in Developing Countries, Publications Division, Ministry of Information and Broadcasting, Government of India, 1979.

A collection of 13 papers. Held in connection with the Seventh International Film Festival of India in New Delhi, 1979.

Vasudev, Aruna ed. *Frames of Mind: Reflection on Indian Cinema*, UBSPD, 1995.

Vasudev, Aruna and Philippe Lenglet eds. *Indian Cinema Superbazaar*, Vikas, 1987.

ADDITIONAL READING

Cameron, Ian and Wood, Robin. *Antonioni*, Studio Vista, 1968.

Detailed analysis of the famous trilogy.

Geduld, Harry M. ed. *Film Makers on Film Making*, Pelican, 1967.

Contains statements by Hitchcock, Resnais, Bergman, Fellini, Welles, Antonioni, Kurosawa on their works. A long discussion with Antonioni (pp. 204–26) is particularly useful for an understanding of *L'Avventura* and *La Notte*.

Georgakas, Dan and Lenny Rubenstein. *Art Politics Cinema: The Cineaste Interviews*, Pluto, 1984.

Indispensable for understanding the political cinema.

Gottesman, Ronald. *Focus on Orson Welles*, Spectrum, 1976.

A brilliant personal estimate by Kenneth Tynan is included.

McCormick, Ruth tr. *Fassbinder*, Tanam Books, 1981.

A collection of six essays with an interview, a documentation on Fassbinder and a comprehensive filmography.

Nachbar, Jack. *Focus on the Western*, Spectrum, 1974.

'Saviour in the Saddle: The Sagebrush Testament' by Michael Marsden is outstanding.

Rayns, Tony ed. *Fassbinder*, BFI, 1980.

Seven essays, five interviews with Fassbinder and an annotated bibliography with documentation.